Delight and Dole

The Children Act 10 years on

Delight and Dole

The Children Act 10 years on

Being

Papers given to the President's Interdisciplinary Conference for judges, directors of social services, mental health professionals, academics, guardians ad litem, panel managers and other professionals, held at the Dartington Hall Conference Centre, Dartington Hall, Totnes, Devon, between 28–30 September 2001, together with a record of the discussions which took place in the plenary sessions of the conference.

Edited by
The Rt Hon Lord Justice Thorpe
and
Catherine Cowton
of Middle Temple, Barrister, Queen Elizabeth Building, Temple

with a Foreword by
Dame Elizabeth Butler-Sloss
President of the Family Division

Family Law
2002

Published by
Jordan Publishing Limited
21 St Thomas Street
Bristol BS1 6JS

British Library Cataloguing-in-Publication Data

A catalogue record for this book is available from the British Library.

ISBN 0 85308 738 5

Typeset in house
Printed and bound in Great Britain by Bell & Bain Ltd, Glasgow

CONTRIBUTORS

Dr Susan Bailey
Gardner Unit, Manchester

Chris Davies
Corporate Director of Social Services, Somerset County Council

Amanda Finlay
Director, Public and Private Rights Directorate, Lord Chancellor's Department

Jane Fortin
Reader in Law, Kings College, London

The Rt Hon Lady Justice Hale

Professor Carolyn Hamilton
Professor of Law, University of Essex, Barrister, 17 Bedford Row, Director, The Children's Legal Centre

Professor Judith Harwin
Department of Health and Social Care, Brunel University

His Honour Judge Mark Hedley
Liverpool Combined Court Centre

Anthony PM Hewson
Chairman, CAFCASS

Pat Monro
Solicitor, Darlington & Parkinson

Morag Owen
Department of Health and Social Care, Brunel University

James Paton
Bill Principal for the Adoption and Children Bill, Department of Health

Vivienne Reed
GALRO Panel Member

Dr Mike Shaw
Consultant Child Psychiatrist, Sutton Hospital

Jenny Stevenson
Chartered Consultant Clinical Psychologist

Rukhsana Farooqi Thakrar
Accredited Social Work Practice Teacher, Children's Guardian, Children and Family Court Reporter, CAFCASS

Dr Arlene Vetere
Academician, Academy of the Learned Societies in the Social Sciences, Chartered Clinical Psychologist, Tavistock Clinic, Principal Lecturer in Systemic Psychotherapy, University of East London

The Hon Mr Justice Wall

... in equal scale weighing delight and dole[1] ...

Hamlet, Act 1, Scene 2

---

[1]   Sorrow.

FOREWORD

Dartington Hall Conference, 28–30 September 2001

The Interdisciplinary Committee of the President of the Family Division organised, at Dartington in Devon, a memorable conference taking stock of the Children Act 10 years on. It was, in every sense, an interdisciplinary occasion and provided a fascinating discussion and interchange of ideas between the judiciary at every level, senior representatives of the Lord Chancellor's Department and the Department of Health, directors of social services, medical consultants, academics and other professionals concerned with child care. It was extremely valuable to meet and together to look back over the life of the Children Act and to look forward to discuss how the provision of services for children can be streamlined and improved.

The papers presented to the Conference deserve a wider audience. The Conference rapporteur, Catherine Cowton from the Family Bar, has collated and edited them and the discussions on them. With her invaluable help, this publication will give an opportunity for others in the field to reflect on the best way forward to provide support for children who come within the family justice system and to give those children as good an outcome as is possible.

Elizabeth Butler-Sloss

Dame Elizabeth Butler-Sloss
President of the Family Division

CONTENTS

EDITORIAL INTRODUCTION

The Rt Hon Lord Justice Thorpe

Before writing this brief introduction I looked back to the introductions to the previous volumes in this series, *Rooted Sorrows, Divided Duties* and *No Fault or Flaw*. That served to emphasise the strength of the thread that binds them. This conference has followed the framework introduced in 1995 and explained by Wall J in his editorial foreword to *Rooted Sorrows*. Again all our work has been informed by the knowledge that we would reach our essential audience not at Dartington but through Richard Hudson's commitment to publish the conference papers and the discussion. For the assembly of the publication material we have again been dependent on the skill of our rapporteur, Catherine Cowton, another in a rain of stars from Queen Elizabeth Buildings. The speed with which she has produced the text means that I write this introduction within 4 days of our departure from Dartington. As yet we could not hope to have received our title but I remain confident that Margaret Wall's prodigious knowledge of English literature will fuel her inspiration.

Every conference engenders an atmosphere and an impetus. We have yet to experience a conference that has fallen flat. The failure of *No Fault or Flaw* as a publication was only that it fell victim to unpredictable shifts in government policy. That cannot be the fate of this next volume. For no statutes are more crucial to the well-being of society than children and adoption Acts. After a decade there can be no doubt of the Government's responsibility and commitment in reviewing the Children Act 1989 to evaluate the need for relatively minor statutory amendment but above all to discover better ways of working to reduce delay and to avoid wastage of resources which are necessarily finite and seldom adequate to meet ever-increasing demands.

The Adoption and Children Bill demonstrates the Government's equal resolve to modernise the law and practice in the sensitive but vital field of adoption. After all, the tools with which we now work were fashioned a generation ago. The timing of the conference was ideal to enable the many disciplines assembled at Dartington to exchange ideas and to unite in formulating a resolution for the consideration of government. Equally timely was the opportunity for the conference with united voice to urge the Government to publish the draft consultation paper on the introduction of an interdisciplinary structure for the family justice system.

The need for such a structure was resoundingly agreed at our previous conference in September 1997. Subsequently, that need was acknowledged and approved by the Lord Chancellor. Since then there have been many expressions of impatience at delay in implementation. The message running throughout the fourth annual report of the Lord Chancellor's Advisory Board on Family Law is clear. The family justice system needs and deserves a support structure. It asks for no more than what has been provided to the criminal and civil justice systems.

Looking back to our previous conferences it is worth recording that much that was argued for in September 1997 has belatedly come to pass as a consequence of the commencement of the Human Rights Act 1998. That eventuality was foretold in my introduction to *Divided Duties*. Seemingly, the decisions of our court in *Re W and B; Re W (Care Plan)* [2001] EWCA Civ 757, [2001] 2 FLR 582 have been the vehicle for change. However, I say seemingly since their validity will be tested in the House of Lords later this term. Beyond that, much will turn on policy decisions that rest with government. There can be no doubt that in our court the determination of the issues was considerably clarified by the work done throughout the 1997 conference and its record in *Divided Duties*.

Finally, I would like to express my gratitude to the Department of Health and the Lord Chancellor's Department without whose support, both financial and general, this conference could never have taken place. I also thank Catherine Cowton for her superb achievement in recording all the discussion so swiftly and so precisely. I thank Malcom Welsh, late of the Judicial Studies Board, whose administration both in advance and at the conference itself was of the highest standard. I thank the staff of Dartington whose hospitality and kindness could not be bettered. Finally, I thank the President for matching the warmth, enthusiasm and kindness shown by her predecessor, qualities so vital to the foundation and growth of the President's Interdisciplinary Committee.

October 2001

CONFERENCE OBJECTIVES

The Rt Hon Lord Justice Thorpe

The Rt Hon Lord Justice Thorpe emphasised in his introductory remarks that the principal objective of the conference must be to produce, by the thinking and discussion of the delegates, something of wider value. It was essential through publication of the conference papers and discussions to reach out to dedicated professionals serving children as well as to policy makers.

His chosen focus of the conference was interdisciplinarity. He recalled the training and preparations for the introduction of the Children Act 10 years ago, and stated that the launch of the Act would not have been the success it was, had various professions not collaborated in making it so.

He reminded the conference of the report prepared by Dame Margaret Booth for the Lord Chancellor in 1996 on delay in public Children Act proceedings. One of the important points highlighted in her report was the initial enthusiastic collaboration of the various relevant professions, which had diminished and in some instances died away in the years since the Act had come into force. She recommended to the Government a revival of interdisciplinary collaboration in areas where it had died. This recommendation has never been implemented.

Lord Justice Thorpe referred to a government consultation paper on interdisciplinary working for which he had written a foreword in January 2001. The focus of the paper was how best to create an interdisciplinary support structure for the family justice system. He was convinced that such a structure held the potential not only to reduce delay but generally to improve standards. Since January 2001 the paper has not been published by the Government.

Lord Justice Thorpe stated that the one resolution he wished to put before the conference was to urge the Government not to underestimate the potential gain across a wide field to be achieved by the creation of such an interdisciplinary structure.

PLENARY ONE

DELAY AND THE CHALLENGES OF THE CHILDREN ACT

Amanda Finlay CBE
*Director, Public and Private Rights Directorate,
Lord Chancellor's Department*

Summary of paper

Amanda Finlay introduced her paper by acknowledging the continual challenge for policy makers of remaining open and alive to the way in which family law was being developed in practice and the changing demands of a changing society. She said that she had found the previous President's Interdisciplinary Conference a very valuable means of finding out what a wide range of professionals working in the Family Justice arena thought was important.

When she took up the post as Director of the Public and Private Rights Directorate in July 1999 the main focus of interest had been on private law children matters and on Part II of the Family Act 1996: the subject of the previous interdisciplinary conference. None the less, it was also important to ensure that public law children matters remained a priority for professionals and for Ministers. As a result, a scoping study of public law Children Act cases had been commissioned which formed the basis of her paper. Because the study had not yet been published, the paper set out its major findings for those working in the family justice system.

Delay

Amanda Finlay emphasised that delay was recognised as damaging for almost everyone caught up in Court Proceedings but it was especially so for children. She acknowledged that on occasion delay could be constructive in allowing people to come to terms with the situation or in working out better ways of dealing with it, but was also necessary to keep an overall eye on the length of time that cases were taking and to consider whether this was appropriate or too long.

The Children Act had been a landmark piece of legislation in a number of significant respects and while tremendous progress had been made in promoting the best interests of children, it was important continually to look at how these cases were being progressed and what remained to be done.

When the Children Act 1989 was introduced it was anticipated that public law Children Act cases would be dealt with within 12 weeks but in 1996 the time taken had increased to an average of 46 weeks and Dame Margaret Booth had been asked to investigate and to make recommendations. The Children Act Advisory Committee, which had been set up to oversee the implementation of the Children Act, had sought to address many of her recommendations in its final report and particularly in its Handbook of Best Practice which was still in use and very relevant today. But despite the efforts of all those involved delay had continued to increase and by the end of 2000 cases were taking 50 weeks on average.

Scoping study

As many of those present knew, a scoping study of Children Act cases had been commissioned in the summer of 2000. She thanked all of those who had been involved in the study, particularly for the candour with which their responses had been given. A draft report was currently with Ministers and it was hoped that this would be published later in the Autumn.

She emphasised that one of the particular difficulties faced in this area was that the Government alone could not provide answers to all the issues identified and that there were many where progress could be made only by the combined efforts of all involved in the Family Justice System. Attending the conference provided an opportunity for her to assess from the discussions in small groups and the feedbacks and the plenary sessions just which issues deserved priority attention, the scope for making things better and the need to avoid making things worse. It was particularly valuable to have the opportunity to hear positive suggestions from those who had been working in detail on how to improve matters.

Experts

The scoping study, in common with Dame Margaret Booth's report, had identified that the use of experts was a major cause of delay. There were many aspects to this, but a particular problem at present was the use of experts to compensate for staff shortages elsewhere. This was an issue which needed to be tackled by all concerned departments, and LCD would be raising it with others. Amanda Finlay also highlighted the problems caused by an apparent lack of trust in social services assessment procedures, often exacerbated by the turnover and inexperience of some staff and the overloading of those staff remaining.

It was particularly helpful that the President's Interdisciplinary Committee had recognised that the issue of experts in Children Act cases needed to be tackled on a broad and interdisciplinary basis. The seminar in November 1999 and the follow up seminar in June 2001 had resulted in a number of initiatives which were being taken forward by the Committee. She also referred to the Law Society's best practice protocol for family cases which encouraged better scrutiny of the need for expert evidence.

Case management

Amanda Finlay referred to the case management protocols which had been developed by a number of courts. It was hoped that these would lead to pilot schemes next year to enable evaluation of their impact. It would be particularly helpful for delegates to consider whether a single nationwide protocol was more appropriate or a variety of protocols to deal with different local circumstances.

There had been early action to improve the case management of adoption cases, particularly through the establishment by the President's Adoption Committee of a nationwide pilot of specialist County Court Adoption Centres. Amanda Finlay thanked the Committee and its Chairman, Mr Justice Holman, for their work

Inflexibility of jurisdiction

Amanda Finlay said that another matter being considered to reduce delay was the introduction of an extended private law jurisdiction for District Judges to enable them to handle contested private law cases in courts where there was not a permanent Circuit Judge present. The scope of this jurisdiction had now been agreed and it was expected that these arrangements would be in place by the end of the year. It also seemed desirable to review the judicial 'ticketing' system to ensure that there were sufficient judges with the necessary experience to do family cases in all areas.

Conclusion

Overall, Amanda Finlay emphasised the value and importance of interdisciplinary working to implement the various proposals necessary to improve the handling and case management of Children Act cases. She hoped that there would soon be consultation on a new model for an interdisciplinary support structure to underlie and promote the changes which were necessary.

Introduction

The President's interdisciplinary conference on the Children Act brings together a wide range of professionals from across the family justice system, and is taking place just under a year after the Human Rights Act 1998 came into force on 2 October 2000.

It provides a timely and welcome opportunity for all of us to think about the extent to which we are giving positive effect to the state's duty to look after the interests of children and their families in the family justice context, and in particular to examine whether we are giving full effect not only to their Art 8 rights under the European Convention for the Protection of Human Rights and Fundamental Freedoms 1950 (ECHR) (relating to the enjoyment of private and family life), but also to their Art 6 rights (relating to the right to a fair and public hearing within a reasonable time).

It is a cliché that justice delayed is justice denied. But clichés may nevertheless be true. Delay may have an adverse effect on litigants or those affected by litigation, whatever their ages. The effect of delay on children may be particularly damaging because of the differences of scale and perspective – an inconvenient delay of 12 months for an adult is literally half a lifetime for a 2-year-old child – and because a young child's development is so rapid and so sensitive to events that damage may sometimes be done even during the time it takes to bring proceedings designed to resolve the child's position and protect him or her from harm. This is aptly summed up in Rowe and Lambert's 1973 paper 'Children Who Wait: A Study of Children Needing Substitute Families':[1]

> 'Waiting on the actions of others is an unsettling and frustrating experience. When one's whole life context may depend on what others do or do not do then the waiting is charged with alarm and trepidation. Add to this a wait which is protracted and which no one seems inclined or able to end with a firm decision. Go further still and imagine you are a child carrying these burdens of uncertainty and anxious doubts and you may gain some inkling of the feelings of the children.'

On the other hand, it can sometimes happen that the passage of time during a case is a necessary factor in enabling it to reach a satisfactory conclusion to which the parties could not otherwise have agreed, or to enable the court to have the information it needs about a case to make the right decision.

The Children Act is now 12 years old, and has been in force for almost 10 years. This is therefore an opportune time to look both at how it has fared over that time, and at how the justice system is delivering those key elements of the Children Act which are of such importance in the human rights context.

The Children Act has proved a landmark piece of legislation. It has:

- put the welfare of children first;
- emphasised through the concept of parental responsibility that the primary responsibility for the care and upbringing of children rests with their parents and carers;
- given children a voice in proceedings concerning their future;
- set parameters for the involvement of the state in the private lives of families;
- introduced case management for children cases.

But while we have made tremendous progress in promoting the best interests of children through the combined efforts of all those professions involved in the family justice system, our job is not done. This paper will focus on delay, as one of the key challenges facing us in delivering a justice system which actively protects and promotes the human rights of children and their families.

---

[1] BAAF, 1973, quoted by Chris Beckett in (2000) 24(2) *Adoption and Fostering* 55.

Making decisions in a reasonable time-frame

How long do cases take?

When the Children Act 1989 was introduced it was anticipated that public law Children Act cases would be dealt with within 12 weeks. The expectation was that this would allow for the identification of any additional evidence requirements and sufficient time to allow for the guardian ad litem to report on the best interests of the child. No target was set for private law cases at the time, acknowledging that often what both parents need is time to come to terms with the relationship breakdown and to agree a way forward, perhaps through mediation. However, the principle enshrined in the Children Act, and supported by Art 6 of the ECHR, that delay is generally considered to be detrimental to the welfare of children, is just as relevant here.

The public law target was only ever met in the first few months of the Children Act's implementation before courts were dealing with a full workload. After 18 months, cases in the county court were taking 23.2 weeks from application to final order. By 1996 this period had increased so that care cases were taking on average 46.1 weeks – almost a year out of a child's life.

What does the ECHR require?

There is no set formula for determining what constitutes unreasonable delay under Art 6. For example, 3½ years has been held to be an unreasonable period in one ECHR case, and 5 years has been held to be reasonable in another. There is no formula which can be used in advance to determine what is a reasonable time.

However, the European Court of Human Rights has laid down some guiding principles to be considered with the circumstances of each case. The reasonableness of the length of the proceedings is to be considered in the light of:

- the complexity of the case;
- the conduct of the applicant and the other parties;
- the conduct of the relevant authorities; and
- what is at stake for the applicant in the litigation.

Complexity. This can include complexities of both fact and law, the number of parties, the amount of evidence and difficulties in obtaining it. The Court indicated in *Glaser v United Kingdom*[2] that the need to be sure that what was done would not harm the children's welfare meant that careful and proper investigation of their needs had to be carried out. In that case, which began in England and moved to Scotland, the Scottish court was held to have been justified in calling for a fresh report on the children. There have been several cases in which the Commission and Court have accepted the need to obtain reports on the children (but see *Bock v Germany*,[3] below). An additional complexity which the Court acknowledged in *Glaser* (although it could also have come under the heading of the conduct of the parties) was the mother's hostility to contact.

Conduct of the parties. Although only delay by the public authority can amount to a breach, if the applicant has contributed to the delay it may weaken his case. Delay caused by other parties may also be relevant and go towards indicating that the public authority cannot be blamed for the overall length of the proceedings. This is quite likely to arise in disputed children cases: in both *Glaser* and *Hokkanen v Finland*,[4] the party who had been awarded custody failed to comply

---

[2]   [2001] 1 FLR 153.
[3]   [1990] 12 EHRR 247.
[4]   [1994] 19 EHRR 139, [1996] 1 FLR 289.

with orders allowing contact to the applicant. Everyone involved in court proceedings has a responsibility for seeing that they are conducted without delay.

Conduct of the authorities. Courts are expected to be proactive in managing their case-loads to ensure that judgment is given in a reasonable time. Even in legal systems where the conduct of proceedings is in the hands of the parties, the authorities still have a role to play in avoiding delay. The European Court has said that states are under a duty to organise their legal systems so as to comply with Art 6.[5] Excessive workload on the courts is only a defence if temporary and remedial steps are being taken to deal with it. It should be noted, however, that too much activism can be harmful. For example, there was held to be a breach of Art 6 in *Bock v Germany*, where the domestic courts had asked for an unnecessary number of reports on the applicant's mental condition in a divorce case.

What is at stake for the applicant. This is an important factor in Children Act cases, since the Court has said, for example in *Hokkanen v Finland*, and reaffirmed in *Glaser*, that custody and contact cases are among those which must be dealt with particularly speedily. The Court has said the same about cases involving irreversibility, such as adoption (see *H v UK*[6]). On the other hand, the Court in *H v UK* also made the point that this principle can mean that cases should not be rushed if they are important. Because adoption is a far-reaching step which should not be sought hastily, on the facts of *H v UK* the prospective adopters' delay in applying was held to be reasonable, whereas that of the local authority was not. There is a further reason to avoid delay, noted in *H v UK*, which is that it can become so great as to become the deciding factor itself. We are familiar with this principle in child abduction cases, in which once a child is settled with parent A, as a result of delays it may be worse to move him or her, even though originally the court would have preferred residence with parent B.

In *Glaser* there had been nearly 4 years' worth of proceedings in a contact case. The Court held that the case was complex, given the need to avoid stress to the children as a result of the attitude of both the parents. The domestic courts had acted reasonably. Although the presentation of a report on the children and the notification to the applicant of the mother's address could both have been done more quickly, the delay was not outside reasonable bounds. The mother had been unco-operative and the authorities had been right to avoid stringent enforcement measures against her without carefully considering their effect on the children. The applicant's own conduct had contributed to delay. The length of the overall proceedings was not unreasonable in the light of the Court's criteria and the facts of the particular case.

The Booth Report

The time taken on Children Act cases was recognised as a problem 5 years ago, and the then Lord Chancellor, Lord Mackay of Clashfern, asked Dame Margaret Booth to investigate and to make recommendations. In her 1996 report on delay in public law Children Act proceedings, Dame Margaret identified the following factors contributing to delay:[7]

- lack of adequate resources;
- poor administration;
- lax procedures on transfer from the family proceedings courts;
- lack of proper court control in the preparation and management of a case;
- difficulties arising with certain aspects of court procedures, particularly the joinder of too many parties, overuse of experts, late and inadequate discovery and waiting times for assessments.

---

[5] *Zimmermann and Steiner v Switzerland* [1983] 6 EHRR 17.

[6] [1988] 10 EHRR 95.

[7] Dame Margaret Booth DBE, *Delay in Public Law Children Act Cases* (Lord Chancellor's Department, 1996).

The Children Act Advisory Committee, set up to oversee the implementation of the Children Act, sought to address many of these issues in its final report and particularly in its *Handbook of Best Practice*. This Handbook is still in use and many of its principles remain just as relevant to case management today.

But despite the best efforts of all those involved, delay has continued to increase. By 1999 the average time from application to final order in the county court had risen again to 48.8 weeks in public law cases, and at the end of 2000 that figure stood at 50.3 weeks.

Children Act scoping study

In recognition of this increasing problem, the Lord Chancellor initiated a scoping study to look again at the reasons for delay and to assess the need for reform. The study was started last summer, and a draft report has been presented to ministers. The study involved surveying all care centres in the country via their designated family judge. In addition, the senior judiciary and professional associations were consulted as to their views on the causes of delay and potential solutions. Twenty areas of the country were then studied in detail, with visits and telephone interviews conducted with judges, magistrates, local authorities and what are now CAFCASS officers. These areas were selected so as to give a reasonably mixed sample of, for example, urban and rural areas, and courts with long and short disposal times. The small team conducting the survey was impressed by and grateful for the candour and enthusiasm with which people responded to the study.

Since the study was completed there has been the decision of the Court of Appeal in *Re W and B; Re W (Care Plan)* [2001] EWCA Civ 757,[8] which raised questions about practice in public law cases, but which is still the subject of an appeal to the House of Lords. Some of the conclusions reached by the study will need to be re-examined in the light of that decision. Nevertheless, some of the main messages which emerged are unaffected by it, and this conference will enable us to reflect on those messages and to consider how they can best be addressed.

Key messages from the scoping study

The study provided an opportunity to take a fresh look at the current state of delay in the family courts. It found, as did Dame Margaret Booth in 1996, that there is a complex web of problems which is difficult to disentangle, particularly as the solutions to one problem may well exacerbate another. The study demonstrated that all those involved in dealing with public law children's cases had a heightened awareness of delay and the need to move cases along as quickly as is consistent with the best interests of the child. However, the study also found a good deal of consistency with the messages of Dame Margaret Booth's research in the problems identified.

The main areas contributing to delay were found to be:

- the culture which has developed surrounding the use of experts;
- deficiencies in case management;
- inflexibility of jurisdiction leading to problems with judicial availability;
- the need for improved inter-agency communication and co-operation.

In addition there were local concerns about levels of resources.

These are not areas where the Government can provide an answer by itself. It is more concerned with the way various professionals handle cases, than with the content of statutes or

---

[8]   [2001] 2 FLR 582.

rules. Where the Government can help, it is crucial that it does so in partnership with the judiciary, the legal profession, CAFCASS officers, social services professionals and other practitioners. This conference will provide an extremely valuable opportunity to explore these issues.

Use of experts

The most frequently cited cause of delay in the study was the lack of available experts, particularly on mental health issues. The President's Interdisciplinary Committee has also identified this as a major concern, after surveying every care centre in the country to assess the extent of provision and local problems of practice and procedure. Both the scoping study and the work of the President's Committee have revealed that this is not a simple matter of resources failing to meet demand.

There has developed what some have called an 'experts' culture' in Children Act cases. Expert evidence is now seen by many as the norm. This may be because the need in individual cases has not been properly explored or because once one party has an expert, another feels that he needs to follow suit to give his case credibility. In addition, some respondents thought that requesting an expert report was a commonly used delaying tactic. The following can be noted:

- experts are being used to compensate for staff shortages elsewhere, particularly in social services departments;
- a lack of trust in social services' assessment procedures is leading to experts' reports being used to check those processes, duplicating effort and contributing to a lack of confidence in some social workers and CAFCASS officers;
- there is evidence of over-reliance on a handful of particularly well-qualified experts, with less-effective use being made of more junior experts, and problems in recruiting new ones;
- there is a lack of training and awareness among experts who are not regularly used as to what is required in producing evidence for the court;
- instructions given to experts are sometimes unclear and not focused on the particular issue on which the experts' views should be sought;
- poor use is made of experts' time at court, with experts having to wait around with little information on when they are to be called to give evidence and little use being made of conferencing/video links.

Against this background, the recognition of the President's Interdisciplinary Committee that the issue of experts in Children Act cases should be tackled on a broad and interdisciplinary basis is timely. In November 1999 the Committee arranged a day seminar inviting representatives of government departments, the Royal Colleges and professional associations, as well as providers and users of forensic expertise. Following that seminar the Committee organised a survey of all care centres and introduced, in collaboration with the Royal Colleges, a scheme for judges to contribute to the training of specialist registrars in court work. The second meeting of this group was convened in June 2001 and a number of initiatives arising out of the day's work are now being taken forward by the Committee. The meeting brought together key players in this field to identify how to make speedy progress, for example in providing improved training, in ensuring that the need for expert evidence is identified earlier and more precisely, and in encouraging the use of jointly instructed experts wherever possible. Both the Lord Chancellor's Department and the Department of Health will be willing partners in this process of change.

The Law Society's best practice protocol for family cases, which was published in draft for comments over the summer, also encourages better scrutiny of the need for expert evidence. In addition, the Court Service's 'Modernising the Civil Courts' programme, referred to in more detail later in this paper, has recognised the need to ensure that the benefits of courtroom technology are extended to the family area, with particular reference to demands on the time of expert witnesses.

In recognising the potential for delivering change through improved practice, the Government is aware that some effort may still be needed to encourage new recruits as experts and that issues such as remuneration may need to be addressed as part of this process. Officials at the Lord Chancellor's Department and the Department of Health will be looking at these issues alongside the matters of practice and aim to update ministers on the need for further action by the end of the year.

Case management

Dame Margaret Booth identified effective judicial case management as the most crucial element in reducing delay. This message was consistently repeated by those consulted in the course of the scoping study.

The following key principles emerged, which the whole range of agencies within the family justice system identified as essential:

- early identification of the issues to be resolved, not just as part of the case management process within the court, but by all the agencies involved;
- identification by the court at an early stage of what extra information and assessments are needed;
- clearly focused instructions to experts to avoid what have been described as 'rudderless foraging expeditions' or attempts by the parties to buy time;
- setting, maintaining and enforcing realistic and achievable timetables for each case to maintain momentum and avoid delay – this requires the effective use of directions appointments and also requires all agencies, not just the courts, to monitor deadlines and report on progress;
- consistent practice and procedure for handling cases, so that at whatever level and by whichever member of the judiciary cases are handled, the principles above are maintained.

Many courts have developed case management protocols to promote consistent inter-agency working. A good example here is the work of the Northern Circuit Children Act Protocol Group, which has brought together judges, lawyers, magistrates, justices' clerks, local authorities and CAFCASS officers among others to devise a standard protocol to improve the handling of Children Act cases. This draft protocol aims to consolidate and promote a more consistent approach to case management. It recognises the potential benefits of a set of working methods which can form the basis of a best practice guide for all players in children cases who have a responsibility for case management and effective timetabling, and builds on the considerable work already carried out by local courts and committees.

The Lord Chancellor's Department is committing resources to commencing case management pilots early next year which will enable us to evaluate the impact of this protocol and the many other local protocols which are already in existence. One of the key tasks before piloting proposals are finalised will be to synthesise the best elements of these protocols. This will provide the opportunity for independent evaluation of the various protocols and will enable us to extract elements of best practice that build on the key principles which have emerged from the scoping study, and translate them into positive steps for action within case management structures. These could include the staging of cases so that at crucial key points during the timetable specific events occur, such as the early filing of evidence, early case management hearings and timetabling, and the early identification of final hearing dates. The Northern Circuit protocol is due to be finalised shortly, and the next stage will be to plan the content of the pilots and where they will take place. All agencies with an interest will of course be involved and consulted as part of this process.

In addition we are working with district judges, lay magistrates and justices' clerks in family proceedings courts to deal with the specific problems affecting case management in magistrates' courts. A working group has been established to look at issues such as the powers of justices' clerks and ways of minimising the delay caused by the need to provide written reasons. The results of this exercise will be fed into the planned case management pilots.

There is, of course, a close relationship between effective case management in public law Children Act cases and the management of adoption cases involving children in care. The early findings of the scoping study have already been fed into Chapter 8 of the White Paper, *Adoption: a New Approach*[9] which was published in December 2000. The Lord Chancellor is grateful to the President and her Adoption Committee, and in particular its Chairman, Mr Justice Holman, for the work they have undertaken in establishing a nationwide pilot of specialist county court adoption centres well ahead of schedule. The pilots will begin across the country on 1 October 2001, with the London Civil Court Group following on 1 November.

These pilots will ensure that adoption cases are dealt with by specialist judges and staff, and are managed at specialist centres, but will still provide flexibility in terms of where cases are actually heard to ensure that the needs of the parties can adequately be taken into account, for example where there are travel difficulties. The specialist adoption centres will operate case management guidance devised by Mr Justice Holman in consultation with all those involved in adoption cases, including the British Association for Adoption and Fostering. The President of the Family Division has consulted the Family Division liaison judges regarding nominations for an informal ticket for both circuit and district judges to deal with work under the pilots, and the Court Service has arranged preparatory training for the court staff involved.

This is an encouraging example of how effective teamwork across a range of disciplines can lead to changes in practice, in support of better outcomes for children. The pilots will be evaluated by the Lord Chancellor's Department on an ongoing basis, not only in relation to their effectiveness in reducing delay, but also in terms of the views of adoptive families on the standard of services provided throughout the process. We expect that a similar approach will be adopted by magistrates' courts committees in due course.

Inflexibility of jurisdiction

Respondents to the Children Act scoping study identified a shortage of judges as a further factor in delay. However, as with the perceived shortage of expert witnesses, this problem does not necessarily require the appointment of more judges.

Further investigation revealed three key problems:

- the under-use of family proceedings courts;
- an overly limited jurisdiction for district judges in the county court; and
- poor use of judicial 'tickets' in the county court.

Family proceedings courts currently deal with two-thirds of care proceedings, and the low appeal rate[10] suggests that they perform their role effectively in the large majority of cases. However, both the scoping study and the Magistrates' Courts Service Inspectorate's thematic

---

[9] Department of Health, *Adoption: a New Approach* (The Stationery Office, 2000).
[10] Only 12 appeals made in the High Court in 2000 (four were upheld): Lord Chancellor's Department, *Judicial Statistics 2000* (The Stationery Office, 2001).

review of family cases has revealed a good deal of inconsistency in the type of cases handled in family proceedings courts and the transfer rate to the higher courts. Both studies concluded that, to maximise available expertise, family work should probably be concentrated in fewer centres. This might enable longer and more complex cases to be handled in family proceedings courts, alleviating the pressure on the county court. The Lord Chancellor's Department will be reviewing the transfer criteria as part of its work on case management. Any decisions in relation to organisational issues affecting magistrates' courts will need to be made in the light of Lord Justice Auld's review of the criminal justice system.

The scoping study also identified that within county courts there was potential for more cases to be handled by district judges, so freeing up circuit judge time to deal with the more complex cases more quickly. In particular there was a need for an extended private law jurisdiction for district judges to enable them to handle contested private law cases in courts where there was not a constant circuit judge presence. The scope of this extended jurisdiction has now been agreed, and it is expected that the nominations for this extended role will be finalised in October 2001 and that the arrangements will be in place by the end of the year.

Ticketing is not only an issue in relation to district judges. Dealing with public law cases is stressful work. The scoping study found examples of some judges facing an unrelenting diet of child abuse cases, while others with family tickets did little if any such work. A frequent criticism by judges themselves is that too many tickets are held by judges who do not necessarily use them. This gives a false picture of the number of judges actually available for family work and so hinders effective resource planning. The awarding and removal of tickets can be handled effectively only through a partnership between the senior judiciary and the Court Service. The President of the Family Division is considering options as to recommended minimum and maximum levels of family work for ticketed family judges to ensure that the right balance is achieved between maintaining expertise in family cases, providing judges with a varied diet, and retaining flexibility in the system. The Court Service is also committed to providing the senior judiciary with better information on the way tickets are used.

Interdisciplinary working

This paper has set out the major factors contributing to delay, and some of the initiatives the Government is taking forward to tackle them. However, the examples given demonstrate clearly that none of these initiatives will work without effective inter-agency communication and co-operation. Good interdisciplinary working is vital to the success of any measures to reduce delay and vital to the welfare of the very vulnerable children within the system.

The White Paper on adoption made clear the Government's commitment to establishing a national mechanism to identify problems in practice and procedure, to devise solutions and to disseminate best practice. Ministers are considering the possibility of consultation on a new model for an interdisciplinary support structure which will build as far as possible on existing mechanisms, support effective inter-agency working and promote best practice and consistency.

It must be recognised that the courts are only one part of a much wider, end-to-end process. There is a need for all those involved in that process to strive to produce and maintain a balanced system in which there are shared aims, mutual trust, confidence and openness of communication in interdisciplinary working between the various key players within the family justice system.

Resources

In identifying the practical issues which need to be resolved to tackle delay the Government does not ignore the fact that resources play their part. However, this is not a straightforward matter. As will be clear from the examples given elsewhere in this paper, there are also issues about how the inevitably limited resources available are best used, for example to ensure that judges are deployed effectively and that we make the best use of expert witnesses' time.

In addition we recognise that we need to work together more effectively with the Department of Health and local authorities in deciding how best to identify changes in workload. We also need to ensure that IT systems support judges and staff in managing cases and that these systems facilitate rather than work against effective inter-agency communication. The Court Service is integrating these issues into its 'Modernising the Civil Courts' programme. In relation to family work, the programme will focus on technology which addresses case management needs and which improves workflow and case progression.

As part of the project, a judicial working group was established to identify from a judicial viewpoint the major defects in the present system and what changes would be needed to remedy these and modernise the system effectively. The report of the working group was published in August and circulated to civil and family judges, and its recommendations will be taken into account in the final project report which is to be completed shortly. Consultation has also taken place with a wide range of practitioners and professionals.

Members of the judiciary will continue to be fully involved in the implementation of the modernisation programme not only through formal advisory structures, but also through membership of the Courts and Tribunals Modernisation Programme Board and other project boards and teams. The Court Service also plans to set up a family advisory board to enable the interests of external stakeholders to be reflected in the implementation arrangements.

CAFCASS

The establishment of CAFCASS in April this year creates a new national body with a national voice, which will give the opportunity to provide an improved, consistent and timely service for all children in the family courts. By bringing together the three different services in one national service it also has the potential to become a more effective champion for children involved in family proceedings. The role of CAFCASS and the challenges of the early days of the new service will be looked at in greater detail in the paper by the Chairman of CAFCASS, Anthony Hewson.

To help the new service in meeting these aims and reducing delay, a group of CAFCASS managers and staff has been established, including a Board member, to develop new national standards to be introduced in 2002, which will establish targets to minimise delay across the spectrum of the court process. CAFCASS will consult widely on early drafts of the new standards. In the meantime, CAFCASS staff will be expected to continue to maintain the standards that were in place previously both for public and private law cases.

Conclusion

The Children Act 1989 is a significant means by which the human rights of children and their families are protected. Other jurisdictions recognise this, and regularly ask for information on the operation of the system in England and Wales so that its key messages can be replicated. The Act, and the procedures, commitment and professionalism which have accompanied it, are a credit to all who work in this area. The implementation of the Human Rights Act 1998 has raised the profile of children's rights, and case-law is developing these rights and our understanding of how best to protect them.

However, we cannot be complacent. In the area of delay particularly we face a challenge we have yet to conquer. It is only through working together that we can tackle the complexity of causes of delay, and this conference provides a significant step along that route.

PLENARY TWO

CHILDREN'S RIGHTS AND THE IMPACT OF TWO INTERNATIONAL CONVENTIONS: THE UNCRC AND THE ECHR

Jane Fortin
Reader in Law, Kings College, London

Summary of paper

Jane Fortin stated that with her paper she could only really scratch the surface of two enormously important international documents, the United Nations Convention on the Rights of the Child (UNCRC) and the European Convention on Human Rights and Fundamental Freedoms (ECHR).

The Conventions had come into being in very different circumstances: the UNCRC was designed to cater for the special needs and vulnerabilities of children, whereas the ECHR was drafted in the aftermath of a major world war, to protect citizens from over-mighty governments. She believed both to be very important in promoting and protecting children's rights. However, the practical use of the UNCRC is limited by it having no direct means of enforcement.

Jane Fortin considered that the ECHR, although on its face not seeming to be a very useful document for children, has been shown in its application by the courts to be an effective and imaginative tool in upholding children's rights. However, she had the following particular concerns about the ability of the ECHR to protect children's rights.

In cases where parents are seeking to take their children back from foster parents, Article 8 of the ECHR could be used to strengthen parents' arguments for return. The courts could find such arguments very difficult to resist.

In claims between adults and teenagers, she hoped that teenagers would bring claims under the ECHR to prevent for example savage discipline by their parents, or their being forced to accept decisions as to religion and education. However, there was very little European case-law on how to reconcile these kinds of children's rights with those of their parents. Jane Fortin felt that this was a wonderful opportunity for the courts to encourage more liberal parenting styles, and that the judiciary should not use Nielsen v Denmark to prevent children from making claims against authoritarian parents.

She would like the courts to retain the ability to force very ill adolescents to undergo life-saving treatment against their will if necessary, but was concerned about how this could be done without infringing their Article 5 rights. In her paper she suggested a way round this, but she was not at all sure that it would work in practice.

Introduction

The Children Act 1989 has undoubtedly had a major impact on the legal principles governing children and families over the 10 years since it was introduced. But it was drafted at a time when the notion of children possessing rights was in its infancy, with the implications of the *Gillick*[1] decision still being slowly digested by academics and the judiciary. By then the work of

---

[1] *Gillick v West Norfolk and Wisbech Area Health Authority and Another* [1986] AC 112, [1986] 1 FLR 224.

the international human rights lawyers, on behalf of children as a group, had not been widely publicised. Relatively few challenges utilising the European Convention for the Protection of Human Rights and Fundamental Freedoms 1950 (ECHR) in favour of children had gone to the European Court of Human Rights.[2] Furthermore, what was to become the United Nations Convention on the Rights of the Child (UNCRC) was still undergoing its decade of drafting and its predecessor, the Declaration of the Rights of the Child 1959, was already very outdated.[3] Given this historical background, it is perhaps not surprising that there was no reference to the concept of children's rights in the 1988 Law Commission's report explaining the reforms it was then recommending, later enacted by the 1989 Act.[4] Since then, more than a decade has elapsed and the importance of children's rights is now widely acknowledged, largely provoked by the need to comply with two important international conventions, the UNCRC and the ECHR.

By the time the Children Bill was drafted, the new UNCRC was nearly complete. Indeed, by a strange coincidence, the progress of the two documents, the UNCRC and the Children Act 1989, marched in parallel. Only a month before the Children Bill was introduced into Parliament in December 1988, the United Nations adopted the UNCRC. The United Kingdom finally ratified the Convention, in December 1991, only 3 months after implementation of the Children Act 1989. Its ratification signalled recognition by the Government that children, as a group, now merited international human rights protection.

Although the two documents, the 1989 Act and the UNCRC, made their debut within months of each other, they were and remain entirely different animals. The 1989 Act makes no pretence of being a code that covers all aspects of children's lives. Meanwhile, the UNCRC contains a long list of 42 substantive rights covering the broad spectrum of children's needs and aspirations. Included are the traditional civil and political rights, such as the right to freedom of expression and religion, and also children's social welfare rights, such as a right to good health care. In the years since its introduction it has become enormously influential, having been ratified by every country in the world, bar the United States and Somalia. The European Commission and Court of Human Rights have increasingly referred to its provisions as being of persuasive authority when reaching their decisions.[5] Equally, the domestic courts have become increasingly confident in referring to its terms to support their decisions.[6]

Since its introduction, we have discovered far more about the way the UNCRC should be interpreted. This knowledge is gained from the reporting process and the activities of the UN Committee on the Rights of the Child. Unlike the ECHR, the UNCRC has no direct means of enforcement; there is no international court to which individual petitioners can complain if their rights are infringed. Countries ratifying the Convention are merely expected to implement its provisions, but are encouraged to do so by their obligation to submit reports to the Committee on the Rights of the Child indicating the progress they are making. The Committee responds to these reports with its own 'Concluding Observations' and it is through the accumulating body of these international responses that the Committee has gradually clarified how the Convention should be interpreted.[7]

At first sight, the UNCRC appears to be a long list of bewilderingly different types of rights, with some, like article 12, reflecting clear philosophical views about children's capacity for autonomy, and others, like article 28, descending into the practical details of children's schooling. Although the UN Committee on the Rights of the Child has stressed that all the articles are inter-related, it has itself elevated 4 articles to the status of general principles, deemed to underwrite the remainder of the Convention. These are: article 2, freedom from

---

[2]   This Convention entered into force in 1953.

[3]   As noted by Thorpe LJ in *Re A (Children: 1959 UN Declaration)* [1998] 1 FLR 354, at p 358.

[4]   *Family Law Review of Child Law Guardianship and Custody*, HC 594 (HMSO, 1988) Law Com No 172.

[5]   Eg *Costello-Roberts v United Kingdom* (1995) 19 EHHR 112, at para [35].

[6]   Eg *Re H (Paternity: Blood Test)* [1996] 2 FLR 65, at p 80, per Ward LJ.

[7]   See P Newell and R Hodgkin (eds), *Implementation Handbook for the Convention on the Rights of the Child* (UNICEF, 1998).

discrimination; article 3, the child's best interests; article 6, the right to life; and article 12, the right to respect for the child's views. It is worth noting that unlike section 1 of the Children Act 1989, article 3 does not make the child's best interests paramount, stating only that it is 'a primary consideration'. Furthermore, article 12 is not about giving children complete autonomy, but giving them the right to express their views, those views being given due weight in accordance with the child's age and maturity.

Although the domestic courts are becoming more adept at referring to certain articles in the UNCRC,[8] many of its articles remain neglected. Perhaps this is because the UNCRC is most well known for the way it urges governments to improve the living conditions of children generally. But the Convention is also an important tool in the context of private family life. It attempts, for example, to find an appropriate balance between maintaining a respect for the parental role, including parents' need for authority over their children, whilst also promoting children's capacity for eventual autonomy. Thus, whilst article 5 respects the parents' right to direct and guide their children, in a manner consistent with their evolving capacities, articles 12, 13 and 14 refer to the child's right to be consulted, to freedom of expression and to freedom of religion. Although there is an obvious tension between these provisions, which may, at times, pull in opposing directions,[9] the Convention acknowledges the need to provide some guidance on the child–parent relationship. The drafting of the Children (Scotland) Act 1995, coming as it did after the ratification of the UNCRC, reflects some of these provisions.[10] Unlike its English equivalent, sections 1 and 2 specify what rights and responsibilities parents have in relation to their children, including the right and duty 'to control, direct or guide them' in a manner appropriate to their stage of development.[11] Furthermore, responding to the requirements of article 12 of the UNCRC, section 6 of the 1995 Act requires parents to consult their children over any major decision involving their upbringing, and presumes that once a child reaches 12, he or she will be sufficiently mature to form a view. The English Children Act 1989 would be improved if it incorporated similar provisions.

It was hoped that the obligation on ratifying countries to produce periodic reports to the UN Committee and the knowledge that they would be subjected to criticisms would encourage states to implement the UNCRC effectively. Countries are expected to be candid over any difficulties they have in reaching the standards required. Unfortunately, the overall impression created by the UK's first[12] and second reports to the Committee on the Rights of the Child is that the Government is relatively untroubled by fear of criticism by the UN Committee.[13] A cynic might argue that a casual approach to the UNCRC will continue until there are improved enforcement procedures. Its lack of teeth means that, in reality, it is legally unenforceable. Its impact would be strengthened significantly were enforcement procedures to be grafted on to it. This would bring the UNCRC in line with the African Charter on the Rights and Welfare of the Child, which incorporates the right of individual petition for all children. Many also consider that the Government should stop dragging its feet over establishing a post of Children's Commissioner for this country. One of his or her tasks would be to promote children's rights and ensure that Convention infringements were investigated and remedied.

Unlike the UNCRC, a lack of an effective enforcement procedure has never hampered the impact of the ECHR. That Convention quickly became immensely influential, largely because it was the first international instrument of its kind to provide a mechanism for its own interpretation and enforcement. The existence of a Commission and Court to adjudicate on

---

[8]   Eg article 7.

[9]   See J Fortin, *Children's Rights and the Developing Law* (Butterworths, 1998), at pp 41–43.

[10]   See *Report on Family Law* (Scot Law Com No 135) (HMSO, 1992), at pp 1–12.

[11]   *Cf* Children Act 1989, s 3.

[12]   Described as being 'dishonest by omission ... without adequate recognition of gaps, inconsistencies and blatant breaches': *The UK Agenda for Children* (Children's Rights Development Unit, 1994), at p xii.

[13]   See the critical form of the *Concluding Observations of the Committee on the Rights of the Child: United Kingdom of Great Britain and Northern Ireland*, CRC/C/15/Add 34 (Centre for Human Rights, Geneva, 1995).

individual petitions rapidly enhanced the Convention's reputation for being one of the world's foremost human rights instruments. Although, by the late 1980s, there was still relatively little Convention case-law involving children, the draftsmen of the Children Act 1989 were well aware of the need to take account of the Strasbourg jurisprudence on the Convention's interpretation.[14] Now, more than a decade later, the case-law has accumulated fast. More significantly, the Human Rights Act 1998 (HRA) has now incorporated the ECHR into English law, giving family and child lawyers a chance to reassess not only the principles established by the Children Act 1989, but also the accrued body of case-law, laid down by generations of judges.

The Court of Appeal's recent decision in *Re W and B; Re W (Care Plan)* [2001] EWCA Civ 757[15] fully substantiates most commentators' view that the HRA would have a radical effect on the principles of law governing children and families. That decision demonstrates that the ECHR can be used creatively to reinterpret legislation fairly radically without waiting for Parliament to introduce amendments to achieve the desired effect. It shows the Court of Appeal avoiding the deliberate intention of the Children Act 1989, which was to maintain a clear division of powers between the courts and local authorities regarding children in care. More particularly, the courts can now read into the legislation a power to intervene in those cases where a local authority has fundamentally failed properly or effectively to pursue a care plan in relation to a child in care, thereby risking an infringement of the child's own rights to a secure family life under article 8.[16]

Although I never doubted that the HRA would have a major impact on the course of the legal system, alongside many others I had severe misgivings about the ability of the ECHR to promote the concept of children's rights particularly effectively.[17] Its limitations are obvious. Unlike the 42 substantive rights spanning children's lives contained in the UNCRC, the ECHR contains a short list of civil and political rights. These make no obvious concessions to the special nature of childhood, nor attempt to protect children's rights, as distinct from those of adults. In particular, none of the articles contain any reference to the best interests principle which underlies most child care legislation throughout the world.

Now that the HRA is implemented, the emerging case-law has shown that some of these concerns were exaggerated. In any event, it was perhaps being slightly unfair to the European Commission and Court for commentators like myself not to give them full credit for their work. Particularly over the last decade, they have interpreted the ECHR in an astonishingly flexible way to accommodate children's special needs. Unlike the UNCRC, the ECHR will never persuade governments to improve children's social and economic rights generally. Nevertheless, one must concede that an imaginative treatment of its awkwardly worded articles has produced remarkably effective, though narrow, forms of protection for children.

It is unlikely, for example, that the draftsmen of the Convention ever considered the need to prevent parental child abuse. Nevertheless, through a combination of articles 2, 3 and 8, it now imposes an obligation on welfare authorities to protect children from abusive treatment.[18] Article 6 ensures that the procedures for dealing with parents and children involved in private and public proceedings are fair.[19] Through a broad interpretation of article 8, the relationships between children and unmarried, as well as married, parents are protected.[20] Equally, despite the absence of a specific reference to procedural fairness within its wording, the European

---

[14]   Eg the decision in *W (and R, O, B and H) v United Kingdom* (1987) 10 EHRR 29 led to the abolition of local authorities' power to pass parental rights resolutions.

[15]   [2001] 2 FLR 582.

[16]   Ibid, at para [79], per Hale LJ.

[17]   See J Fortin, 'Rights Brought Home for Children' (1999) 62 MLR 350; and J Herring, 'The Human Rights Act and the Welfare Principle in Family Law – Conflicting or Complementary?' [1999] CFLQ 223.

[18]   See *X and Y v The Netherlands* (1985) 8 EHRR 235; and *Z and Others v United Kingdom* [2001] 2 FLR 612.

[19]   Eg *Elsholz v Germany* [2000] 2 FLR 486; and *McMichael v United Kingdom* (1995) 20 EHRR 205.

[20]   Eg *Marckx v Belgium* (1979) 2 EHRR 330.

Court asserted that article 8 guarantees fairness in any procedures infringing family life.[21] It even secures for children the right to obtain any information about themselves, held by public agencies, which enables them to know and understand their childhood and early development.[22]

The ECHR's ability to promote children's rights has also been immeasurably strengthened through the notion of positive obligations attaching to many of its provisions.[23] These not only compel states to abstain from interfering with the rights they protect, they require them to take active steps to secure these rights effectively. States must not, therefore, merely refrain from the intentional and unlawful killing of a child under article 2, they must also take appropriate steps to safeguard his or her life.[24] State agencies, such as social service departments, must also fulfil their positive obligations under article 3 to protect children effectively from abusive parental behaviour amounting to inhuman or degrading treatment.[25] They must not stand back and allow abuse to continue once they are aware of it. Article 8 also carries positive obligations.[26] The courts themselves, as public authorities, are under a positive obligation to intervene on a child's behalf, if, as in *Re W and B; Re W (Care Plan)* [2001] EWCA Civ 757,[27] a local authority is infringing the child's own rights to a secure family life under article 8.

Even the absence of the best interests formula had been dealt with reasonably effectively by the time the HRA was implemented in October 2000. The Strasbourg institutions had very obviously taken full account of the widespread commitment amongst European countries to this criterion. Their response was to formulate a way of accommodating the criterion within the terms of article 8.[28] As the Court of Appeal has itself noted,[29] private disputes can be dealt with in a way which is fully consistent with the requirements of section 1 of the Children Act 1989. A court can justify infringing a parent's rights to family life by reference to article 8(2), supported by evidence regarding the child's own rights and by issues revolving around his or her welfare.

The Strasbourg institutions responded in a similar vein when dealing with parents' complaints about the actions of welfare agencies in removing their children from their care. Starting with its decision in *Johansen v Norway*,[30] the European Court repeatedly stressed the crucial importance attaching to the best interests of the child, which, depending on their nature and seriousness, could override those of the parent.[31] This case-law enables the domestic courts to deal very effectively with parents' challenges in public law cases. They can now achieve an identical outcome to that obtained under the Children Act 1989 prior to October 2000, but with the reasoning and language used in their judgments complying with Convention requirements. A decision should maintain a satisfactory balance between the needs of the parents and of the child and ensure that the intervention is proportionate to its legitimate aim – so giving the impression that the exclusivity of children's rights has disappeared.[32]

One might assume from these comments that I am now reasonably confident that the ECHR can promote children's rights very effectively. It certainly provides an extremely valuable tool for enabling the courts to reassess the principles of case-law and legislation governing children and their families. Nevertheless, I retain serious reservations and will refer to some of these briefly, in the hope that you will consider them and produce your own views in response.

---

[21]   *W (and R, O, B and H) v United Kingdom* (1987) 10 EHRR 29.

[22]   *Gaskin v United Kingdom* (1989) 12 EHRR 36, sub nom *The Gaskin Case* [1990] 1 FLR 167.

[23]   See U Kilkelly, *The Child and the European Convention on Human Rights* (Ashgate, 1999), esp pp 12–13.

[24]   *Osman v United Kingdom* [1999] 1 FLR 193, at para [115].

[25]   See *Z and Others v United Kingdom* [2001] 2 FLR 612, at para [74].

[26]   *Marckx v Belgium* (1979) 2 EHRR 330.

[27]   [2001] 2 FLR 582.

[28]   Eg in *Hoffmann v Austria* (1993) 17 EHRR 293; and *Glaser v United Kingdom* [2001] 1 FLR 153.

[29]   *Payne v Payne* [2001] EWCA Civ 166, [2001] 1 FLR 1052.

[30]   (1997) 23 EHRR 33.

[31]   Ibid, at para [78]. See also *Scott v United Kingdom* [2000] 1 FLR 958, at p 968.

[32]   See, eg the language used by Hale LJ in *Re C and B (Care Order: Future Harm)* [2000] 1 FLR 611, at paras [33] and [34].

The first relates to the important evidential differences between the requirements of the European Convention and the paramountcy principle established by the Children Act 1989. As Herring points out, under the Children Act 1989 the starting point in a parental dispute was to determine any dispute in a way which fulfilled the child's best interests.[33] Now, the starting point may be a parent's claim that the proposed order would infringe (or fulfil) his own article 8 rights. If maintainable, this will effectively trump everyone else's claim, unless and until the order can be justified under article 8(2). Although the outcome will often be the same, there is a risk that such arguments may start revitalising outdated notions of parents' rights and powers over their children. This would undermine the Children Act's efforts to promote a more liberal approach to the parent–child relationship by employing the term 'parental responsibilities'. Will this difference of approach, for example, affect the outcome of disputes between birth parents and third parties – over whether a child should return to a birth parent or remain in the care of a relative or foster carer? Will it reinforce what amounts to a presumption in favour of birth parents, thereby increasing the evidential difficulties of their opponents, possibly at the expense of the child, who may be thriving in his or her new home?[34]

A further concern is that, unlike the UNCRC, the ECHR contains no guidance on how to reconcile parents' rights to freedom from state interference, with children's own rights to fulfil their potential and to develop a degree of independence from their parents as they mature into adulthood.[35] Even taking account of the case-law on corporal punishment,[36] there is no Convention article or decision which protects children adequately from repressive parents. The wording of article 8 suggests that family privacy ensures happiness for its members and that family regulation can be safely entrusted to parents. Whilst family privacy may protect brutal and bullying parents, an adolescent may need disciplining. How, for example, will the domestic courts deal with a father's claim that, by refusing to return his runaway teenage daughter home, by force, if necessary, the social services department is infringing his own article 8 rights? Note that Convention case-law is ambivalent about recognising the child's own right to privacy, as opposed to that of his or her parents.[37]

At first sight, one might have assumed that teenagers with authoritarian parents would gain assistance from article 5 of the ECHR, in so far as it appears to provide children, like adults, with protection against deprivation of liberty. Nevertheless, the decision of the European Court of Human Rights in *Nielsen v Denmark*[38] confuses matters since it suggests that all parental decisions reached for 'a proper purpose' over how their children spend their time are protected by article 8 and are therefore completely outside the ambit of article 5 of the ECHR.[39] The European Court did not clarify the boundaries between parents' rights to family privacy and autonomy under article 8 and children's rights to freedom from unreasonable restrictions under article 5.

---

[33] J Herring, 'The Human Rights Act and the Welfare Principle in Family Law – Conflicting or Complementary?' [1999] CFLQ 223, at p 231. See also J Fortin, 'The HRA's impact on litigation involving children and their families' [1999] CFLQ 237, at p 253.

[34] See discussed more fully in J Fortin, '*Re D (Care: Natural Parent Presumption)* Is blood really thicker than water?' [1999] CFLQ 435. Note also Munby J's view in *Re X and Y (Leave to Remove from the Jurisdiction: No Order Principle)* [2001] 2 FLR 118 that all presumptions in family proceedings are ruled out by s 1(5) of the Children Act 1989.

[35] Discussed more fully at n 9 above, pp 357–359.

[36] Eg *A v United Kingdom (Human Rights: Punishment of Child)* [1998] 2 FLR 959.

[37] *X v Netherlands* (1974) (Application No 6753/74) (1975–76) 1–3 DR 118, in which the European Commission dismissed the complaints of a 14-year-old Dutch runaway that her rights under article 8 had been infringed by the welfare authorities returning her home unwillingly. Such action was justified to protect her health and morals under article 8(2). But see *X v Denmark* (1978) (Application No 6854/74) (1977–78) 7–9 DR 81, in which the European Commission rejected the claim that the Danish welfare authorities had infringed the parents' rights under article 8 by refusing to force their 14-year-old daughter to return home against her will.

[38] (1989) 11 EHRR 175.

[39] Ibid, at para [69].

The *obiter* remarks of Judge LJ and Butler-Sloss P in *Re K (Secure Accommodation Order: Right to Liberty)*[40] suggest that the domestic courts will not hesitate to withdraw article 8 protection from parents who behave in an outrageously over-authoritarian manner. But what of the father who claims that it is perfectly reasonable to lock his teenage daughter into her bedroom every evening to prevent her joining her 'unsuitable friends'? Would a court consider that such behaviour falls within 'ordinary acceptable parental restrictions upon the movements of a child',[41] and therefore outside the ambit of the girl's own article 5 rights?

Finally, what of the intelligent adolescent who refuses to undergo life-saving treatment? I would oppose the courts losing their ability to force unwanted life-saving treatment on minor patients.[42] But how is a court to gain its authority to force such a patient to undergo medical treatment without itself infringing article 5? A court might perhaps argue that since a minor's rights under the Convention sometimes inevitably conflict, notably his or her rights under articles 2 and 5, it is entitled to find an appropriate balance between them. Furthermore, since article 2 imposes a positive obligation on all public authorities, including the courts, to take all reasonable steps to preserve life,[43] the court cannot ignore its duty to save the life of a desperately ill adolescent.[44]

It is difficult to do full justice to the UNCRC and the ECHR – two enormously important international human rights documents which promote the rights of British children in very different ways. Despite its weak enforcement mechanism, the UNCRC remains the Convention which will nudge the Government into ensuring that children's lives are improved by better services. Now that the ECHR has become part of domestic law, it may have a more practical and immediate impact on the legal principles applying to individual children on an everyday basis. Both Conventions enhance children's chances of being treated as individuals, with rights of their own.

---

[40]   [2001] 1 FLR 526.

[41]   Ibid, at para [28], per Dame Elizabeth Butler-Sloss P.

[42]   *Re R (A Minor) (Wardship: Medical Treatment)* [1991] 4 All ER 177, [1992] 1 FLR 190; and *Re W (A Minor) (Medical Treatment)* [1992] 4 All ER 627, sub nom *Re W (A Minor) (Consent to Medical Treatment)* [1993] 1 FLR 1.

[43]   *Osman v UK* [1999] 1 FLR 193, at paras [115]–[116].

[44]   See discussed more fully in J Fortin, 'Children's rights and the use of physical force' [2001] CFLQ (forthcoming).

INTERFACE OF CHILDREN INVOLVED IN CRIMINAL MATTERS. VULNERABLE AND A RISK TO OTHERS – THE DOUBLE CHALLENGE

Dr Susan Bailey
Gardner Unit, Manchester

Summary of paper

Dr Bailey stated that with her paper she was seeking to bring some practice reality. The mental health, welfare and legal rights of young offenders were to be set in the context of what was known of the demographics and the service responses of the jurisdictions of health, justice, care and education to the needs of every child in our society. The issues she particularly wished to highlight were the following:

- *More resources should be put into the youth justice system, particularly in developing a proper, mental health based screening process for young offenders. Twenty-six per cent of those in secure accommodation had significant learning difficulties and she queried why they were entering the system at all.*
- *The use of secure accommodation orders for girls intent on self-destruction, who proceeded to carry out such self-destruction when in secure accommodation, was a concern. She felt that there was a need for gender sensitive, intensive community services.*
- *She welcomed the availability of district judges in youth courts, thus preventing some cases from having to go to the Crown Court. She felt that all young defendants, including those charged with serious offences, should be tried in youth courts (with permission for adult sanctions for older youths if certain conditions were met), thus enabling a mode of trial for young defendants to be subject to safeguards which can enhance understanding and participation.*
- *She considered that the maturity of young defendants should be assessed before a decision was made as to the venue and mode of trial for their offence. At present she was aware of very different practices across the country.*
- *Recruitment to medical schools could still take place without representation by psychiatrists at selection interviews. Recruitment and retention in psychiatry, and child and adolescent psychiatry in particular, was difficult. In some areas of the country there were no child psychiatrists in post and everywhere else child psychiatrists were overloaded with competing priorities arising from sheer weight of referrals and recent Government initiatives.*
- *Experts sometimes found the court process intimidating. She encouraged schemes such as those involving experts training with judges to improve this situation. She referred to three initiatives which the Royal College of Psychiatrists were taking forward:*

  - *to continue and build on the excellent training for Children Act proceedings provided by clinicians such as Dr Sturge;*
  - *through a Department of Health grant, to offer consultant child and adolescent psychiatrists section 12 approval training, shaped to their work with adolescents;*

        – to develop adolescent forensic mental health training to assist child psychiatrists asked to work with young offenders, with pilot training now in Salford and at the Maudsley Hospital.

- *In the family justice system, the solicitors who represented children had specialist training and were on childcare panels. She queried why this was not the same for those representing juveniles in the criminal justice system, some of whom in her view had little understanding of their young clients.*
- *She had grave concerns about the new Mental Health Act, particularly the scope of the Act which could cover any mental disorder, including conduct disorder and ADHD.*
- *She felt that there was much work to be done but that the opportunity to share thoughts and ideas at such events as this Conference formed sure foundations for effective delivery of care and justice in the future.*

Introduction

Since 1997, in England and Wales a new era of youth justice is now in place. The creation of multi-professional youth offending teams in every local authority has changed the face of youth justice procedures. The introduction of detention and training orders, parenting orders and child safety orders should have meant a reduced time in custody for established young offenders and an alternative option for courts for those just starting their criminal career. At the time of writing all forms of secure accommodation, whether detention (secure) training centres (D(S)TCs), local authority secure care beds commissioned by the Youth Justice Board, and young offender institutions are full, with huge pressure on the system to find appropriate beds for those with 'vulnerability'.

There is still, again at the time of writing, no national strategic framework for the equitable development of specialist adolescent forensic mental health teams and needs-led inpatient bed provision. The Youth Justice Board has been charged with the formidable task of tackling and reducing youth crime. Its recent focus, working with the Department of Health on physical and mental health issues, has to be welcomed. All these initiatives should be thought through in terms of the implications for the working of the diverse legal frameworks: the Children Act, the Mental Health Act (current and future), the Crime and Disorder Act, the common law and the inherent jurisdiction, and now the Human Rights Act 1998. The risk is that service provision could be led by legal test cases, eg instead of holistic, child-centred approach to 'children' who are also young offenders.

Context

The mental health, welfare and legal rights of young offenders must be set in the context of what we know of the demographics and the service responses of the jurisdictions of health, justice, care and education to the needs of each and every child in our society (Bailey, 2000).

Population figures

Children and teenagers make up one-quarter of the 56.8 million population of the United Kingdom, a similar percentage to other European countries (Coleman and Schofield, 2001). Six-and-a-half per cent of the population comes from an ethnic minority background, but there are wide variations in the age distribution of different populations. This is most marked in the Pakistani/Bangladeshi group where 37% of the population is under 16, as compared, for instance, with 20% in the white community. Such figures clearly have considerable significance for education and family life.

Family composition

Changes in family composition between 1971 and 1999 have been dramatic. The number of couple families with 'dependent' children (up to the age of 16) has decreased from 92% to 75% during this period. There has been a concomitant increase in families headed by a lone parent from 8% to 25% of all families over this time-span. This represents a major social change, that must have implications for child care, the welfare state, legal systems and indeed the very nature of parenthood. A common assumption is that the greatest number of the lone parents are teenage parents. This is far from the case. Only 14% of all lone mothers fall in the 16–24-year age group, while there are hardly any lone fathers under the age of 30.

Children and young people in care/looked after

Children and young people looked after by local authorities are a significant minority, recognised as vulnerable. From 62,000 in 1989, the number went down to 49,000 in 1994, but has now risen to 58,000. The increase cannot be explained by social workers being tougher and seeking more care orders. Coleman (2000) suggests it is to do with wider changes in society, in particular higher levels of poverty and deprivation.

Boys have always outnumbered girls in this group. The snapshot study (DOH, 1999) of age distribution of children and young people being looked after in England in 1999 showed that by far the greatest number are in the 10–15-year age group, but this type of study masks the rapid throughput which is more heavily weighted towards younger children. In comparison with other ages, teenagers are more likely to be placed in residential care.

Education

Of the total exclusion in 1998/99, 83% were from secondary schools, and 13% from primary schools; 83% of exclusions are male, reflecting the preponderance of boys involved in antisocial and challenging behaviour. Exclusion rates for white pupils was 0.15%, and the rate for black Caribbean pupils was 0.58%. Gender differences are similar across ethnic groups, with girls doing better in every cultural group.

Health of young people

Particular groups of young people whose health is problematic include those growing up in poverty, those in public care and those in custody. Apart from infancy, death rates among children and adolescents are highest in the 15–19-year age group, primarily because of increase in injury, poisoning and transport accidents.

Studies such as those of McCann et al (1996) have shown high rates of classifiable mental health problems in young people in residential care (see Table 1).

Table 1: Prevalence of psychiatric disorders among adolescents in the care system

	% In care	% Controls
Prevalence rate of disorder	67	15
Conduct disorder	28	0
Anxiety disorder	26	3
Major depressive disorder	23	3
ADHD	14	2
Functional psychosis	8	0

(Source: McCann et al, 1996)

The Office for National Statistics Study of 10,000 children and adolescents in Great Britain (Meltzer et al, 2000) showed that emotional disorders are higher in girls, whilst conduct disorder is substantially higher in boys. Rates of disorder are higher among black young people and very much lower among Indian adolescents. Disorders are distributed across social class categories reaching rates of over 25% in 11–15 year olds whose family social class rests in the 'never' worked category.

Attempted and completed suicide

In the United Kingdom as a whole, 571 young men between the ages of 15 and 24 took their own lives in 1998. Of these, 83 were in Scotland, and 461 in England and Wales. The numbers of suicides and undetermined deaths increase steadily during the adolescent years but there are still a significant number of 16 year olds taking their own lives (Kelly and Bunting, 1998). Hawton's Study (2000) shows that the numbers of young men and young women who attempt suicide and are referred to hospital varied considerably between 1985 and 1995. However, there has been a moderate increase in both genders and the gender differential remains as it was in 1985. Kerfoot (1996) reports a ratio of 4:1 girls to boys.

The nature of young offenders

Delinquency, conduct problems and aggression all refer to antisocial behaviours that reflect a failure of the individual to conform his or her behaviour to the expectations of some authority figure, to societal norms, or to respect the rights of other people. The 'behaviours' can range from mild conflicts with authority figures, major violation of societal norms, to serious violations of the rights of others (Frick, 1998). The term 'delinquency' implies that the acts could result in conviction, although most do not do so. The term 'juvenile' usually applies to the age range extending from a lower age set by the age of criminal responsibility, and an upper age when a young person can be dealt with in courts for adult crimes. These ages vary between, and indeed within, counties and are not the same for all offences (Justice, 1996; Cavadino and Allen, 2000).

The need to control a small group of very persistent, recalcitrant children is perennial. Specific methods have been available since at least the eighteenth century (Hagell, Hazel and Shaw, 2000). In the eighteenth and nineteenth centuries children were seldom distinguished from adults and were placed with adults in prison. In the England of 1823, boys as young as 9 were held in solitary confinement for their own protection in ships retired from the Battle of Trafalgar. In the nineteenth century, legislation regarding children's rights was tied into the need for labour. There have been periodic reactions against convicting, imprisoning and punishing young people. The pioneers who sought to rescue both young offenders and those children offended against, provided the beginnings of youth justice, care and child protection. Both community and secure residential innovations in youth justice have been characterised by a pattern of reforming zeal, followed by gradual disappointment fuelled by the results of research evaluations.

Of relevance to multi-agency treatment responses is the emerging pattern of persistent offenders displaying more educational problems, a lack of social integration, more disruptive family backgrounds, experience of institutional care and a group that is more likely to have developmental difficulties including hyperactivity. The increased recognition of the heterogeneity of serious antisocial behaviour is leading to the development of possible key differentiations that should in turn inform the direction and development of treatment programmes for a group of young offenders who commit particular crimes (Rutter, Giller and Hagell, 1998).

Longitudinal research suggests that at least two main groups can be delineated. The more common group involves 'adolescent limited' antisocial behaviour involving a quarter or more of the general population (Moffitt, 1993). 'Life course persistent' antisocial behaviour is different in having both an unusually early age of onset and a tendency to persist into adult life.

The greater male involvement in crime is a universal finding that applies across cultures over time and is evident on all types of measure. However, over the last 40 years the sex ratio for crime has fallen from about 11:1 to 4:1, with the peak age of offending being 18 for young men and between 14 and 19 for young women. Rates differ by country and by type. Violent crimes form a small proportion of known offending by young people (about 10%), but most frequent offenders will have a violent offence on their record.

Ethnic minorities are over-represented in official statistics but do not appear to be more antisocial on self-reports. This discrepancy between official statistics and self-report data leads to questions about how law enforcement agencies deal with young people from diverse cultural and ethnic backgrounds.

Findings from a second sweep of the Youth Lifestyle Survey (YLS) (Home Office, 2000) provides a recent snapshot of admissions of offending among 12–30 year olds, confirming previous findings. The YLS study showed that poor parental supervision, having delinquent friends and acquaintances, persistent truanting and exclusion from school were all predictive of offending. It also showed the importance of lifestyle factors as a link to higher offending rates for males. Drug use was highly predictive across the full 12–30 year old age range, and heavy drinking was predictive for 18–30 year olds.

Early interventions

There are four types of prevention and early intervention that can reduce juvenile offending (Tonry and Farrington, 1995):

- criminal justice prevention – deterrence, incapacitation and rehabilitation strategies operated by law enforcement and criminal justice agencies;
- situational prevention – designed to reduce the opportunities for antisocial behaviour and to increase the risk and difficulty of committing antisocial acts;
- community prevention – interventions designed to change social conditions and social institutions that influence antisocial behaviour in communities;
- developmental prevention – interventions designed to inhibit the development of antisocial behaviour in individuals by targeting risk and protective factors that influence human development.

Lipsey (1995) suggested the importance of three strategies:

- primary population-based preventative intervention;
- secondary interventions focused on high risk groups;
- programmes centred on tertiary treatment.

Overall factors influencing successful outcomes of community programmes for established young offenders include:

- avoidance of indiscriminate choice of treatment foci;
- the use of more structured and focused treatments;
- the inclusion of a cognitive component that includes tackling the attitudes, values and beliefs that support antisocial behaviour;
- interventions that are conducted in the community. Residential programmes, however, can be effective when structurally linked with community-based interventions (Hollin, 1993).

However, official reconviction rates show that custody is relatively ineffectual in reducing juvenile offending. The way in which an institution is run affects outcomes for young people. Rutter, Giller and Hagell (1998) found that, whereas deterrent and incapacitation effects of incarceration were negligible, beneficial effects derived from:

- education and training that could open up new opportunities on release from custody;
- help with drug abuse/misuse, with no access to drugs during custody;
- the maintenance of a pro-social ethos with good relationships and models for behaviour;
- the enhancement of self-efficacy.
- the encouragement of strong, regular links with families.

Family participation in the residential experience and co-operation with community agencies are important factors in successful outcomes.

Young offenders and mental health

Studies of juveniles presenting to juvenile courts in North America and Europe have all shown high levels of psychiatric disorder, family psychopathology and inadequate resources to deal with these problems (Doreleijers et al, 2000; Vermeiren et al, 2000; Dolan et al, 1999; Doob et al, 1995). Nicol et al (2000) found marked similarity in the level of need in adolescents, whether in penal or welfare establishments. Studies of incarcerated adolescents in England and Wales (Maden et al, 1995; Lader et al, 2000) have all demonstrated high rates of psychiatric disorder, particularly in those facing the stress of incarceration whilst awaiting trial. Studies have highlighted the particular needs of adolescents from diverse ethnic groups (Lockman, 1994), and of the difficulties faced and posed by adolescent female offenders (Jasper et al, 1999; Lenssen, 2000). The overall rate of psychopathology in delinquents is substantially raised. Its clinical implications will depend, amongst others things, on the extent and type of comorbidity, the degree of chronicity and the developmental impact.

Medico-legal assessment of young offenders (Bailey, 2002)

There are common core principles that should be applied to medico-legal assessments of juveniles. Key questions concern the young person's 'fitness to plead' and capacity to 'effectively participate in the proceedings' (Grisso and Schwartz, 2000). The European Court of

Human Rights has made it explicit that the right of an accused to a fair trial has to include children. Two key suggestions for practice emerge from a review of international practice.

- All young defendants, including those charged with serious offences, should be tried in youth courts (with permission for adult sanctions for older youths if certain conditions are met). This should enable a mode of trial for young defendants to be subject to safeguards that can enhance understanding and participation.
- The maturity of a young defendant's cognitive and emotional capacities should be assessed before a decision is taken about venue and mode of trial.

One fundamental distinction in the criminal law is between conditions that negate criminal liability and those that might mitigate the punishment deserved under particular circumstances. Very young children and the profoundly mentally ill may lack the minimum capacity necessary to justify punishment. Those exhibiting less profound impairments of the same kind may qualify for a lesser level or deserved punishment even though they meet the minimum conditions for some punishment. Immaturity, like mental disorder, can serve both as an excuse and as a mitigation in the determination of just punishment. Capacity is sometimes thought of as a generic skill that a person either has or lacks. However, that is not so. To begin with, it is multifaceted, with four key elements:

(1) the capacity to understand information relevant to the specific decision at issue (understanding);
(2) the capacity to appreciate one's situation as one is confronted with a specific legal decision (appreciation);
(3) the capacity to think rationally about alternative courses of action (reasoning); and
(4) the capacity to express a choice among alternatives (choice).

The second key point is that capacity is a feature that is both situation-specific and open to influence – as brought out in discussions of the assessment in relation to children's consent to treatment (British Medical Association, 2000), participation in research (Royal College of Psychiatry, 2001), and criminal responsibility (Justice, 1996). Young children may well appreciate the difference between right and wrong but yet not understand the seriousness of some forms of irresponsible behaviour. With respect to their ability to understand legal procedures (as distinct from their crime), much can be done to aid their understanding (Ashford and Chard, 2000).

Any evaluation of competence (Grisso, 1997) should include assessment of possibly relevant psychopathology, emotional as well cognitive understanding, the child's experiences and appreciation of situations comparable to the one relevant to the crime and to the trial, and any particular features that may be pertinent in this individual and this set of circumstances. The clinician should also be alert to possible treatment needs, and should be aware of how these might be met for the individual, given the forensic situation. Before the evaluation it is important to be sure that the rules and limits of confidentiality for the evaluation are clear and that the child and the family understand them (Bailey, 2000). The appropriate level of clinical thoroughness and detail will vary with the intrinsic clinical complexity of the case, the specific legal context and the consultant's role in the legal system. The general principles to be used in the assessment are broadly comparable to those employed in any clinical evaluation. However, particular attention needs to be paid to developmental background, emotional and cognitive maturity, exposure to trauma and substance misuse. The likely appropriate sources for obtaining clinical data relevant to assessment of a juvenile's competence to stand trial will include a variety of historical records, a range of interviews and other observations and, in some cases, specialised tests.

Records of the child's performance at school, a clinical assessment, treatment history and previous involvements with the law all need to be obtained. In coming to an overall formulation, there should be particular focus on how both developmental and psychopathological features may be relevant to the forensic issues that have to be addressed.

Evaluation of functional capacities

Here, the main focus is on the youth's ability to understand and cope with the legal process. This comes from three sources: direct questioning of the defendant; inferences from functioning in other areas; and direct observation of the defendant's behaviour and interaction with others. It is useful to enquire about the youth's expectations of what the consequences of court involvement might be. Because the course of juvenile proceedings can vary so widely, with consequences ranging from the extremely aversive to extremely beneficial, rational understanding will necessarily involve a high degree of uncertainty.

Potentially relevant problems include inattention, depression, disorganisation of thought processes that interferes with the ability to consider alternatives, hopelessness, such that the decision is felt not to matter, delusions or other fixed beliefs that distort the understanding of options (or their likely outcomes), maturity of judgement, and the developmental challenges of adolescence.

Gudjonsson (1992) (see also Gudjonsson and Singh, 1984) found that adolescents are more prone than adults to offer inaccurate information to persons in authority when they are pressured. Younger adolescents are significantly more likely to change their stories to give answers that are less accurate than their original descriptions. This has practical implications for interviewing by police and lawyers. The ability to take another person's perspective is important for effective communication, an ability that has matured by middle adolescence but is less reliably found in early adolescence.

Sometimes concerns about a youth's conduct may be raised as potentially significant to his competence (Barnum, 2000). A youth may be impulsive, loud, angry or disruptive during trial and it may be suggested that these tendencies could undermine the formality or integrity of the proceedings. In addressing this question, it is important to be clear about the general clinical basis for any expected functional problems, and even more important to be clear about specific implications of potential disruptiveness for the relevant features of competence. If a youth's impulsiveness may be expected to interfere with his attention to the proceedings in court, and if his attention to those proceedings actually matters to his understanding and his effective collaboration with counsel, then it will be important to characterise these expectations or implications. For instance, if the youth is so angry and disruptive that he seems unable to sit and confer with his legal advisers, this may have important implications for his ability to understand the issues and respond helpfully to them. The clinician therefore needs to attend to these issues and show how they stem or do not stem from clinical disorder or developmental deficit.

In providing information to the court, written reports have the advantage of a standard format that helps the consultant to be sure that he or she has considered all the relevant questions; it also provides a familiar structure for readers of the reports. In essence, for the sake of consistency and clarity, competence reports need to cover the following areas:

(1) identification of information and referral questions;
(2) description of the structure of the evaluation including sources and a notation of the confidentiality expectations;
(3) provision of clinical and forensic data;
(4) discussion and presentations of opinions.

The assessment of competence to stand trial presents challenging questions. Child and adolescent consultants need to appreciate the systems implications of competence questions and must be able to provide opinions and recommendations that match the legal and systems circumstances of individual cases. This area is full of uncertainty, and the complexity of these challenges can sometimes seem overwhelming. However, in responding carefully and thoughtfully to questions posed, consultants can contribute to the development of a potentially important aspect of legal and clinical practice (Zimring, 2000).

Key issues to take forward

A better understanding of the process of moral development through childhood and adolescence will inform interventions with young offenders. Risk and offence reduction (Dolan and Doyle, 2000) is most likely to be achieved through a comprehensive needs assessment (Kroll et al, 1999) linked into an integrated standardised review of pro-social and antisocial behaviour that includes the internal attributional thinking of the young person.

Young offenders have a right to a full range of mental health services. The right of 'children' to be involved in decisions about their own treatment for either physical or mental illness is set within complex child care, mental health, criminal and European human rights legislation. Governments will continue to demand cost-effective youth justice services. Prevention and early intervention programmes to reduce rates of offending in young people may take a minimum of 10 years to demonstrate direct results. Denying mental health and social services benefits to children and adolescents today to save money will only ensure that the prison population grows (Bailey, 1999).

The major challenge of altering the trajectories of persistent young offenders has to be met in the context of satisfying public demands for retribution, together with welfare and civil liberties considerations.

Treatment of delinquents in institutional settings has to meet the sometimes contradictory need to control young people, to remove their liberty and to maintain good order in the institution, at the same time as offering education and training to foster future pro-social participation in society and meeting the delinquents' welfare needs. At least in England and Wales, the recent legislative overhaul of youth justice (Crime and Disorder Act 1998) has mandated practitioners to bridge the gap between residential and community treatments and to involve families using youth offending teams (YOTs) to meet this complex mix of needs.

Over the last 30 years there has been a gradual shift in opinion regarding effectiveness of intervention with delinquents, from the 'nothing works' approach to a 'what works' approach. The jury is still out for 'what works' in the long term, but the evidence base that can be placed before the jury is growing (McGuire, 1997, 2000). In practice, the pressure from politicians and the public will remain for a quick fix solution to problems that span cultures, countries and generations. The most important childhood predictors of adolescent violence include troublesome and antisocial behaviour, daring and hyperactivity, low IQ and attainment, antisocial parents, poor child rearing, harsh and erratic discipline, poor supervision, parental conflict, broken families, low family income and large family sizes (Farrington, 2000). Important policy implications are that home visiting programmes, parent training and skills training programmes, singly and in combination, should be implemented at an early stage to prevent adolescent high risk behaviour and offending. The best knowledge about risk factors has been obtained in longitudinal studies, and the best knowledge of effective programmes has been obtained in randomised experiments.

Provision of appropriately designed programmes can significantly reduce recidivism amongst persistent offenders. The mode and style of delivery is important; high quality staff and staff training are required, together with a system for 'monitoring integrity'. Where comparisons are possible, effect sizes are higher for community-based than institution-based programmes. In prison settings, the strongest effects are obtained when programmes are integrated into the institutional regimes. Multimodal programmes such as multisystemic therapy, adopting a cognitive behavioural approach, delivered intensively and, if needed, repeated over time, show most promise (Hengeller, 1999).

Our knowledge of true prevalence rates of mental disorders in a young offending population has to be developed further (Kazdin, 2000) so that mental health issues can be addressed. Child and adolescent mental health practitioners have the skills to set the understanding of delinquency in a developmental context (Bailey, 2002) and to assess those young offenders with mental disorders. Many young offenders have already experienced the looked after, care pathway; those with mental illness have not always had their needs met by mental health and reach the Mental Health Act following a journey down the criminal justice pathway. The implications of custody for 10–14 year olds are yet to be seen, whilst waiting in the wing is a new Mental Health Act that subsumes any 'disorder' including 'any disorder in a child' (Harbour and Bailey, 2001).

References

Ashford M and Chard A, *Defending Young People in the Criminal Justice System* (Legal Action Group, 2nd edn, 2000).

Bailey S, 'The Interface between mental health, criminal justice and forensic mental health services for children and adolescents' (1999) 12 *Current Opinion in Psychiatry* 425.

Bailey S, 'European Perspectives on Young Offenders and Mental Health' (2000) 23 *Journal of Adolescence* 237.

Bailey S, 'Confidentiality Myths and Realities in Confidentiality', in C Cordess (ed), *Confidentiality and Mental Health* (Jessica Kingsley, 2000).

Bailey S, 'Treatment of Delinquents', in M Rutter and E Taylor (eds), *Child and Adolescent Psychiatry: Modern Approaches* (Cambridge University Press, 4th edn, 2002).

Barnum R, 'Clinical and Forensic Evaluation of Competence to Stand Trial in Juvenile Defendants', in T Grisso and RG Schwartz (eds), *Youth on Trial: A Developmental Perspective in Juvenile Justice* (University of Chicago Press, 2000), pp 193–224.

British Medical Association, *Health Care for Children and Young People: Consent Rights and Choices* (British Medical Association, 2001).

Cavadino P and Allen R, 'Children who kill. Trends, Reasons and Procedures', in G Boswell (ed), *Violent children and adolescents. Asking the question why* (Whurr Publishers, 2000), pp 16–17.

Coleman J and Schofield J, *Key Data on Adolescence* (Trust for Study of Adolescence, TSA Publishing, 2001).

Coleman J, 'Young people in Britain at the beginning of a new century' (2000) 14 *Children and Society* 230.

Dolan M and Doyle M, 'Violence Risk Prediction. Clinical and Actuarial Measures and the Role of the Psychopathy' (2000) 177 *British Journal of Psychiatry* 303.

Dolan M, Holloway J and Bailey S, 'Health status of juvenile offenders. A survey of young offenders appearing before the juvenile courts' (1999) 22 *Journal of Adolescence* 137.

Doob AN, Manners V and Varma KN, *Youth crime and the Youth Justice System in Canada. A research perspective* (Centre of Criminology, University of Toronto, 1995).

Doreleijers TAH, Moser F, Thijs P, Van England H and Beyaert FHL, 'Forensic assessment of juvenile delinquents: prevalence of psychopathology and decision-making at court in the Netherlands' (2000) 23 *Journal of Adolescence* 263.

Farrington DP, 'Adolescent Violence. Findings and Implications from the Cambridge Study', in G Boswell (ed), *Violent Children and Adolescents. Asking the Question Why* (Whurr Publishers, 2000), pp 19–35.

Frick PJ, *Conduct Disorders and Severe Antisocial Behaviour* (Plenum Press, New York, 1998), pp 9–20.

Grisso T and Schwartz RG, *Youth on Trial. A Developmental Perspective on Juvenile Justice* (University of Chicago Press, 2000).

Grisso T, 'The Competence of Adolescents As Trial Defendants. Psychology' (1997) 3 *Public Policy and Law* 32.

Gudjonsson G and Singh K, 'Interrogative Suggestibility and Delinquent Boys. An Empirical Validation Study Personality and Individual Differences' (1984) 5 *Journal of Adolescence* 425.

Hagell A, Hazel N and Shaw C, *Evaluation of Medway Secure Training Centre* (Home Office, 2000), pp 1–13.

Harbour A and Bailey S, 'Reforming the Mental Health Act. What are the implications for children' (2000) 45 *Young Minds Magazine* 12.

Harbour A and Bailey S, 'Acting Lawfully: Children and Reform of the Mental Health Act' (2001) *Young Minds Magazine* 14.

Hawton K et al, 'Deliberate self-harm in adolescents in Oxford 1985–1995' (2000) 23 *Journal of Adolescence* 47.

Henggeler SW, 'Multisystemic therapy. An overview of clinical procedures, outcomes and police implications' (1999) 4 *Child Psychology and Psychiatry Review* 2.

Jasper A, Smith C and Bailey S, 'One hundred girls in care referred to an adolescent forensic mental health service' (1999) 21 *Journal of Adolescence* 555.

Justice, *Children and Homicide. Appropriate Procedures for Juveniles in Murder and Manslaughter Cases* (Justice, 1996).

Kazdin AE, 'Adolescent Development, Mental Disorders, and Decision Making of Delinquent Youths', in T Grisso and RG Schwartz (eds), *Youth on Trial, A Developmental Perspective on Juvenile Justice* (University of Chicago Press, 2000), pp 33–65.

Kelly S and Bunting J, 'Trends in suicide in England and Wales, 1982–1996' (1998) 92 *Population Trends* (Summer).

Kerfoot M, 'Suicide and deliberate self-harm in children and adolescents' (1996) 10 *Children and Society* 236.

Kroll L, Woodham A, Rothwell J, Bailey S, Tobias C, Harrington R and Marshal MM 'Reliability of the Salford needs assessment schedule for adolescents' (1999) 29 *Psychological Medicine* 891.

Lader D, Singleton N and Meltzer H, *Psychiatric morbidity among Young Offenders in England and Wales* (Office for National Statistics, 2000).

Lenssen SAM, Doreleijers TAH, Van Dijk ME and Hartman CA, 'Girls in detention: what are their characteristics? A project to explore and document the character of this target group and the significant ways in which it differs from one consisting of boys' (2000) 23 *Journal of Adolescence* 287.

Lipsey MW, 'What do we learn from 400 research studies on the effectiveness of treatment with juvenile delinquents?', in J McGuire (ed), *What works: Reducing offending* (Wiley, 1995).

McCann et al, 'Prevalence of psychiatric disorder in young people in the care system' (1996) 313 *British Medical Journal* 1529.

McGuire J, 'Psycho-social approaches to the understanding and reduction of violence in young people', in V Varma (ed), *Violence in children and adolescents* (Jessica Kingsley, 1997).

McGuire J, *Working with Young Offenders in Secure Settings*, paper presented (University of Sheffield, 2000).

Maden A, Taylor C, Brooke D and Gunn J, *Mental Disorder in Remand Prisoners* (Institute of Psychiatry, London and Home Office, 1995).

Meltzer H, *Mental health of children and adolescents in Great Britain* (Office for National Statistics and Stationery Office, 2000).

Moffitt TE, 'Adolescence limited and life course persistent antisocial behaviour. A developmental taxonomy' (1993) 100 *Psychological Review* 674.

Nicol R, Stretch D, Whitney I, Jones K, Garfield P, Turner K and Stanion B, 'Mental health needs and services for severely troubled and troubling young offenders in an NHS Region' (2000) 23 *Journal of Adolescence* 243.

Royal College of Psychiatrists, *Guidelines for Researchers and for Ethics Committees on Psychiatric Research Involving Human Participants* (RCP, 2001).

Rutter M, Giller H and Hagell A, *Antisocial Behaviour by Young People* (Cambridge University Press, 1998).

Tonry M and Farrington DP, 'Strategic approaches to crime prevention', in M Tonry and DP Farrington (eds), *Building a safer society: strategic approaches to crime prevention* (University of Chicago Press, 1995), pp 1–20.

Vermeiren R, De Clippele A and Deboutte D, 'A descriptive survey of Flemish delinquent adolescents' (2000) 23 *Journal of Adolescence* 277.

TROUBLED CHILDREN AND CRIMINAL JUSTICE

His Honour Judge Mark Hedley
Liverpool Combined Court Centre

Summary of paper

His Honour Judge Hedley explained that his paper was a personal reflection, in answer to the question of why the British tend to be particularly penal in dealing with young people in trouble. He emphasised that it was a personal response.

He felt that three matters were fundamental to the whole issue of children and the criminal justice system:

- *That one had to recognise the fundamental difference in culture between the family justice system and the criminal justice system.*
- *That there was a need within the criminal justice system for two quite different processes to take place. The first which was almost entirely objective, was whether the young person had committed the offence, with the requisite intent. On a human rights level, one had to be careful that there was the same quality of fact-finding for juveniles and adults. Once the first process had been concluded, then the court had to look subjectively at the culpability of the young person, their needs and how to address these within the system.*
- *That in the family justice system it was axiomatic that the welfare of the child should be the court's paramount consideration. This view was one not shared by everyone when talking about the criminal justice system. His Honour Judge Hedley referred to the explosive cocktail of fear surrounding youth crime, and felt that we were in dire danger of disconnecting ourselves from a substantial group of the population and their perceptions, if we were unable to demonstrate on an outcomes basis that in the long term a welfare-based approach was better than penal sanctions. He wished to encourage thought along these lines.*

Introduction

There is a perception that we in England and Wales are much more punitive in our response to the misdoings of children than are the rest of Europe. It is said that our low age of criminal responsibility and our increasing resort to the criminal justice system contrasts unfavourably with European systems in which welfare is the primary consideration. That response may indeed be well founded provided the question is asked as to whether the current official European response carries the consent of the person on the Lyons or Munich omnibus, any more than the liberal response of our system in the second half of the last century won approval in Clapham.

I would, however, like to respond personally as to why this might be and how it might be addressed. I do so not only from the perspective of a professional lawyer but as a sometime foster parent and someone with 30 years' involvement in youth work in central Liverpool. I stress that this response is personal, it has not been discussed with others, and in so far as it may turn out to represent any judicial view or policy, that will be mere coincidence.

The English upper and middle classes have long been notorious for their approach to their children. Mediaeval scholars complained bitterly that men would lavish resources on their stables that they would never consider for their schoolroom. Those with the care of children ranked low in the list of importance. As with every generalisation there were many exceptions and it would be foolish to press the matter too hard, but the witness of history and literature inescapably gives substance to it. No doubt John Aubrey was going a little too far when he said in 1670:

> 'The gentry and citizens had little learning of any kind and their way of breeding children was suitable to the rest. They were as severe to their children as their schoolmasters; and their schoolmasters as masters of the house of correction. The child perfectly loathed the sight of his parents as the slave his torture.'

John Aubrey did not have a happy childhood. John Ruskin, however, did (or so he believed) and his account may be all the more revealing for being seen in that context. He wrote of the 1820s:

> 'Nor did I painfully wish, what I was never permitted for an instant to hope, or even imagine, the possession of such things as one saw in toyshops. I had a bunch of keys to play with, as long as I was capable of pleasure in what glittered or jingled; as I grew older, I had a cart and a ball; and when I was five or six years old, two boxes of well cut wooden bricks. With these modest, but as I still think, entirely sufficient possessions, and being always summarily whipped if I cried, did not do as I was bid, or tumbled on the stairs, I soon attained secure and serene methods of life and motion ...'

No doubt Ruskin was unusual, but there is no reason to think that his experience or his views were altogether unusual. Boyhood, at least, was regarded as a serious matter in which future welfare was learned at the hands of harsh experience.

It is not easy to trace why this should have been so. Some have tried to blame the religion of the Reformation with its talk of Original Sin. Some justification for this can be found in some of the more extreme statements of that position. In 1535 John Calvin thundered:

> 'Yea, and very infants themselves bring their own damnation with them from their mother's womb. Who, although they have not yet brought forth the fruits of their iniquity, yet have the seed thereof enclosed within them. Yea, their whole nature is a certain seed of Sin, therefore it cannot but be hateful and abominable to God.'

Certainly that gives no child much of a start in the eyes of the older generation, and it is not surprising that many saw it as a great work of good to beat the Satan out of children. But that cannot be the complete answer, for within English culture there has always been a deep strain of sentimentality over the innocence of childhood. Writing in the nineteenth century, Mary Hewitt expressed it thus:

> 'God sends children for another purpose than merely to keep up the race – to enlarge our hearts, to make us unselfish, and full of kindly sympathies and affections; to give our souls higher aims; and to call out all our faculties to extended enterprise and exertion; to bring round our fireside bright faces and happy smiles and loving tender hearts. My soul blesses the Great Father every day, that He has gladdened the earth with Little Children.'

I am tempted to the view that Ms Hewitt had never been a full-time carer. Perhaps it is because those two strands are part of our cultural psyche and have never been resolved that accounts for our ambivalence to difficult or troubled children.

The approach of our society historically to crime has almost always been essentially punitive and, in that approach, children have not been spared. It is not that long ago that age did not spare a child from the gallows let alone the birching stool. Traditionally, we have in fact, whatever public pronouncements may have been, punished the crime rather than the wrongdoer, or perhaps we have assumed that the offender must have seen the offence in the same light as did those who punished it and, in that, small allowance has traditionally been made for age.

What I fear is also true is that we find strong echoes of our history and of our ambivalent approach to childhood in our own society today. The public hysteria (especially in Liverpool) over Thompson and Venables, which made no concessions to their age or life experiences and the 'name and shame' debate that surrounds every Crown Court conviction of a juvenile, are but examples of an approach to children in trouble that our ancestors would have recognised. If you listen to the talk on the streets of our urban priority areas where the concerns are not of grave but rather low tariff crime (vandalism, rowdyism, public order, etc), the tone remains profoundly punitive, relieved only occasionally by an 'I blame the parents'. Our society abolished Doli Incapax and maintained the age of criminal responsibility and, in doing so, I believe, read the broad popular mood aright.

I have queried whether the populist mood in Europe is different to here and I am not qualified to offer an answer. However, other cultures which are credited with a more child-friendly approach can also be quite punitive. I worked for a year in a rural township in Northern Sudan and have a number of close African friends. We would find their views on child-rearing (to put it mildly) old-fashioned and yet we would at the same time applaud the stability in which those children were reared.

I have for a long while sought to reflect on this, and have two observations to offer. Both may be obvious, even trite, and yet it seems to me that they encapsulate much of what conditions our approach to difficult children when compared to the approach of others.

The first is that in the foreign system I know, like our culture traditionally, difficulties caused by children are seen as the province of the family and school rather than the criminal justice system. Sanctions may (or may not) still be stern, but they are capable of being seen in a context which is restorative rather than merely punitive. Moreover, where the problems posed by the child are seen as beyond home or school to handle, it is possible to see a need then for intervention that is other than punitive. However, there is a case for arguing that today in this country we have disempowered home and school and cast on to the criminal justice system responsibilities that it was neither intended nor is able to handle.

The second reflection is that our perspective on a child's behaviour is closely related to the extent that we knew them as people before the happening of their offensive behaviour. In stark contrast to the hue and cry over Thompson and Venables is told the story of the 6 year old who killed two children in a Norwegian town and was dealt with on a welfare basis and readmitted to the community. I would not rule out any such thing happening in a small, close English community where everyone was known by everyone else before catastrophe struck. The problem was that Jamie Bulger died in a great urban sprawl. Thompson and Venables were unknown to their vilifiers and it is so much easier to demonise the unknown rather than the troubled child next door whose nice side you have seen from time to time.

One of the reflections from youth work in central Liverpool is how much more readily children respond to leaders they see on the street, in the shops, at the parents' room at school, as well as in the club. Those leaders may be just as determined (sometimes more so) to insist on good behaviour as the visiting leaders and are often harsher in enforcement, but the secret lies in their knowing and valuing the young people, and in the young people's own acceptance that they are known and valued. We had trouble with drugs in clubs recently. The offenders readily understood an approach which said 'the judge has said no drugs in here because if we allow it we, the leaders, will be in trouble'. Of course the spliffs were then found along the outside wall! The reactions on both sides were, however, conditioned by mutual knowledge and acceptance.

The growth of urbanisation has paradoxically made for greater distance between people, not less. It allows an anonymity which undermines trust and results in a defensive punitiveness, rather than a concern to bring about change. Moreover, it breeds a climate of fear. If you listen on our urban priority streets you will find anger about difficult children inextricably bound up in a real fear of them. Anger and fear make an explosive cocktail when it comes to dealing with young people. It is, I believe, in this context that we need to understand popular sentiment towards young people in trouble, a sentiment which is expressed rather than resisted by government, which might reasonably argue that that is a price of democracy.

Furthermore, we need, as professionals, to recognise how we are seen. Those who only see troubled children in the context of professional life may sometimes not see the whole picture. You cannot ignore the perspective created by having been burgled, having your disabled son knocked over in an attempt by others to rob his mother, having your car vandalised or stolen or your house windows threatened if you complain. Having had all that experience I think that I am beginning to understand why there is an undercurrent of public mistrust of liberal values in relation to children in trouble and why that mistrust (even if misplaced) should be taken seriously. I am not surprised (even if I am saddened) by a widespread, populist spirit of negative punitiveness to children in trouble, nor am I surprised that government of whatever shade feels under acute electoral pressure to give expression to it.

How, then, do I think our criminal justice system ought to respond to children in trouble? First, and most importantly, we should be clear about what we are and are not entitled to expect from the system. It exists to protect society and to uphold its values (in so far, of course, as common values can still be said to exist) by the detection, prosecution, conviction and punishment of offenders. That is its traditional role and much of that is conceptually inconsistent with accepted principles of caring for children. We do not use drawn out, formal procedures for dealing with children at home or in school or clubs. At the same time we do not want the full panoply of state powers to be unleashed on a child who has not had at least the same official safeguards as an adult. So at once we are drawn into irreconcilable conflicts of priority which illustrate the difficulties of dealing with children through the criminal justice system. I am very guarded in my expectations of how well the criminal justice system can deal with children. It may be both necessary and effective in dealing with the highly dangerous and those who commit grave crime, but these comprise a tiny proportion of children in trouble and an even smaller proportion of those against whom public ire is actually directed.

It seems to me that those of us who favour a welfare-centred approach to children in trouble have to win the argument that that is an effective way of making these youngsters easier to live with than they were before. It is no longer enough simply to assume the obviousness of a welfare-centred approach; most of our compatriots do not actually believe it, and no government can afford to ignore that view. It is now necessary to demonstrate that welfare outcomes yield better conclusions than punitive ones. No one who knows Feltham YOI (and a host of others) could believe that it generally discharges better people than it takes. But whilst you could set Peperharow up in contrast to an approved school, the evidence of today's equivalent is less well known. At least for as long as he's in a YOI he's not burgling me, is an argument requiring an answer.

Accordingly, we need not only to confront public opinion with the inadequacy of the criminal justice system in dealing with young people in trouble (other than grave offences or the downright dangerous), but we need also to make the case both that the criminal justice system is conceptually alien to the needs of these young people and also (and most importantly) that demonstrably more effective options exist.

Personally I hold some, no doubt rather old-fashioned, views about keeping children out of the system by re-empowering parents, restoring morale in education and rediscovering the value of youth provision in its widest sense. For me, things that trouble children arise from their domestic and social experiences and should be addressed in that context, and I have been part of it sufficiently, albeit in one tiny corner, to base my convictions on evidence. I do not believe in the innate goodness of humanity – all the evidence is against it – but I do believe that every human being is stamped with the image of God so that none is beyond reclaim or redemption.

The issues are: how to do it and how to convince others that welfare succeeds over punishment. People with different values, radically different even, can, however, combine to advocate a common cause. My simple point is that it is no longer sufficient to assume the rightness of a welfare approach and the wrongness of a punitive one. The point now has to be argued, and if it is to be won, it has to be won not only on philosophical grounds but on practical ones evidenced by positive outcomes.

WHEN YOUNG PEOPLE REFUSE TREATMENT: BALANCING AUTONOMY AND PROTECTION

Dr Mike Shaw

Consultant Child Psychiatrist, Sutton Hospital

Summary of paper

Introducing his paper, Dr Shaw suggested that the Law's approach to young people refusing treatment was an evolving area which benefited from interdisciplinary discussion.

Given the conference theme, he took the Children Act 1989 as his starting point. The Act encourages competent young people to participate in decision-making subject to their welfare. Whereas a competent adult has the absolute right to refuse treatment, the competent young person's refusal can be overridden in pursuit of their welfare.

He referred to the cases of Re R (A Minor) (Wardship: Medical Treatment) [1992] 1 FLR 190 and Re W (A Minor) (Medical Treatment) [1993] 1 FLR 1 and the decision in each case that the child's parents had an independent right to consent to treatment on behalf of their children. Dr Shaw stated that the application of these cases means that competent young people who refuse treatment could have their refusal effectively bypassed by the consent of their parents. In his view this approach stepped outside the framework of the Children Act 1989.

Dr Shaw was concerned that the law provides only limited protection for young people deprived of their right to refuse. This contrasted with both the strict rules and safeguards in the Children Act's approach to restriction of liberty, and the Mental Health Act 1983 where a second opinion has to be sought, clear timeframes are set out, and there is the opportunity to have the decision reviewed by an independent body.

Dr Shaw felt that no young person should be treated against his or her wishes unless discussion of alternatives had been exhausted, and without treatment the young person was likely to suffer significant harm. He recognised that society places a high value on young people's lives and that some would need treatment against their wishes. However, he believed that doctors should approach welfare in a straightforward way, not 'fudge' the issue by setting an unrealistically high level of competence or by bypassing the young person in favour of their parent.

The questions he posed for the conference were:

- *whether one can dispense with the independent right of parents to consent to treatment on behalf of a competent child;*
- *if so, whether it is possible to borrow the framework from the Mental Health Act or otherwise to provide guidance.*

Introduction

The Children Act builds on the *Gillick* ruling (*Gillick v West Norfolk and Wisbech Area Health Authority and Another* [1986] 1 FLR 224) by including competent young people in decision-making. For example, 'the ascertainable wishes of the child concerned (considered in the light of his age and understanding)' is part of the so-called 'checklist' (s 1(3) in regard to s 8 and Part IV orders). But the central premise of the Children Act is that 'the child's welfare shall be the court's paramount consideration': s 1(1). As a result the competent young person's wishes can be overruled in pursuit of his welfare.

Two important rulings by the Court of Appeal (*Re R (A Minor) (Wardship: Medical Treatment)* [1992] 1 FLR 190 and *Re W (A Minor) (Consent to Medical Treatment)* [1993] 1 FLR 1) have reinterpreted the *Gillick* ruling and significantly curtail a young person's ability to refuse treatment. Some argue that these decisions upset the balance between autonomy and protection intended by the Children Act (Devereux et al 1993; Freeman 1993).

Ten years after the Children Act came into force the British Medical Association has called for a review of the law on young people's involvement in health care decisions (BMA 2001, p 40):

> 'The BMA's view is that there is a need for clarity about when it is acceptable to override a young person's wishes and when it is not. The legal issues could be clarified by the courts or statute, and would be an appropriate subject for consideration by the Law Commission particularly in the light of the Human Rights Act which may have implications for young people's refusal of treatment.'

This paper considers how the legal framework might be improved.

Competence

Introduction

Competence is fundamental to the law's approach to consent. Only a competent person can give a valid consent. Whether or not a young person is competent to make a particular treatment decision varies with the availability of information and time, their level of understanding, the complexity and gravity of the decision, their ability to think about the issues and the presence of factors which enhance or impair these capacities (see A Competence Checklist, p 52 below).

Providing information and time

Competence is only possible in the presence of adequate information. The General Medical Council (1999) and British Medical Association (2001) stress the importance of providing information. The value of information will be increased by an opportunity to ask questions and time to 'sleep' on a decision (in the absence of an overriding need to act).

Commenting on *Re L (Medical Treatment: Gillick Competency)* [1998] 2 FLR 810 and *Re E (A Minor) (Wardship: Medical Treatment)* [1993] 1 FLR 386, McCafferty (1999) argues that L and E were denied an opportunity to make a competent choice because they were not given enough information.

Future decisions are likely to be guided by s 10 of the Human Rights Act 1998, which provides a right 'to receive and impart information'. The BMA (2001, p 100) recommends doctors only withholding information from young people in 'exceptional cases, where the harm of disclosure outweighs the value of seeking a competent decision'.

Understanding

Ruling in the *Gillick* case Lord Scarman linked competence to 'sufficient understanding and intelligence' to allow a young person 'to understand fully what is proposed'. Understanding 'fully' includes understanding the nature of the condition/illness, the investigation and treatment procedures, the treatment options, the benefits and risks of treatment, and the outlook with or without treatment.

The level of understanding that is 'sufficient' will vary with the complexity and gravity of the decision. Of particular importance are the relative benefits, risks and burdens of treatment options. Greater understanding is expected if the burdens are heavy, the risks high, or the benefits uncertain.

A higher level of understanding is required if young people refuse treatment. As Pearce (1994) argues:

'The consequences of withholding consent to treatment are usually much more significant and potentially dangerous than simply giving consent ... A more stringent test should therefore be applied when assessing a child's ability to refuse consent than when assessing competence to consent.'

Building on understanding

Lord Justice Thorpe's decision in *Re C (Refusal of Medical Treatment)* [1994] 1 FLR 31 broadens the *Gillick* concept of competence. C was a patient at Broadmoor Hospital suffering from schizophrenia who refused amputation of his gangrenous foot. Ruling that C should decide for himself, the court defined competence as:

'... first comprehending and retaining information, secondly, believing it and thirdly, weighing it in the balance to arrive at a choice.'

In this context 'believing' means that a young person appreciates the importance of information and sees how it applies to him or her. The young person may weigh the information differently from his or her parents or doctor, and unwise choices are permitted.

When evaluating young people's competence it is important not to set a higher standard than would be expected for adults. This will be assisted by making a clear distinction between competence and welfare. Downie (1999) has argued that:

'Where the life of the teenage patient is in danger, it is difficult to disagree with the conclusion that he should not be allowed to bring about his own death ... The court will base its decision on its view of the child's welfare; and it may, therefore, be preferable to avoid the process of finding him incompetent in order to legitimise such a decision, especially when this process can involve tortuous reasoning tending to make the concept of *Gillick* competence ever more obscure.'

Enhancing competence

Young people's competence will be enhanced if they feel valued and supported. Most people prefer to discuss important decisions with a family member or friend. Equally, discussion with health professionals will be more productive when the relationship is founded on trust and respect. The BMA guidance on consent in young people (2001, pp 101–103) provides an excellent list of practical ways to enhance competence.

Threats to competence

Competence can be temporarily impaired by certain mental or physical states. Lady Justice Butler-Sloss's ruling in *Re MB (Medical Treatment)* [1997] 2 FLR 426 is important in this regard. MB was a pregnant woman declared incompetent when a needle phobia led to her refusing a Caesarean section. The judgment drew attention to:

'The 'temporary factors' mentioned by Lord Donaldson MR in [*Re T (An Adult) Consent to Medical Treatment)* [1992] 2 FLR 458] (confusion, shock, fatigue, pain or drugs) may completely erode capacity but those concerned must be satisfied that such factors are operating to such a degree that the ability to decide is absent.'

Another such influence may be panic induced by fear. Again, careful scrutiny of the evidence is necessary because fear of an operation may be a rational reason for refusal to undergo it. Fear may also, however, paralyse the will and thus destroy the capacity to make a decision.

Mental illness may impair a young person's judgment sufficiently to render them incompetent. But it is important not assume that all (or even most) mentally ill people are incompetent (Grisso and Appelbaum 1995).

Finally, competence can be undermined by coercion from peers, family or even health-professionals.

Assessing competence

Judgments about competence can only be made case-by-case, taking account of the individual, the type of decision and other circumstances, as Rutter (1999) points out:

> 'Often there is a wish, by courts and by researchers, that there be a suitable simple criterion or measure of competence that could be applied in a standardised fashion. Unfortunately, not only is no such test available but … it is highly unlikely that such a test could be devised. That is because there is no universally acceptable level of competence that applies to an individual child. Rather, the question is of a child's competence in a particular context, for a particular type of decision, given particular circumstances.'

Judgements about competence are strongly influenced by the attitudes of society, as Roth et al (1977) say:

> 'In practice, judgements of competency go beyond semantics or straightforward applications of legal rules; such judgements reflect social considerations and societal biases as much as they reflect matters of law and medicine.'

In the absence of benchmarks the clinician's preference for a particular treatment could cloud his or her assessment of the patient's competence. As Devereux et al (1993) put it:

> ' … the catch 22 by which patients whose competence is in doubt will be found rational if they accept the doctor's proposal but incompetent if they reject professional advice.'

Even where young people are judged not to be competent their preferences and misgivings about particular treatments need to be considered in making decisions on their behalf.

In complex cases it is best practice for an independent clinician to advise on competence and vital to document the factors contributing to any judgment of competence.

Consent

Introduction

Other than for emergencies or in the circumstances described in Part IV of the Mental Health Act 1983, consent is a necessary prerequisite to the treatment of any young person. The Department of Health's Mental Health Act 1983: Code of Practice (1999) gives the following definition of consent (para 15.13):

> '"Consent" is the voluntary and continuing permission of the patient to receive a particular treatment, based on an adequate knowledge of the purpose, nature, likely effects and risks of that treatment including the likelihood of its success and any alternatives to it. Permission given under any unfair undue pressure is not "consent".'

The General Medical Council guidance (1999) on consent places particular emphasis on providing patients with adequate information and freedom from pressure.

A person with parental responsibility (including a local authority having a care order) can give consent on behalf of the young person (before their eighteenth birthday). However this power is subject to a number of qualifications.

16 and 17 year olds

The Family Law Reform Act 1969 lowered the age of majority to 18 years and gave 16 and 17 year olds the same right of consent as adults. Sections 8(1) says:

> '... the consent of a minor who has attained the age of sixteen ... shall be as effective as it would be if he were of full age; and where a minor has ... given an effective consent to any treatment it shall not be necessary to obtain any consent for it from his parent or guardian.'

This means that if a 16 or 17 year old consents it is unnecessary to seek consent from a person with parental responsibility.

Under 16 years

As described above, the competence of a young person under the age of 16 years is considered in light of the *Gillick* decision. As is well known, this case examined the circumstances in which it would be lawful to give contraceptive advice to a young person under the age of 16 years without his or her parents' permission. In his judgment Lord Scarman said:

> '... the parental right to determine whether or not their minor child below the age of sixteen will have medical treatment terminates if and when the child achieves a sufficient understanding and intelligence to enable him or her to understand fully what is proposed.'

This ruling gives under 16 year olds with sufficient understanding ('*Gillick*-competent') an independent right to consent to treatment.

However, even with a *Gillick*-competent young person (under the age of 16 years) it is good practice also to seek consent from a person with parental responsibility. In his ruling in the *Gillick* case Lord Fraser set out five preconditions that would justify a doctor prescribing contraceptives to a young woman under the age of 16 years without her parents' consent:

(1) that the girl (although under the age of 16 years of age) will understand his advice;
(2) that he cannot persuade her to inform her parents or to allow him to inform the parents that she is seeking contraceptive advice;
(3) that she is very likely to begin or to continue having sexual intercourse with or without contraceptive treatment;
(4) that unless she receives contraceptive advice or treatment her physical and mental health or both are likely to suffer;
(5) that her best interests require him to give her contraceptive advice, treatment or both without parental consent.

Lower age limit

Although there is no lower age limit, Bailey and Harbour (1999) suggest that it would rarely be appropriate for a young person under the age of 13 years to consent to treatment without his or her parents' involvement.

Alderson (1993) interviewed 120 young people (8–15 years old) undergoing elective orthopaedic surgery; she also spoke to their parents. Surgery was being undertaken for relief of chronic pain, disability or deformity, and on average they had already had five operations. The young people were asked, 'How old do you think you were or will be when you're old enough to decide?' (about surgery). Their parents were asked, 'At what age do you think your child can make a wise choice?'. The two groups gave a very similar mean age (14.0 years for the young people and 13.9 for the parents). But the girls and their parents thought they would be ready to decide 2 years earlier than boys and their parents (girls 13.1, their parents 12.8; boys 15.0, their parents 14.9).

Other reasons for involving young people in decision-making

There are many reasons for informing young people and gaining their co-operation over and above obtaining valid consent. Alderson (1993) cites the following reasons: out of respect for the child; to answer questions and help the child know what to expect; to reduce anxiety; to help the child make sense of their experience; to warn about risks; to prevent misunderstanding or resentment; to promote confidence and courage; and to increase compliance.

Refusal

Introduction

A competent adult has a right to refuse treatment 'for reasons which are rational or irrational, or for no reason' (Sidaway, 1985). The Children Act explicitly gives competent under-16 year olds the right to refuse assessment and treatment in the very limited circumstances of care proceedings (which can be overridden by the court). (There are five provisions in the Act where 'if the child is of sufficient understanding to make an informed decision he may refuse to submit to a medical or psychiatric examination or other assessment' (ss 38(6), 43(8), 44(7), and Sch 3, paras 4(4)(a) and 5(5)(a)) and one provision where the child can refuse medical or psychiatric treatment (Sch 3, para 5(5)(a)). The Act and accompanying guidance and regulations place considerable emphasis on taking account of the child's views. But the central premise of the Children Act is that 'the child's welfare shall be the court's paramount consideration' (s 1(1)). Unlike the competent adult, the competent child's views may be overruled in pursuit of his welfare.

Limitations on a young person's right to refuse

Two rulings by the Court of Appeal (*Re R (A Minor) (Wardship: Medical Treatment)* [1992] 1 FLR 190 and *Re W (A Minor) (Consent to: Medical Treatment)* [1993] 1 FLR 1) have significantly curtailed a young person's ability to refuse treatment. They concern R, a 15-year-old young woman refusing anti-psychotic medication, and W, a 16-year-old young woman with anorexia nervosa refusing transfer to another treatment centre. In the case of R, Lord Donaldson argued that in the *Gillick* ruling:

> '... Lord Scarman was discussing the parent's right to determine whether or not their minor child below the age of 16 will have medical treatment ... a right of determination is wider than a right of consent ... I do not understand Lord Scarman to be saying that, if a child was 'Gillick competent' ... the parents ceased to have a right of consent as contrasted with ceasing to have a right of determination, i.e. a veto. In a case in which the 'Gillick competent' child refuses treatment, but the parents consent, that consent enables treatment to be undertaken lawfully.'

In both cases the court ruled that treatment could lawfully proceed with the consent of either a competent young person or a person with parental responsibility, and that the consent of a person with parental responsibility will bypass the refusal of the young person (whether or not he or she is competent).

Mason and McCall Smith (1999) argue that s 8(3) of the Family Law Reform Act 1969 upholds the right of someone with parental responsibility to consent on behalf of a minor when it says:

'Nothing in this section shall be construed as making ineffective any consent which would have been effective if this section had not been enacted.'

But the judgments in *Re R* and *Re W* have been criticised for undermining the *Gillick* decision, and departing from the principles of the Family Law Reform Act, the Children Act and the United Nations Convention on the Rights of the Child (Devereux et al 1993; Freeman 1993). For example, the Children Act encourages the competent young person to decide, but will overrule his wishes in pursuit of his welfare; whereas the Court of Appeal's decision makes the competent young person's ability to decide depend, not so much on his welfare, as on an algorithm linked to whether he consents or refuses and what his parents decide.

Doubts have been raised about the logic of the rulings. Balcombe LJ's judgment in *Re W* admits:

' ... in logic there can be no difference between an ability to consent to treatment and an ability to refuse treatment.'

While Bainham (2000, p 279) points out:

'Lord Donaldson's distinction between determination and consent cannot overcome the essential reality that, where a doctor is aware of a disagreement between parent and child, he must, of necessity, choose between the opposing views. If he elects to comply with what the parent wants, then he effectively gives to that parent a veto over the child's wishes, and this would appear to conflict directly with the decision in Gillick.'

The judgments in *Re R* and *Re W* add to the complexity of the law. Competence is the only hurdle to a valid consent; by comparison, refusal is labyrinthine. Where a young person is refusing treatment the test for competence will be more stringent (see Pearce's argument above). A competent young person's refusal can be bypassed with the consent of someone with parental responsibility. For the same reason the local authority can bypass the refusal of a competent young person in its care. Finally, the court can use its inherent jurisdiction to overrule the refusal of a competent young person. As a result, the law favours consent over refusal and protection over autonomy.

Scottish law is more straightforward and even-handed. The Age of Legal Capacity (Scotland) Act 1991, s 2(4) says:

'A person under the age of 16 years shall have legal capacity to consent on his own behalf to any surgical, medical or dental procedure or treatment where, in the opinion of a qualified medical practitioner attending him, he is capable of understanding the nature and possible consequences of the procedure or treatment.'

Involving the court

In *Re W* the Court of Appeal recommended that competent young people withholding consent should be subjected to invasive treatment only with the court's authority. However, in *Re K, W and H (Minors) (Medical Treatment)* [1993] 1 FLR 854, the High Court criticised a hospital's application as 'misconceived and unnecessary'. The British Medical Association believes there is 'uncertainty about the extent to which it is necessary to seek court approval' (2001, p 38).

In cases involving sterilisation or abortion the court's guidance should always be sought. If neither the young person nor any other person can give a valid consent, the authority of the court must be sought, unless emergency treatment is required.

It is often inappropriate for a parent who has abused his or her child to give consent on that child's behalf. Where the young person is not already in care the court's authority should be sought.

Protecting young people treated against their consent

In cases not brought to court, the law provides no specific protection for the young person whose refusal has been bypassed. By contrast, the Children Act sets strict safeguards for the 'restriction of liberty'. Restricting a young person's liberty for more than 72 hours in any consecutive 28 days requires the authority of the court (Children (Secure Accommodation) Regulations 1991, reg 10(1)) and the young person must have the access to legal representation in any proceedings (s 25(6)).

The Mental Health Act

The Mental Health Act 1983 can be used to treat people of all ages. With its requirement for a second opinion, time-limited application and opportunity for independent review, the Act goes further to protect the rights of young people treated against their wishes. The Government's White Paper for reforming the Mental Health Act (2000) indicates:

> '... in the new legislation a 16–18 year old person who does not consent, and who meets the conditions for care and treatment under compulsory powers, will only be treated under compulsory powers and will thereby be protected by the safeguards ...'

My own view is that across the age range, the Mental Health Act should be preferred in situations to which it applies.

Human Rights Act

The Human Rights Act 1998 incorporates the European Convention on Human Rights into domestic law. Section 8 of the Act deals with the right to 'private and family life' and could form the basis for a challenge to the court's existing approach to young people refusing treatment.

Difficult cases in clinical practice

Sometimes young people refuse treatment despite the most sensitive and skilled approach of staff and parents. Pearce (1994) suggests:

> 'Every effort should be made to reach a consensus, however protracted this process may be – so long as this does not involve taking unacceptable risks with the child's future health ... It is usually better to delay treatment until attitudes and relationships have changed – which could just as easily be the professional's attitude as the patient's.'

The British Medical Association (2001) recommends an independent health professional act as an arbiter and attempt to negotiate an agreement.

I believe that no young person (competent or otherwise) should be treated against his or her will unless he or she is more likely than not to suffer significant harm without treatment. Even when overruling a young person's refusal it will often be possible to give limited choices.

The *Guidelines for Good Practice on Consent* (p 53 below) tries to build on the best features of existing law and guidance.

Refining the legal framework further

I believe that there is great integrity in the Children Act's approach to young people's participation in decision-making. Competent young people should be encouraged to take decisions even if they sometimes act unwisely. Their choices should be overturned only where welfare is threatened. It is unfortunate that the Court of Appeal's decisions in *Re W* and *Re R* have come to dominate the law. I think that we can dispense with a parents' independent right to consent when their competent child refuses. Young people's refusal may still have to be overruled on the basis of their welfare. Balancing autonomy against protection in a straightforward way is to be preferred. It is more respectful than setting an unrealistically high standard for competence, or using parental consent to bypassing the young person. It may also do less damage to the development of the young person's sense of autonomy and respect for authority.

At the moment the courts are the only independent authority in these difficult cases. It would be helpful to have a range of options. We might develop a body to review young people treated against their wishes along the lines of the new mental health tribunals (as outlined in the Government's White Paper, 2000). Alternatively, children's guardians might be appointed to provide the young person with independent advice. The courts would continue to handle the very difficult cases.

A competence checklist (adapted, with permission, from Shaw, 2001)

Young people are more likely to be competent and contribute to decision-making:

(1)   In the presence of:

- a supportive and affectionate parent–child relationship;
- trust and confidence in the doctor–patient relationship;
- adequate information presented in an appropriate way.

(2)   Free from:

- pressure;
- panic;
- pain;
- or other 'temporary factors' that could impair judgment.

(3)   Understanding:

- that there is a decision to make;
- that decisions have consequences;
- the nature and the illness;
- the nature of the recommended intervention and any alternatives;
- the risks and benefits of interventions or no intervention;
- the longer-term consequences of each option.

(4)   Able to:

- retain an understanding;
- appreciate its importance;
- see how it applies to them;
- weigh the issues in the balance;
- arrive at a decision.

The level of understanding required for competence:

- will vary with the complexity and gravity of the situation;
- may be higher if the young person refuses treatment;
- should not be higher than what would be expected for adults.

Guidelines for good practice on consent (modified, with permission, from Shaw, 1998)

(1)   Parents and young people (whether or not they are competent) need to be informed and involved as much as possible in treatment decisions.

(2)   Treatment can proceed with the consent of a person having parental responsibility and the incompetent young person's agreement, or the competent young person's consent.

(3)   If either the parent or young person refuse, treatment should be delayed for more discussion, modification of the treatment plan, or the help of an independent arbiter.

(4)   Treatment may proceed with the consent of one person having parental responsibility (Children Act 1989, s 2(7)) even if there is opposition from another. The onus is on that person to obtain a prohibited steps order under s 8.

(5)   If there is no person having parental responsibility willing to consent to a necessary action or treatment programme for a child who is not competent, consideration must be given to obtaining a specific issue order or asking the local authority to seek a care order.

(6)   Overruling the refusal of any young person (competent or not) should be considered only if:

   (a)   discussion and modification of the treatment has been exhausted;
   (b)   (and) the parents are in favour, or the authority of the court is obtained;
   (c)   (and) the young person is more likely than not to suffer significant harm without treatment.

(7)   Before treating a young person against his or her will:

   (a)   consider whether treatment under the Mental Health Act is indicated;
   (b)   alternatively the decision should be confirmed by a second opinion;
   (c)   (and) a time limit should be set for reviewing the decision;
   (d)   (and) the reasons for the decision should be recorded in the notes.

(8)   If it is considered necessary to overrule the refusal of consent by a competent child, legal advice should be taken on whether to rely on the consent of a person having parental responsibility, if available, or whether to seek the authority of the court.

(9)   Parents or the young person can withdraw consent at any time.

(10) Staff need to be aware of the service's policy on consent.

(11) Staff will need training and ongoing support to achieve an appropriate balance between autonomy and protection.

References

Alderson P, *Children's Consent to Surgery* (Open University Press, 1993).

Bailey P and Harbour A, 'The law and a child's consent to treatment (England and Wales)' (1999) 4 (1) *Child Psychology & Psychiatry Review* 30.

Bainham A, *Children: The Modern Law* (Family Law, 2000).

British Medical Association, *Consent, Rights and Choices in Health Care for Children and Young People* (British Medical Association, 2001).

Department of Health, *Reforming the Mental Health Act (Part 1: the new legal framework)* (The Stationery Office, 2000).

Department of Health and Welsh Office, *Code of Practice: Mental Health Act 1983* (HMSO, 1999).

Devereux JA, Jones DPH and Dickenson DL, 'Can children withhold consent to treatment?' (1993) 306 *British Medical Journal* 1459.

Downie A, 'Consent to medical treatment – whose view of welfare' [1999] Fam Law 818.

Freeman M, 'Removing rights from adolescents' (1993) 17 *Adoption & Fostering* 14.

General Medical Council, *Seeking Patients' Consent: The Ethical Considerations* (General Medical Council, 1999).

Gillick v West Norfolk and Wisbech Area Health Authority [1986] AC 112.

Grisso T and Applebaum PS, 'The MacArthur treatment competence study III. Abilities of patients to consent to psychiatric and medical treatments' (1995) 19 *Law and Human Behaviour* 149.

McCafferty C, 'Won't consent? Can't consent! Refusal of medical treatment' [1999] Fam Law 335.

Mason JK and McCall Smith RA, *Law and Medical Ethics* (Butterworths, 1999).

Pearce J, 'Consent to treatment during childhood: the assessment of competence and avoidance of conflict' (1994) 165 *British Journal of Psychiatry* 713.

Re C (Adult: Refusal of Medical Treatment) [1994] 1 FLR 31.

Re E (A Minor) (Wardship: Medical Treatment) [1993] FLR 386.

Re K, W and H (Minors) (Medical Treatment) [1993] 1 FLR 854.

Re L (Medical Treatment: Gillick Competency) [1998] 2 FLR 810.

Re MB (Caesarean Section) [1997] 8 Med LR 217, (1997) 38 BMLR 175, CA.

Re R (A Minor) (Wardship: Medical Treatment) [1992] Fam 11, [1991] 4 All ER 177, CA.

Re W (A Minor) (Wardship: Medical Treatment) [1993] Fam 64, [1992] 4 All ER 627, CA.

Roth LH, Meisel A and Lidz CW, 'Tests of competence to consent to treatment' (1977) 134 *American Journal of Psychiatry* 279.

Rutter M, 'Research and the family justice system: What has been the role of research and what should it be?', 3rd Annual Lecture of The National Council for Family Proceedings and reprinted in its newsletter (1999), pp 2–6.

Shaw M, 'Childhood, mental health and the law', in J Green and B Jacobs, *In-patient Child Psychiatry Modern Practice, Research and the Future* (Routledge, 1998).

Shaw M, 'Competence and consent to treatment in children and adolescents' (2001) 7 *Advances in Psychiatric Treatment* 150.

Sidaway v Board of Governors of the Bethlem Royal Hospital and the Maudsley Hospital [1985] AC 871.

PLENARY THREE

ADOPTION

James Paton
Bill Principal for the Adoption and Children Bill, Department of Health

Summary of paper

James Paton in introducing his paper focused particularly on the Adoption and Children Bill which was introduced to Parliament in March 2001, and has been remitted to Select Committee for further consideration. He confirmed that it was the Government's intention that the Bill would become legislation during this session of Parliament, although the precise timing was not at present clear.

The Bill was intended to replace the Adoption Act 1976 for England and Wales, and incorporate most provisions of the Adoption (Intercountry Aspects) Act 1999, providing a full framework for adoption. It also included some amendments to the Children Act 1989.

James Paton highlighted three main areas of the Bill to the conference:

- *Bringing adoption law more closely in line with the Children Act 1989, with the paramount consideration for adoption becoming the child's welfare. In addition the Government's intention was to include a checklist of factors for the court to have regard to, similar to the s 1(3) Children Act checklist, but tailored to the particular circumstances of adoption cases. He stated that the Government's current view was that the welfare principle should also apply to dispensing with birth parents' consent to adoption although this went against the recommendations made in the 1992 interdepartmental review of adoption law. The reason for the Government's stance was that it seemed more logical not to make an exception to the welfare principle just in this case, and that the amendments made to the proposed checklist included taking into account the birth parents' views. It was considered that such an approach was compatible with the European Convention on Human Rights, as the court would have an eye to Convention rights when performing the balancing act required by the checklist factors. However, James Paton acknowledged that this was a key area for further debate and discussion and emphasised that the Government had not closed its mind to further amendment at this stage.*

- *Changes to the structure and operation of adoption services, including a better framework for post-adoptive support services, a new independent review mechanism for adopters who feel they are being turned down unfairly and a National Adoption Register to enable authorities and agencies to pool available resources in matching children with adoptive parents.*

- *Changes to the process of placement for adoption: James Paton explained that the Bill involved a comprehensive remodeling of the adoption process, with the key aim being to try to ensure that substantive decisions were taken at a much earlier stage than currently as to placement for adoption, the consent of the birth family and whether any refusal to consent should be overridden. At present it was felt that too much was left until the final adoption hearing, which was not in the interests of the child or adopters. It also contained potential unfairness for birth families since, by the time of this hearing, the child had often been placed with the potential adopters for such a long time that the hearing could be effectively a 'fait accompli'. The intention was to try to get a decision if possible before the child was placed. James Paton stated that, in consultation, broad support for the changes had been received although certain concerns had been raised, particularly about the discrepancy between the need to satisfy the threshold criteria in care proceedings and the need just to consider the child's welfare for a placement order. He stated that these concerns were being given active consideration.*

James Paton emphasised that the Government wanted to get the Bill right, and that he wanted to use the conference to gather further ideas and suggestions as to amendments before the provisions of the Bill were finalised.

Introduction

This paper is intended to provide a brief review of major developments in the adoption field since the implementation of the Children Act in 1991. A great deal has happened during this time; what follows is inevitably selective. It is also primarily a 'view from the centre'. The period concerned has been characterised by an increasing focus by government on adoption policy and practice and on reform of the legislative framework, with the intensity of scrutiny and pace of change both picking up considerably over the last 18 months, as a direct result of the Prime Minister's Review. The paper aims to put these ongoing developments in context, to highlight the key themes that have emerged and to look ahead to the further changes in prospect.

The paper examines developments in three main areas:

- adoption policy and practice, concentrating particularly on public law adoption;
- intercountry adoption;
- adoption law reform.

The section on adoption law reform highlights for discussion some of the key issues that have arisen in response to the current Government's proposed new adoption legislation, in anticipation of the reintroduction of the Adoption and Children Bill in the forthcoming Parliamentary session.

Adoption policy and practice

The 1990s saw a continuation of the gradual fall in the overall number of adoptions in England that began in the early 1970s, reflecting the decline of private law adoption as a result of wider social changes, principally the reduction in the number of mothers relinquishing babies for adoption. The total number of adoptions in England fell from around 6,700 in 1991 to about 4,000 in 1999.

Over the same period the number of 'looked after' children adopted from local authority care fell from around 2,500 at the beginning of the 1990s to a low of 1,900 in 1997. It has been suggested that this fall in numbers from the early 1990s may have been due to a more hesitant approach to the use of adoption by local authorities immediately following implementation of the Children Act, in the belief that courts would be less prepared under the new legal framework to endorse adoption as a placement option.[1] In the later 1990s the numbers picked up, rising to 2,700 in 1999/2000. As a result, public law adoptions now make up over half of the total numbers of adoptions in England, compared to under 40% in 1991.[2] In terms of the proportion of the overall 'looked after' children population, the numbers adopted represented around 4% during most of the 1990s, rising to 5% in 1999/2000.

---

[1]   Parker (ed), *Adoption Now* (Wiley, 1999), at p 3.

[2]   All figures from Office for National Statistics, *Marriage, Divorce and Adoption Statistics* (1991).

Thanks to an improved research effort over the last 10 years we now know much more about the characteristics of 'looked after' children adopted.[3] The average age at adoption is now 4 years 4 months, down from 5 years 9 months in 1995. Over 60% of 'looked after' children adopted are now aged under 5 years, and less than 5% are over 10.[4] Many of these children have special needs or have become looked after as a result of abuse and neglect.[5] Finding suitable adoptive placements for them can prove difficult for social services departments, and meeting their particular needs can pose challenges for adopters, raising important questions about the support available to adoptive families.[6]

From the mid-1990s there has been a concerted effort on the part of government to improve the performance of local authorities in delivering their adoption services. Social Services Inspectorate reports in 1996 and 1997 raised concerns about the variable quality of local authority adoption services, and the relatively low priority accorded to this service at local level.[7]

In response, the Government issued a Local Authority Circular, *Adoption – Achieving the Right Balance*,[8] which was intended to achieve two principal objectives: first, to counteract any perceived relative neglect of adoption services by emphasising to local authorities that adoption was an important and beneficial option in the care of children, and one that was wholly consistent with the framework of duties and obligations under the Children Act; and, secondly, to set out a number of steps for local authorities to take to improve their planning for individual children and their management of the adoption service as a whole, the latter aimed at 'bringing adoption back into the mainstream of children's services'.

The emphasis on connecting adoption work more closely with children services generally and promoting improved local management of the adoption service continued with the launch, in 1999, of the comprehensive Quality Protects (QP) programme for improving children's social services as a whole. One of the specific objectives of the programme is to 'maximise the contribution that adoption can make to provide permanent families for children in appropriate cases'.[9] More recent Social Services Inspectorate surveys and the evaluation of the QP programme have found evidence of improvements at local level as a result of these efforts, but have also confirmed that performance continues to vary and that many stages of the adoption process are subject to undesirable delay.[10]

This was the background to the Prime Minister's announcement in February 2000 that he would lead a major review of the use of adoption as an option for 'looked after' children. As a first stage the Prime Minister commissioned the Performance and Innovation Unit (PIU) in the Cabinet Office to conduct a rapid review of the evidence, explore the options for action and make recommendations to the Government.

The PIU report was published for consultation in July 2000.[11] It reported that there was scope to make substantially greater use of adoption as an option that would benefit 'looked after' children. It also identified a range of obstacles that were preventing full realisation of the potential of adoption:

---

[3] See especially Ivaldi, *Surveying Adoption* (BAAF, 2000), and Ivaldi, *Children Adopted from Care* (BAAF, 1998).

[4] Figures from Ivaldi, 2000 and 1998, ibid; and Department of Health, *Children Looked After By Local Authorities, Year ending 31 March 2000* (Department of Health, 2001).

[5] Ivaldi, 2000, n 3, pp 21–23.

[6] Parker, n 1, chapters 3, 4 and 7; Lowe and Murch et al, *Supporting Adoption – Reframing the Approach* (BAAF, 2000); Quniton, Rushton, Dance and Mayes, *Joining New Families* (BAAF, 1998).

[7] *For Children's Sake: An SSI Inspection of Local Authority Adoption Services* (Department of Health, 1996); *For Children's Sake – Part II: An Inspection of Local Authority Adoption Services* (Department of Health, 1997).

[8] LAC(98)20 (Department of Health, August 1998).

[9] *The Government's Objectives for Children's Social Services* (Department of Health, 1999), paras 1–3.

[10] *Adopting Changes – Survey and Inspection of Local Councils' Adoption Services* (Department of Health, 2000).

[11] *Prime Minister's Review – Adoption* (Performance and Innovation Unit, July 2000).

- local authority performance in planning for children and delivering adoption services was patchy and inconsistent;
- too often decisions about how to provide a safe, stable and secure family life for 'looked after' children, including the use of adoption, were not addressed early enough, focused clearly enough or taken swiftly enough;
- where plans for adoption were made, delays in local authorities and the legal system meant that they were often not delivered quickly enough, bearing in mind the appropriate timescale for the child;
- there was a shortage of suitable adopters and recruitment activity was sporadic, poorly co-ordinated and of variable quality;
- post-adoption support services were inadequate, bearing in mind the challenging characteristics of many 'looked after' children adopted.

Notwithstanding the progress that had been made in improving local adoption services, the PIU advised that many of the problems identified needed action by central Government if they were to be tackled effectively. It recommended that the Government develop and implement a comprehensive national programme of action.

The Government's White Paper, *Adoption – a new approach*,[12] published in December 2000, built on the PIU report and set out a wide-ranging strategy for promoting the greater use of adoption as a placement option where it would benefit 'looked after' children, and for improving adoption services. Key elements of the strategy include:

- setting new National Adoption Standards for adoption agencies, so that all parties could be clear what they should expect from the adoption services. These would include timescales for planning and decision-making in respect of children, and for key elements of the adoption process;
- a comprehensive effort to improve local authority performance, including establishing an Adoption and Permanence Taskforce to identify and spread best practice and to work with authorities to help them achieve the standards of the best performers;
- alongside the National Adoption Standards, further efforts to tackle delay, including a new National Adoption Register to help speed the matching of children and families, and improvements to the court system, including case management pilots and the development of specialist adoption centres;
- improved recruitment of adopters and better, more consistent, post-adoption support services, delivered according to a new national framework;
- reform of existing adoption legislation to underpin the whole programme.

The programme is supported by over £66 million of investment over 3 years. Taken together, the aim is that this programme will transform local adoption services and enable hundreds more 'looked after' children to benefit from adoption where this is in their best interests. The Government has set a Public Service Agreement target of delivering at least a 40% increase in the numbers of 'looked after' children adopted by 2004/05.

It will take several years to put in place all the measures in the programme, but the pace of progress has been rapid. The Adoption and Permanence Taskforce has now been up and running for just over a year, the contract for the National Adoption Register was signed in July and the final National Adoption Standards were issued at the same time. Over the coming year, while local authorities and voluntary adoption agencies begin to implement the Standards, the Government will be consulting on and developing the new national frameworks for post-adoption support and adoption allowances, as well starting work on the fundamental review of the adopter assessment process and piloting new adoption legislation through Parliament.

---

[12] *Adoption – A New Approach*, Cm 5017 (December 2000).

Intercountry adoption

The 10 years since the implementation of the Children Act have seen unprecedented attention focused on intercountry adoption. Prior to the 1990s, intercountry adoption featured very little in the United Kingdom, with an estimated 50–60 children brought into the United Kingdom for adoption through official channels and a further 60 to 70 arriving without prior entry clearance.[13] However, over the 2 years following the Romanian revolution in 1990, over 400 children from Romania were brought into the United Kingdom for adoption. The numbers from Romania declined following the conclusion of a bilateral agreement on adoption in 1993, but the overall number of intercountry adoptions recorded through official channels has increased from the mid-1990s level of around 200 per year, to over 350 in 2000, and is continuing to grow. Adoptions from China now account for over 50% of the total. In addition, there are an estimated 100 cases per year of people avoiding the adoption procedures.

The influx of Romanian children raised the profile of intercountry adoption and highlighted a number of concerns about how the process worked. Over the rest of the period under review the Government took action to put in place a sound framework for intercountry adoption, focused on the welfare and interest of the child. In 1993 the Government signed the Hague Convention on the Protection of Children and Cooperation in Respect of Intercountry Adoption. This aimed to provide a legal framework for intercountry adoption, to ensure that it took place in the child's interest. Sending states must ensure that adoption overseas is in the best interest of the child, while receiving states are responsible for ensuring that adopters are properly assessed as suitable. Convention adoptions are to be channelled through central authorities and their accredited bodies, and activity confined to non-profit-making organisations. Measures to allow the United Kingdom to ratify the Convention became law following the passage of the Adoption (Intercountry Aspects) Act 1999. The Act also clarifies local authorities' duty to provide an intercountry adoption service and introduces sanctions to deal with acceptable practices in intercountry adoption.

Sections providing that only registered adoption societies may conduct 'home study' suitability assessments and introducing controls on bringing children into the United Kingdom for the purposes of adoption have already been brought into effect. It is intented to commence the remainder of the Act over the coming year, to allow the United Kingdom to ratify the Convention in 2002. Following the recent high profile intercountry adoption case involving the Kilshaws, the Government has confirmed that the next version of the Adoption and Children Bill will include further measures aimed at ensuring that those adopting children from overseas follow the correct procedures. National Standards for intercountry adoption are also being developed. So while intercountry adoption looks set to continue to grow over the coming years, there can be greater confidence that a legislative and regulatory framework will be in place to ensure that the welfare and interests of children are protected.

Adoption law reform

The process of adoption law reform has been long and convoluted, spanning the entire period since the implementation of the Children Act. The previous Government launched an interdepartmental review of adoption law, in co-operation with the Law Society, in 1989. The review reported in 1992.[14] It recommended that the Government should not make fundamental changes to the nature and effect of adoption in English law on the grounds that the current model was effective and well understood. But the review recommended that comprehensive legislative change was needed to align the framework of adoption law with the Children Act

---

[13] *Adoption Law Review: Discussion Paper 4* (Department of Health, 1992), para 27.

[14] *Review of Adoption Law – Report to Ministers of an Interdepartmental Working Group* (Department of Health and Welsh Office, October 1992).

and to reshape the legal process for placing children for adoption to make it fairer for all parties and to promote improved decision-making. The review also recommended that there needed to be a new legal framework for intercountry adoption.

The Government's 1993 White Paper[15] broadly accepted the review's proposals, but committed the Government to further consultation on the new concept of placement in advance of legislation. A draft Bill was eventually published for consultation in March 1996[16] but did not progress any further. However, the Prime Minister's Review imparted new momentum into the legislative reform process; in July 2000 a firm commitment was made that there would be new legislation in 2001. The Adoption and Children Bill was duly introduced in March 2001 and referred to a Select Committee for consultation and scrutiny. While it fell at the General Election, the Queen's Speech in June this year confirmed that the Bill would reappear in the legislative programme this session. At present we are preparing the Bill for reintroduction, and, in particular, are working through all the various issues raised during the Select Committee process.

The Adoption and Children Bill builds on the earlier draft Bill, includes some significant changes as a result the 1996 consultation and incorporates a range of new measures stemming from the December 2000 White Paper. Its key elements include:

- provisions aligning adoption law with the Children Act to make the child's welfare the paramount concern in all decisions on adoption;
- a range of changes to the adoption services to deliver the White Paper commitments, including improved post-adoption support and a National Adoption Register;
- improvements to the legal process of placing a child for adoption, including a new system of placement and placement orders;
- strengthened safeguards for adoption, including improved legal controls on intercountry adoption, making arrangements for adoption, and advertising children for adoption, including over the internet;
- a number of amendments to the Children Act, including the introduction of a new 'special guardianship' order to provide security and permanence for children where adoption is not suitable.

Many of these areas could fruitfully be discussed at length, but I would like briefly to highlight two of what I think have been the most significant areas of debate since the publication of the Bill.

Clause 1 – child's welfare paramount

The first is clause 1 of the Bill. This is a key overarching provision. It brings adoption legislation explicitly into line with the Children Act by making the child's welfare the paramount consideration for a court or adoption agency making any decision relating to the adoption of a child. As with s 1 of the Children Act, it includes a 'checklist' of issues clause that courts and agency's must consider in determining the child's welfare. But the clause is specifically tailored to adoption. It is the child's welfare in childhood and beyond that the court must consider, in recognition of the lifetime impact of adoption. In addition to the issues set out in the Children Act equivalent, the welfare checklist also includes the impact on the child of becoming adopted and ceasing to be a member of his or her original family, the relationship the child has with his or her parents and relatives, including the likelihood of any such relationship continuing, the value to the child of it doing so, the wishes and feelings of the relatives regarding the child, and their ability to provide the child with a stable and secure home.

Debate since the Bill's publication has focused on the fact that the Bill would make the

---

[15]   *Adoption: The Future*, Cm 2288 (November 1993).

[16]   *Adoption – A Service for Children* (Department of Health and Welsh Office, March 1996).

child's welfare the paramount consideration in dispensing with birth parents' consent to adoption, a departure from the 'unreasonably withholding consent' test in s 16 of the 1976 Act. The suggestion has been made that this inappropriately shifts the balance away from the birth family, or even shuts their views and interests out from consideration.

The Government does not believe that this is the case. As set out above, in applying the clause 1 checklist the court will have to consider the impact on the child of becoming adopted and ceasing to be a member of his or her original family, the relationship the child has with his or her parents and relatives, including the likelihood of any such relationship continuing, the value to the child of it doing so, the wishes and feelings of the relatives regarding the child and their capacity to care for him or her. The court must also consider all the alternatives it has available under adoption legislation and the Children Act 1989 when it is considering whether to make an adoption order. The court will exercise its discretion as to whether to make an adoption order after considering all the facts of the individual case and weighing up the interests of all parties in line with European Convention for the Protection of Human Rights and Fundamental Freedoms 1950 (ECHR) case-law. The Government considers that the clause sets the right structure within which these interests should be balanced, with the child's welfare at the centre. But we can no doubt expect debate on this issue to continue in Parliament.

Placement for adoption

The second set of provisions that have attracted attention are those concerning placement for adoption. The Bill establishes new legal processes for placing a child for adoption through an adoption agency. There are two routes:

- birth parents can give consent to placement;
- the adoption agency can secure a placement order from the court.

Parents may consent to placement with specific adopters or consent to allow placement with adopters whom the agency selects. They must agree to parental responsibility being given to the adoption agency and being shared with the prospective adopters once the child is placed. The birth parents retain parental responsibility up to the final adoption order, but their ability to exercise it is limited. Where a child is placed with consent, the birth parents can, at any time up until the point that an application for an adoption order has been made, request the return of their child. The agency and the prospective adopters must comply. Following an application for an adoption order, the court's consent is required for the removal of the child.

Where a parent has consented to placement for adoption, he or she may only oppose the final adoption order with the leave of the court, and the court may only give leave if there has been a change of circumstances since the parents gave consent to placement.

Where an adoption agency is satisfied that a child should be placed for adoption, but the parents do not consent to placement or have withdrawn consent, the agency must apply for a placement order.

Where a child is subject to a care order and the care plan recommends adoption, the local authority may apply for a placement order or, if the parents consent to placement, the parents themselves can go down that route.

A court may make a placement order only if it is satisfied that the parents consent, or that their consent should be dispensed with, for example on the grounds of the child's welfare. Where a child is under a care order, this is suspended for the duration of the placement order, but would automatically revive if the placement order were revoked.

Placement orders authorise the adoption agency to place a child with any adopters it may select. The agency need not go back to court if an initial placement falls. Once a placement order is made, parental responsibility is given to the adoption agency and, once the child is placed, to prospective adopters also. The birth parents retain parental responsibility up to the final adoption order, but their ability to exercise it is limited.

Placement orders last until an adoption order is made, or the child reaches 18, or the order is revoked. Courts can revoke orders on the application of the adoption agency or the birth parents. The parents may not apply to revoke the order unless a year has passed since the order has been made, the child has not been placed and the court gives leave. The court may give leave only if the birth parents' circumstances have changed since the order was made.

Where a child has been placed under a placement order, the birth parents may oppose the final adoption order only with the leave of the court, and the court may give leave only if there has been a change of circumstances since the order was made.

The idea of formalising placement for adoption flowed from the Adoption Law Review. The aim was to ensure that substantial decisions around whether adoption was the right option for the child and whether the parents consented were taken earlier in the adoption process, with court involvement where necessary. The current system was felt to leave too much to be resolved at the final adoption order stage. Focusing decisions around the placement of children was intended to:

- provide greater certainty and stability for children by dealing, as far as possible, with the bulk of issues around consent to adoption before they had been placed;
- minimise the uncertainty for prospective adopters, who possibly face a contested court hearing at the adoption order stage;
- reduce the extent to which birth families are faced with a 'fait accompli' at the final adoption hearing since the child had by that time been placed for a considerable period;
- improve decision-making, by ensuring court involvement at an appropriately early stage in this significant decision about the child's future.

The placement provisions are also intended to replace the legally unsatisfactory freeing provisions as a means to allow birth parents voluntarily to relinquish their children for adoption. To that end the Bill also allows birth parents to give advance consent to the final adoption order, either at the same time as they give consent to placement or at any time afterwards, as a means of allowing people voluntarily to give up their children for adoption.

This consent cannot be withdrawn. But if they change their minds the birth parents can apply to the court for leave to contest the final adoption order. The court may give leave only if there has been a significant change of circumstances since the consent was given.

While the placement provisions have been broadly welcomed (in particular the emphasis on making key decisions on a fairer basis earlier in the process), a number of concerns have been raised. Perhaps the most pressing of these is whether the bases for the making of placement orders against the parents' wishes fits appropriately with the threshold for intervention in family life set out in the Children Act, particularly those for care orders. The Government has found the consultation process valuable and is currently giving active consideration to these issues. Again, we can expect further debate and discussion in Parliament.

Conclusion

It has been possible only to provide a brief overview in the space available and I am conscious that there are many areas of policy and practice that I have not even touched on (for instance the question of openness and contact in adoption, or of taking full and proper account of children's views). But I hope that what I have set out has been helpful in terms of giving a central government perspective on developments since the implementation of the Children Act, and in setting out the latest state of play in the long-running saga of adoption law reform.

A STUDY OF CARE PLANS AND THEIR IMPLEMENTATION AND RELEVANCE FOR RE W AND B AND RE W (CARE PLAN)

Professor Judith Harwin and Morag Owen[1]
Brunel University

Summary of paper

Judith Harwin stated that the major focus of the study was not the court process, but the implementation of care plans after orders had been made and the welfare outcomes of the children. Nevertheless a study was also made of developments to the plan before the order. The particular points which she highlighted in introducing her paper were:

- *Social workers valued the chance to discuss the care plans with guardians ad litem; the initial plans were generally not set in stone.*
- *The worst rates of plan fulfilment after 21 months were found where children had been placed at home. One of the matters she asked the conference to focus on was whether children should be placed at home if the situation was serious enough for a care order to be made.*
- *Parental substance abuse was a major factor in bringing cases to court. If alcohol misuse and all types of drug misuse are combined, they are much more significant than learning difficulties, mental health or domestic violence. She referred to the difficulties that all agencies were found to have in responding to and monitoring alcohol abuse. In some cases where substance abuse was a factor, no experts' reports had been commissioned on this issue: she asked the conference to consider whether this was the right or wrong approach.*
- *Different placement options had different strengths and weaknesses. She believed that placements should be judged by their capacity to handle children's initial difficulties and to improve children's prospects. Some placements (eg foster care) were found to be very good at taking on children with many difficulties, but less good at bringing about improvement. Good welfare outcome results were found with adoption, but she felt this was likely to be because the adoption system generally screened out children with particular difficulties, sibling groups and most children over the age of 3.*
- *Placing children with relatives was an underused option. Although the children in such placements were found to have high rates of initial difficulties, 78% of the placements endured.*

Judith Harwin also referred to the recent judgments in Re W and B; Re W (Care Plan) [2001] EWCA Civ 757, [2001] 2 FLR 582. She queried the numbers of cases which were likely to come back to court, and was concerned about the wider implications of the judgments. In particular she referred to the possibility that more defensive care planning practices would grow up, with social workers aiming for more realisable and achievable care plans rather than seeking an outcome which was better for the child but less easily achievable. She also queried the court's expectations as to plan fulfilment. She believed it important to be careful to avoid an over-simplistic conclusion that plan fulfilment always brings the best welfare result for

---

[1] Department of Health and Social Care, Brunel University.

the child. She referred to children whose plans were changed for good reasons and urged the courts to distinguish carefully between justifiable changes by social services and real breaches of human rights.

Introduction

Aims

This paper has two main aims. First, it draws out for the courts the main results of a Department of Health (DH)-funded study of care plans[2] and their outcomes in respect of 100 children from 57 families placed on care orders in 1997. The children came from five local authorities and were followed up for 21 months.[3] Secondly, it considers some implications of the findings with special reference to the recent Court of Appeal judgment *Re W and B; Re W (Care Plan)* [2001] EWCA Civ 757.[4]

The study set out to answer three main questions:

- To what extent are care plans implemented according to the agreed care plan?
- What factors influence fulfilment or non-fulfilment?[5]
- What is the relationship between plan implementation and welfare outcome?

The development of the plan prior to the care order was also studied in order to understand its history and antecedents.

Care plan formation and the role of the court

Care plans were analysed in terms of their recommendations with regard to placement, contact and services, as these three elements were deemed the core of the plan. At the time of the first interim care order, the key issue was whether the child should remain or return home. The particular form of substitute care was much less of an issue, to be clarified later in relation to criteria such as age, contact needs, availability of carers and the child's wishes and feelings. A number of the plans were quite open-ended and seemed to suggest that social services were looking for the court to supervise the assessment and to help firm up the future direction of the case.

The court process did indeed change a significant number of care plans. As can be seen from Table 1, the biggest changes that took place were in respect of plans for reunification and adoption.

---

[2]   For full details, see report to the Department of Health, *A Study to Investigate Care Orders made under the Children Act 1989* (2001); and J Harwin, M Owen, R Locke and D Forrester, *Making Care Orders Work: a Study of Care Plans and their Implementation* (The Stationery Office, forthcoming, 2001). The study also had the support of the Lord Chancellor's Department.

[3]   The data were derived from analysis of court files and interviews with social workers, guardians ad litem and local authority solicitors at the start point. Analysis of social service files was carried out at 21 months, and second stage interviews were held with social workers and with 18 birth parents, 44 current carers and 26 children aged 7 or over.

[4]   [2001] 2 FLR 582.

[5]   The definition of fulfilment was that at 21 months the child was living in the placement type specified in the care plan for the court. Implemented plans refer to those put into effect according to the court care plan, although some of these broke down. (Successful implementation and fulfilment are used synonymously in the text for variety.)

Table 1: Changes during care proceedings: the development of placement plans for the sample children

	Initial plans	*Final plans*
Home placement	39	22
Kinship care	18	18
Adoption	19	33
Long-term fostering	19	22
Residential care	5	5
Total	100	100

The 39 children for whom placement at home was the dominant initial plan came from 21 families and included a large number of singletons. By the final hearing, just 10 families were left with a home placement plan and nearly all involved sibling groups. As the numbers of plans for home placement dropped, so the final care plans for adoption swelled. Ten of the 17 children diverted to substitute care had final plans for adoption, while four were to remain in foster care and three were to live with relatives.

The drop in the numbers of plans for home placement came about as a result of assessments carried out by social services and family centres during the proceedings, the advice of guardians and reports from experts. A number of key turning points could be identified in relation to the 17 children whose initial plans changed to substitute care, as follows:

- parents withdrew from the assessments;
- the assessment showed that parents were making insufficient progress;
- rehabilitation failed;
- parents failed to acknowledge the risk of physical and/or sexual abuse;
- previous concerns about the child's safety were seen in a new light.

The influence of the guardian ad litem on changes to initial plans for rehabilitation was strong. Guardians most typically emphasised risk to the child where social workers were more inclined to take a more optimistic view of the likelihood of parental change.

Of particular interest is the group of 22 children for whom the initial plan for home placement remained unchanged at the final hearing. Twelve of these children never left home, while a further 10 were removed temporarily to foster care but all but two were back home prior to the making of the care order. We might ask how it was possible for a home placement to be recommended when the making of the care order by definition indicated that these children were at significant risk from their parents. In some cases a dangerous partner had left the house. If the main threat had been removed, was a care order necessary? But more commonly, the main threat was neglect by the mother. In these cases, how would a placement at home be monitored? Kempe reminds us that 'if a child is not safe at home, he cannot be protected by casework'.[6]

The decision to recommend placement at home in the care plan at the final hearing caused the most worry to social workers, guardians and solicitors, and at interview these placements were sometimes rated as standing no more than 50% chance of success. This uncertainty did not come out in proceedings and it may have been obscured by the lack of contest by parents, who often agreed to the order on the condition that the child would remain at home.[7] Furthermore, although home placement was sometimes chosen for positive reasons (nearly always because

---

[6]   Quoted in *A Child in Trust* (Brent, 1985), p 288.

[7]   Only one home placement was contested at final hearing. This was the lowest rate of contest of all placement options.

the strength of attachment was deemed to outweigh possible risk), it also reflected in a number of cases a view by the solicitor that there was insufficient evidence to justify removing the child. This applied to two types of case in particular:

- new born babies and young children whose elder siblings had been harmed, but for whom evidence of harmful parenting did not exist in relation to the baby;
- cases of chronic, long-standing neglect which lacked any trigger event to the proceedings where sometimes risk had been greater at an earlier point (eg from a dangerous partner who had moved out).

Occasionally, unease was also echoed in the court arena, and in one case the plan was endorsed only on the grounds that the parent had not been formally warned previously by social services of the possibility of removal.

However, it seems unlikely that greater certainty would have been achieved by extending the use of interim care orders in these home placement cases, which commonly involved parental alcohol misuse, learning difficulties and dangerous partners. First, expert reports or assessments from specialist resources such as family centres were usually available to the courts. Insofar as these particular parental difficulties are unpredictable in nature, likely to pose different kinds of risk over the duration of childhood and vary in impact, and seem therefore to fall into the category of 'chronic or inevitable uncertainty'.[8] Moreover, prediction of risk needs to take account of many issues. In all these cases, the parental difficulty needs to be judged in relation to a range of factors, including the child's behaviour, the social supports available within the family network and the nature and extent of support from agencies.

Could other types of uncertainty have been eliminated by the opportunity to delay the final care order in options other than home placement? In one kinship care case, the order was made before the medical report was available when suspicions of alcohol misuse were known during proceedings. In another kinship care case the assessment was hurried and both plans foundered. In both these cases it might have been an advantage to have been able to make further interim orders to ensure that the plan was viable, but no other cases were found where this would have been beneficial.

There were, however, other ways in which the final care plans presented to the court could have provided greater certainty on a wide range of important issues. By the time of the final hearing all the plans had been firmed up with regard to aims and placement choice.[9] But timescales were missing in 49% of the cases, and the likely duration of the placement was absent in 68%. Reunification was rarely stated as an aim, except where the child had left home briefly in home placement cases. Even though there were five or six fostering cases where interviews confirmed that the child returning home had not been ruled out at a later stage, reunification was still not targeted in these care plans. Contact arrangements with adults were far more common than with siblings – the long-term plans for siblings (even including 'indirect contact') were missing for approximately half the children. The role given to parents in day-to-day arrangements tended to emphasise their marginality: only one plan stated that the parent was to be involved in the introduction to long-term foster carers and given the opportunity to help develop the links. Only 25% of the plans mentioned arrangements for notifying disagreements. Finally and importantly, only 28% of the plans included adequate information on contingencies were the plan to break down while 27% omitted altogether a contingency plan.

---

[8]   *Re W and B; Re W (Care Plan)* [2001] EWCA Civ 757, [2001] 2 FLR 582, at para [29].
[9]   These findings derive from a content analysis of the 100 plans submitted to court in the final hearing. It was based on the key elements to be included in care plans set out in Department of Health, *Children Act 1989 Guidance and Regulations* (HMSO, 1991), Vol 3, 'Family Placements', at para 2.62. Although this format was subsequently revised in Local Authority Circular, *Care Plans and Care Proceedings under the Children Act 1989*, LAC(99)29 (Department of Health, 1999), the information requested in Vol 3 is common to both versions.

Given that the available government guidance[10] specified the importance of this information, we may ask why it was not required more frequently: an opportunity was undoubtedly lost here for the court arena to be used to full effect.

Implementation

Sixty of the 100 placement plans were implemented successfully according to the agreed care plan at the 21-month point. As can be seen from Graph 1 below, fulfilment rates varied with the type of placement chosen.

Although the numbers vary for each placement type, plan fulfilment was highest for children placed with relatives (78%) and lowest for those placed at home (41%) (the numbers for whom residential care was chosen were too small to generate meaningful results and have only been included for completeness). The kinship placements (which included placement with fathers who had not previously had care of the children) were noteworthy. In contrast to successfully implemented adoption and placement at home plans, children placed with relatives had high numbers of initial problems;[11] these were well managed by carers and welfare outcomes were favourable.[12] The adoption figures deserve special comment. Only

Graph 1: Placement plan recommendations at the final hearing for the sample children and fulfilment at 21 months

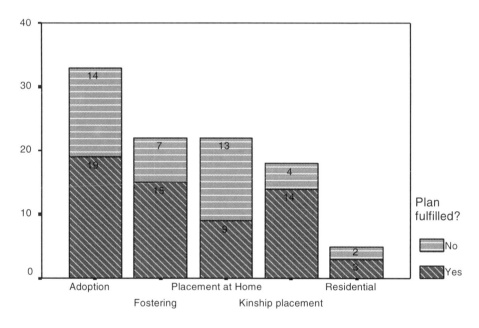

10   Above, n 9; and see also J Plotnikoff and R Woolfson, *Reporting to Court under the Children Act* (HMSO, 1996). The guidance in the Children Act Advisory Committee, *Handbook of Best Practice in Children Act Cases* (LCD, 1997) would not have been available in the time period to practitioners.

11   The study used the Looking After Children framework for classification of child difficulties. See especially H Ward (ed), *Looking After Children: Research into Practice* (HMSO, 1995). This framework encompasses seven domains of child well-being: health, education, family and social relationships, identity, emotional and behavioural difficulties (including offending), social presentation and self-care skills.

12   EJ McFadden, 'Kinship Care in the United States' (1998) 22(3) *Adoption and Fostering* 7. This review notes that children placed in kinship care in the United States have fewer placement changes than children placed with unrelated foster carers and are viewed more favourably by relatives although their welfare needs are no less than other children in need of public care.

58% of these plans were fulfilled within the 21-month period, and the majority of these children were under the age of 2, but a sibling group of four children was shortly to enter an adoptive placement. This reminds us that our findings present a snapshot of a constantly moving picture. Efforts to implement the plan were made in all cases.

Certain factors were statistically associated with placement plan fulfilment or non-fulfilment. With regard to child factors, children with higher numbers of initial problems were less likely to have their placement plans fulfilled: educational needs and developmental delay mentioned in the court reports were particularly associated with non-fulfilment. Somewhat unexpectedly, age itself was not a predictor of plan fulfilment, partly because its influence was mediated by the child's initial problems and by the type of placement sought. Gender had no significant effect on implementation, while the small numbers of children from ethnic minorities precluded statistical analysis.

Alcohol abuse was the only parental difficulty which almost reached statistical significance in influencing the prospect of placement plan fulfilment. Mental illness, domestic violence and drug abuse had no effect. The most likely reason for this finding is that alcohol abuse was seen as a lesser risk factor for child well-being than other forms of parental difficulty. Children of alcohol-abusing parents were more likely to be left at home for longer periods prior to legal proceedings. When a care order was made, they were also more likely to be placed at home, or to maintain contact with parents whose drinking difficulties could disrupt the placement.

The final factor that was statistically correlated with successful implementation was the tier of court. Plans presented to the higher courts were more likely to be fulfilled (see Table 2). The most striking differences were found in relation to placements at home and adoption, although the numbers for each option were small. (The numbers in this and Table 3 represent plans for individual children. Since many of the children were in sibling groups, the number of families represented here is considerably fewer; but within one family different placements were sometimes recommended for individuals or sibling pairs.)

Table 2: Placement plans at the final hearing and the numbers fulfilled at 21 months by tier of court

Placement option	Family proceedings court		County court		High Court	
	Plans	Fulfilled	Plans	Fulfilled	Plans	Fulfilled
Adoption	14	6 (43%)	17	11 (65%)	2	2
Fostering	12	7 (58%)	9	8 (89%)	1	
Placement at home	11	1 (9%)	11	8 (73%)		
Kinship	6	5 (83%)	12	9 (75%)		
Residential	2	1*	3	2 *		
Total	45	20 (44%)	52	38 (73%)	3	2*

* Numbers too small to generate meaningful percentage calculations.

There was, however, no clear relationship between the duration of proceedings and plan fulfilment (see Table 3). This is hardly surprising given that many other factors influence the length of the hearing. But it should be noted that 71% of cases were completed in 9 months or less, and there was considerable concern to speed up proceedings to avoid the damaging effects of delay.

Table 3: Time from first application to final hearing by court for final hearing and placement plan fulfilment rates

	Family proceedings court		County court		High Court	
	Total no of plans	Fulfilled	Total no of plans	Fulfilled	Total no of plans	Fulfilled
Less than 6 months	18	13	10	6		
6–9 months	19	6	22	15	2	2
9–12 months	4	1	6	6	1	
12–18 months	4		11	11		
More than 18 months			3			
Total	45	20	52	38	3	2

The study did find a relationship between the quality of the care plan and the likelihood of placement fulfilment, although this was not explored statistically. On the basis of the content analysis of all the care plans previously described, four items each had above-average success rates (60% or more) in terms of placement fulfilment provided they were recorded in detail. These were:

- type and details of the proposed placement;
- arrangements for contact and reunification;
- how the children's needs might be met;
- services to be provided by the local authority.

It is easy to see why these particular headings were linked to placement plan fulfilment. Detailed completion of the parts of the plan relating to placement, contact and services demanded positive forward planning and also invited action to ensure that the necessary arrangements would be in place.

The above results are based on the research criterion of children being in the placement type set out in the court plan at 21 months. The study also tracked how long it took the children to reach the placement of choice. On average it took just under 10 months for children to enter their adoptive placements[13] and 6.5 months to reach a foster placement.[14] As would be expected, children moved to relatives much faster – on average within approximately 2 months of the order. Placements were also analysed to assess the degree of permanency they provided the child. Using a six-point permanency scale[15] ranging from placements which had been officially

---

[13]   Thirteen of the 19 children were placed in one year or less. The average time to entry into the placement was 3 months longer than found in the BAAF survey 1998/89, cited in *Prime Minister's Review of Adoption* (PIU, 2000), p 85. Matching timescales were similar.

[14]   Just under half the children whose fostering plans were successfully implemented were living in their foster placements at the time of the order. Some of these were short-term placements which were subsequently re-designated as long term, but the change in status had not been ratified in many. The advantage to the child of remaining in the same placement was that it reduced the number of moves required, but the failure to alter the status of the plan meant that the placement had no official permanency.

[15]   The degree of permanence was classified into six categories as follows: permanence of the current placement has been agreed and officially ratified (by court or by local authority panel); permanence has been applied for; placement is considered permanent and treated as such; the current placement is not permanent but new carers have been identified; there is a possibility that the current placement may become permanent; the placement is not permanent (it is definite the child will have to move on but no new carers have been identified).

ratified to those which were definitely short term, only 50% of the children were in a placement considered permanent by the 12-month point (see Graph 2).

At the end of the study, 40 children were living in placements that had not been planned when the care order was made. Foster care emerged as the main collecting ground when placement plans for younger children ran into difficulties, with 27 extra children ending up in foster care for whom it had not been planned originally. For six of these, the likelihood was that they would spend a substantial – if not the greater part – of their childhood in foster care.

Extent of court activity in the implementation period

There was a considerable amount of court activity in the implementation period (see Table 4). A number of points emerge from post-order intervention by the courts. First, Table 4 suggests that a not inconsiderable number of cases were scrutinised by the courts post-order – the table includes some applications made on behalf of several children. Secondly, in so far as a goal of planning for children on care orders is to help them leave the care system altogether, it is worth noting that 15 children had formally exited from the care system through adoption, discharge of the care order and residence orders by 21 months. More were on their way to doing so when the study finished. Thirdly, parents' applications for discharge of the care order and extension of contact were singularly unsuccessful: none succeeded. Fourthly, no children applied for discharge of the care order, although three adolescents with foster care plans had contested the making of the care order and were unhappy about its continuation.

Applications to discharge the care orders, when brought by the local authorities, raised a number of difficult issues. One was the problem of applying for discharge where the care order was not working, typically in cases of wayward adolescents who were frequently missing. Local authorities usually considered that the courts would be unwilling to discharge the order in these circumstances, and this acted as a deterrent to making the application. Another problem arose when parents mistakenly considered that precise specification of a timescale was tantamount to a promise to fulfil it. In one case of this sort the care plan at the final hearing specified a timescale for return to court to discharge the order; but when the case was adjourned for further assessments, relations between the social services and the family sharply deteriorated. The effect of such difficulties was to discourage the local authority from seeking discharge of the order unless the outcome was more or less certain.

Graph 2: Numbers of children who were in a placement considered permanent by length of time post-care order

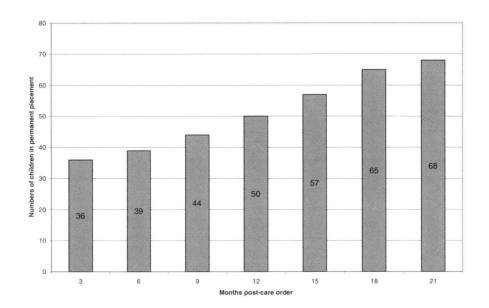

Table 4: Applications to court following the making of the care order

Type of application	Number of applications	Pending	Granted	Refused	Adjourned	Withdrawn
Discharge of care order (brought by LA)	5	2	1	0	1	1
Refusal of contact (brought by LA)	3	0	1	0	1	1
Parental application for contact variation and discharge of CO	5	1	0	3	0	1
Parental application for contact only	2	0	0	2	0	0
Freeing for adoption	2	0	2	0	0	0
Adoption order	13	4	9	0	0	0
Residence orders	9	0	4	2	2	1
Recovery orders	2	0	2	0	0	0

Why were placements not fulfilled?

Understanding reasons for non-fulfilment is crucial for both practitioners and policymakers. There were two main reasons for failure of the plan: the child did not reach the placement, or the placement broke down. Incidence varied according to placement type, but the predominance of non-entry in unfulfilled adoptions and the breakdown of all placements at home were especially noteworthy. The obvious influence of resource shortages on adoptive placements was striking, but the child's profile also affected placement prospects. Children were least likely to find an adoptive placement if they were over 3 years of age at the time of the court hearing,[16] had developmental delay or disability, or belonged to large sibling groups.[17] Fostering was least likely to be achieved:

- if a specialist resource was required;
- if the child was aged 9 or older;
- if the child had educational and behaviour difficulties, learning difficulties or other educational needs identified at the time of the final hearing;
- if the child had not fully agreed to the plan at the time of the final hearing.

By contrast to all other placement options, children placed at home tended to have few initial difficulties, and this held true whether the placement continued or disrupted. Placements at home were more likely to break down if the child was a member of a sibling group but the most distinctive feature of these breakdowns is that they were social-work led.

---

[16] The average age of the children whose adoption plans were fulfilled was 1.37 years, and 15 of the 19 children were aged 2 or less.

[17] Nine of the 14 children who failed to find adoptive families within the study's timescales came from just two families. Delay was the main factor hindering adoption rather than total failure to find a placement. The child characteristics that were associated with non-implemented plans are also found in J Hunt and A MacLeod, *The Best-Laid Plans: Outcomes of Judicial Decisions in Child Protection Proceeding* (The Stationery Office, 1999).

Relationship between plan implementation and welfare outcome

Of the 60 children whose plan was fulfilled, 39 (65%) made good progress; but in the 40 cases where the plan was not fulfilled, only 16 (40%) made good progress. Fulfilment of the placement plan therefore had a significant effect on welfare outcome. Children who made satisfactory progress and who obtained the best standard of welfare at the end of the study were more likely to be living in the placement type specified in the care plan, and vice versa. When the data were controlled for the number of initial difficulties, plan fulfilment still exerted an influence, although it was much weaker. Carrying out contact arrangements in agreement with the original plan was less clearly related to welfare outcome, but it did significantly increase the chances of good family and social relationships and a positive sense of identity. It was not possible to study the statistical relationship between provision of services and child well-being because there was a great variety of services and these were provided on an ad hoc basis with more being suggested at reviews than were initially recommended in the plan.

Discussion and implications of our findings for *Re W and B* and *Re W*

Two important changes to the operation of the Children Act 1989 (CA 1989) have been put forward as a result of the two cases heard recently by the Court of Appeal which tested the relationship between the CA 1989 and the Human Rights Act 1998 in respect of care plans for the court. The judgments were first, that the trial judge should have wider discretion to defer making the final order through use of interim care orders in appropriate cases 'where the care plan seems inchoate' or where 'an uncertainty is neither inevitable nor chronic'. Secondly, a system of 'starred milestones' should operate. These milestones would be drawn up by the parties (or by the court in the event of failure to agree) and comprise those elements of the plan deemed to be fundamental to its success with specific timescales attached for their implementation. As well as reactivating the multidisciplinary process that led to the care plan, failure to achieve the starred milestone would trigger a duty for the local authority to report to the guardian and, if not available, directly to the court for directions. Both local authority and guardian would have the right to apply to court for directions. The court would have a power to review the case where there was considered to be an actual or potential breach of human rights. Starred milestones were described by the Court of Appeal as the more radical proposal because they would redraw boundaries under the CA 1989 between the judiciary and executive.

Can our study shed any light on how starring of essential milestones could work in practice or on the likely numbers of applications that could involve a duty to report? It has been suggested that placement plan fulfilment is a crucial ingredient of the plan and that more children made good progress if their plan was fulfilled. This finding provides some incentive for the starring process to focus on achieving placements within particular timescales. As has already been made clear, in our own study precise timescales for placement implementation were rarely built into the care plan to enable accurate projections of default. But 40 children were not in the placement type agreed with the courts at the end of the study, despite efforts to implement plans in every case. Would there have been a duty to report on all of these? If non-fulfilment of placement were the only criterion, the Court of Appeal projection of 200 applications[18] per annum looks likely to be a considerable underestimate. We should also remember that our own cases were collected over 6 months from only five local authorities in England, and the criterion for judging success was whether the plan had been implemented at 21 months. If a shorter timescale had been adopted, many more plans would have been deemed non-implemented. This would suggest that the demands on court time, including that of the guardian ad litem could be greater than envisaged in the judgment.

---

[18]   *Re W and B; Re W (Care Plan)* [2001] EWCA Civ 757, [2001] 2 FLR 582, at para [31](ii).

However, it is clearly over-simplistic to equate non-fulfilment of the placement with violation of rights that may justify a need to apply to the court for directions. Our study also found that plans that were varied could have good results. Sixteen children made good progress, although their plans were not achieved during our timescale. They had become attached to foster carers, or preferred a residential placement to foster care despite the view at the time of the order that the latter was in their best interests. Conversely, 15 children whose plans were successfully implemented made poor progress. This suggests that it is dangerous to equate placement non-implementation with failure and implementation with success, although the latter is more likely. Difficult decisions will need to be made on a case-by-case basis as to when variation is justified, in the absence of any clear framework for determining what will constitute breach of human rights. There is also a need to determine how far resource constraints faced by local authorities[19] should be taken into consideration and mediate those rights.

The starring proposal in *Re W and B; Re W (Care Plan)* [2001] EWCA Civ 757 is attached to the achievement of essential milestones in the care plan.[20] What these are will depend on the case but, as already indicated, we could expect them to be issues such as adoption placement, long-term fostering placement or return home, as the case may be. The Court of Appeal has expressly stated that it is difficult at this stage to comment on how timescales will work in practice. In this regard, our study has raised some issues which are pertinent to both the practice and policy issues. As a minimum it has provided some indication of the likely time taken to reach placements. But there is a risk that timescales focus largely on short-term goals and may become too rigid. Were they also to incorporate longer-term objectives, then this would have repercussions for the likely length of time guardians would need to remain involved post-order. Finally, although those plans that provided detailed timescales were more likely to be fulfilled, the study found no correlation between time to placement and welfare outcome. By contrast, the degree of permanence was correlated with welfare outcome. Placement stability rather than delay may therefore be a more sensitive measure of effective post-order intervention.

Perhaps the most basic question to be posed by *Re W and B; Re W (Care Plan)* [2001] EWCA Civ 757 is to ask what would be the role of the court in any post-order supervision. The judgment does not specify the kinds of directions the court would be able to make. But the bigger question is what the court would be able to achieve? In our own 40 cases, as already discussed, 15 children did not enter the designated type of placement, and a further 25 experienced placement breakdown. For the 15 children who never reached their placement, the main problem was a resource shortage. Efforts had been made to find placements in all cases. It is hard to see what the courts could have achieved beyond what the local authorities were striving for. The real need is substantially to expand the numbers of adopters able to take sibling groups, older children and those with particular welfare needs. As important is the urgent need to build up a cadre of high-quality foster carers. Some of the delays in adoptive placements might also be reduced by greater readiness to split up large sibling groups.[21]

With regard to placement breakdown, our study has drawn attention to the particularly disappointing results of placements at home. Although the numbers involved are small,[22] they are in line with Hunt's study of court care plans[23] and these cases also raise issues of principle. In our report we argued for a new approach. We suggested that supervision orders should be used where a child is considered to be safe at home. Where the risk is considered too great to leave the child at home, a care order should be made involving out-of-home care as a prerequisite whether or not reunification is planned for later. This would make it clear to all

---

[19]   *Re W and B; Re W (Care Plan)* [2001] EWCA Civ 757, [2001] 2 FLR 582, at para [32].

[20]   Ibid, at para [30].

[21]   In our authorities, practice varied on this matter.

[22]   In 1998 placements at home comprised 11% of all placement options for children looked after (*Children Act Report 1995–1999* (Department of Health), p 13).

[23]   Op cit, n 17.

concerned that a care order envisages removal of the child as necessary, while still permitting home on trial at a later date. Unless the 'apparent paradox'[24] of allowing children to remain at home under care orders is resolved, it is possible that birth parents may consider using the Human Rights Act 1998 to challenge the making of the care order on the grounds of disproportionate interference in family life.

An important point made in the *Re W and B* and *Re W (Care Plan)* cases is the lack of a mechanism to protect children who are too young to challenge the local authority through Children Act 1989, s 26 powers and whose interests by parents and the authority are not being met. In our study, the reviewing mechanism worked reasonably well, albeit sometimes tardily, but when placements required change, additional planning contexts were used, such as legal planning meetings. However, in approximately half of all adoption cases, the period of contact prior to the adoptive placement was shortened and the goodbye visit was brought forward. This meant that some young children were in foster homes for a considerable period without family contact of any kind and without independent visitors to monitor their well-being. Would these cases constitute breach of Art 8 of the European Convention for the Protection of Human Rights and Fundamental Freedoms 1950? There was also a small group of older children who were on the run, whose whereabouts were not always known to the local authority and who needed protection. The need to put in place an independent mechanism to protect children in these circumstances seems right and proper, judged from the viewpoint of children's rights. But the extent to which the guardian ad litem could remain available whenever there is a question of return to court, as contrasted with the passing of a starred milestone, requires debate.

Conclusion

The study was commissioned against a background of some concern about the willingness and capacity of social services to implement care plans agreed with courts. Its results should dispel doubts about the likelihood of capricious changes of plan by local authorities, but resource issues certainly constrained planning, most particularly for adoption but also for specialist foster care and residential care where a therapeutic resource was needed.

Probably the main lessons from this inquiry are first, that the Children Act 1989 was right to make care planning for the courts a more stringent process on the grounds of child rights, welfare prospects and social services accountability. It has been found that the court process plays a valuable role in helping firm up and improve plans, and to change those that appear ill-judged, although sometimes at the cost of a lengthy process. It has also been shown that all agencies, courts and social services could work to improve the quality of planning before the final hearing, thereby decreasing the likelihood of expensive and time-consuming litigation in the post-order period.

---

[24] J Pinkerton, *In Care at Home: Parenting, the State and Civil Society* (Avebury, 1994) .

PLENARY FOUR

EXPERT EVIDENCE 10 YEARS AFTER THE IMPLEMENTATION OF THE CHILDREN ACT 1989: WHERE ARE WE?

The Hon Mr Justice Wall

Summary of paper

Starred milestones

In introducing his paper, Mr Justice Wall referred to the recent Court of Appeal decision in Re W and B; Re W (Care Plan) [2001] EWCA Civ 757, [2001] 2 FLR 582. He expressed his concern that the Court may have been optimistic about the number of cases in which it expected the duty to report and power to review would arise, ie some 200 per year. He thought the true number of cases would be many more.

Whilst welcoming the decision of the Court of Appeal in Re W and B; Re W (Care Plan) [2001] EWCA Civ 757, [2001] 2 FLR 582, Mr Justice Wall was concerned that the Children Act 1989 did not provide a mechanism for post care order judicial intervention, and an absence of jurisdiction to make substantive orders in these circumstances remained. This, he thought, should be remedied by legislative amendment, which he considered of vital importance.

Expert evidence

Mr Justice Wall referred the conference to the ADSS position statement, the contents of which he supported.

He expressed disagreement with the suggestion made by Pat Monro that it should be possible for a party to use an expert in Children Act matters whose evidence was not disclosable. He felt this ran completely counter to the Family Division's clear, up-front approach to the use of experts.

Northern circuit expert witness initiative

Mr Justice Wall drew the attention of the conference to this Initiative which he considered to be an amazing achievement for a group of practitioners. He hoped it would prove a model for others.

Kathryn Hughes, a committee member of the Northern Circuit Expert Witness Initiative, gave the conference a brief report on their local initiative to strengthen forensic services for family justice in the North West.

Introduction

This paper is designed to raise a number of questions for discussion. It follows on in particular from the day conference held by the Committee on 29 June 2001 at the Principal Registry, and aims to pick up issues discussed on that day. It is being written without any idea of what my colleagues in Plenary 4 are going to say. It will be interesting to see what common ground exists.

Much of this paper will, I fear, cover familiar territory.[1] However, the issue of expert evidence in children's cases remains one of particular importance and continuing difficulty. It should, therefore, in my view, be an objective of this conference to address the outstanding issues in a clear and direct way, and to formulate some positive and practical proposals both by way of resolutions and recommendations. At the end of this paper I will set out some suggestions which I hope will be discussed.

Definitions

The very term 'expert evidence' causes a degree of difficulty. As I shall consider later in this paper, witnesses such as social workers and children's guardians who have professional qualifications usually have expertise within the area of those qualifications. But they have not been accorded 'expert' status for the purposes of care proceedings. For present purposes, therefore, I propose to use the terms 'expert witness' and 'expert evidence' in a narrow sense, and as applicable to persons who are external to the proceedings and whom the court invites in, to enable them to advise the court on specific issues in the proceedings relating to the interests of the child. Whether we should continue to use the phrase 'expert witness' in this context is arguable: I use it here purely for identification purposes.

I suggest that the outstanding substantive issues we need to address are the following:

(1) Are we too prodigal in our use of expert evidence in care cases?

(2) (a) If the answer to question (1) is 'yes', why is it that judges and magistrates are permitting expert evidence in so many cases?
     (b) Why is there in particular an apparent reluctance to rely on the social work assessments of the local authority and the investigation by children's guardian?

(3) Why is there a shortage of available expertise in the various disciplines required to give expert evidence in the cases which require it?

(4) What can we do about the shortage of experts?

(5) There is plainly a need for local psychiatric and psychotherapeutic services for children within the care system (a) before any application for a care order is made, (b) during the pendency of the proceedings, and (c) post-care order. Why is there apparently a lack of such facilities? And why is there such delay and difficulty involved in gaining access to them where they exist?

(6) Why are some doctors so reluctant to become involved in the forensic process?

(7) How do we address the delay involved in obtaining reports from the limited pool of experts?

(8) What do we do with the partisan expert?

I include question (8) partly by way of footnote, but also because, as will be apparent later, the point is both of importance and of topical interest.

---

[1] For an historical perspective reference can be made to Mathew Thorpe's paper, 'The Impact of Psychoanalytic Practice on the Family Justice System', in *Rooted Sorrows* (Family Law, 1997). My own paper in the same publication, 'Issues Arising from the Involvement of and Expert Evidence given by Psychiatrists and Psychologists in Proceedings involving Children', and its various appendices, set out the law as I saw it in 1995.

Within the eight issues I have identified there are areas where I think we have made progress since the introduction of the Children Act; there are, however, areas where we have made no progress or even gone backwards. It is for this reason that I say it should be a major objective of this conference to put forward a strategy to identify what we can and should be doing to improve the deficiencies in the system.

Where we begin: the need for independent expert evidence in the appropriate case-areas in which we have made progress

The multi-disciplinary nature of family proceedings renders it inevitable that in difficult cases the court will require expert evidence to assist it reach its conclusions. As Butler-Sloss LJ (as she then was) put it in *Re M and R (Child Abuse: Evidence)* [1996] 2 FLR 195, at p 205:

> 'In cases involving children, expert medical and psychiatric evidence from paediatricians and allied disciplines is often quite indispensable to the court. As Parker LCJ said in *Director of Public Prosecutions v A and BC Chewing Gum Ltd* [1968] 1 QB 159, 165A, when dealing with children, the court needs "all the help it can get". But that dependence in no way compromises the fact that the final decision in the case is the judge's and his alone. '

This is but one example of many expressions of the same opinion which can be found in the books. As a judge who regularly hears and has to decide complex cases involving children, I wholly endorse the passage I have cited from *Re M and R*, as I am sure do all my colleagues.

Reference is regularly made to the substantial increase in the volume of expert evidence in proceedings relating to children since the implementation of the Children Act in 1991. Properly used, I regard this use of expert evidence as a very healthy development. I am in no doubt that the quality of the court's decision is directly related to the quality of the advice it receives.[2] Like all my colleagues, I regularly find myself heavily dependent on expert opinion on a large range of topics. These are all very familiar.[3] The problem lies in identifying the cases which need expert evidence in the sense defined in para 3 above and those which do not.

As a judge, therefore, the perspective from which I approach the question of expert evidence is that it is an invaluable tool. But in each case I have to ask myself, on the facts of that case, whether or not I need expert evidence; and if I do not, how I can best harness the available expertise (in the broad sense) from the other disciplines already operating within the case to help me reach a decision.

Progress

Acknowledging the criticism that we may admit expert evidence too readily, the judiciary has, I think, nonetheless made progress in relation to most procedural and administrative issues concerning expert evidence. If bad practice continues to exist, it is not from want of telling. There is practice guidance for lawyers, judges and doctors in the law reports, in journals and in

---

[2] A recent example of the manner in which expert advice has assisted the judiciary is in the area of domestic violence. The decision of the Court of Appeal in *Re L, V, M and H (Contact: Domestic Violence)* [2000] 2 FLR 334 was plainly informed by the report written for it on the instructions of the Official Solicitor by Claire Sturge and Danya Glaser.

[3] Obvious examples are the causation and timing of serious and sometimes quite subtle physical injuries to children, including: poisoning; the strength and significance of parental relationships with their children; assessments of the therapeutic needs of children; proposed treatment of the mental states of children and adults; whether or not a child has been sexually abused; and the likely effect on children on their placement inside or outside their natural families.

my own handbook, a copy of which was, I hope, given to all members of the Committee.[4] So we all know – or should know – what our respective duties and responsibilities are. Doctors should be being better treated – both in and outside court. The idea that a doctor can be asked to turn up and hang around for a day in order to be asked to come back on another day – to take one example – or that appearances in court are some kind of gladiatorial combat where the naked doctor armed only with net and trident is torn to pieces by legal lions waving machetes whilst the judge smilingly gives the thumbs down – these ideas ought to have gone.

It should also perhaps be remembered that at the time of the 1995 conference, we were debating whether or not doctors should be permitted to give evidence as to the credibility of children, and that the law then was that an expert's opinion on that subject was both inadmissible and capable of being highly prejudicial. This was a position altered by the Court of Appeal as *Rooted Sorrows* went to press.[5]

So I do think that the decks are pretty much cleared. The structure and ground rules exist for the court properly to be given unbiased expert evidence. It is from this point that we have to assess the use we currently make of such evidence and tackle the outstanding issues.

Question 1: Are we too prodigal in our use of expert evidence in care cases?

I accept, of course, that control over the use of expert evidence in Children Act cases is the court's responsibility.[6] I also accept that it may well be that judges and magistrates have not been sufficiently rigorous in identifying the cases which do not need outside expert evidence; that granting permission for a second opinion or another assessment has become too much of a matter of routine, with the consequence that valuable resources are being used unnecessarily and the delays already inherent in the system exacerbated.

In *Re G (Minors) (Expert Witnesses)* [1994] 2 FLR 291, I suggested guidelines for the manner in which expert evidence should be obtained. It never occurred to me, I have to say, that it was necessary to spell out to the legal profession that consideration of expert evidence arose only if that evidence were necessary for the proper determination of issues in the case. I thought it sufficient to say that as part of the process of granting or refusing permission for the papers to be shown to an expert, the advocates had a positive duty to place all relevant information before the court; and the court had a positive duty to enquire into it. In particular, amongst other things, the court and the parties had to have regard to 'the relevance of the expert evidence sought to be adduced to the issues arising for decision in the case'. It seemed to me that if expert evidence was not required, or if it did not address the issues in the case, there was self-evidently no need to consider how it should be obtained.

That mistake on my part has since been rectified. In *Re F (A Minor) (Care Proceedings: Directions)* [1995] 3 FCR 601 at 607 justices refused an application by a child's guardian for a psychological assessment of the child. The guardian appealed to Connell J, who upheld the justices' decision. Commenting on my guidelines, Connell J said that it was implicit:

---

[4]	*A Handbook for Expert Witnesses in Children Act Cases* (with His Honour Judge Iain Hamilton) (Family Law, 2000).

[5]	See *Rooted Sorrows* (Family Law, 1997), p 39. The position now is that such evidence is admissible: see *Re M and R (Child Abuse: Evidence)* [1996] 2 FLR 195.

[6]	However, the court has no power over a local authority which tells it that it is going to contract out the social work assessment which the court would normally expect to be undertaken by the local authority social workers. In my experience the reason given for this is the need to avoid a sense of bias on the part of the family: it can also be due to chronic shortage of staff.

'... that the relevance of the expert evidence sought to be adduced to the issues arising for decision in the case must be carefully considered before an expert's report is directed. In this case, there is, as I have already indicated, no live issue to which that report can go.'[7]

It appears that Connell J's message needs repeating. My first proposition for the conference's consideration, therefore, is that there needs to be a statement of good practice[8] re-emphasising that when considering the directions to be given in every case, the court should give permission to instruct outside expert evidence only if that evidence is relevant to a particular issue in the case and necessary for the proper disposal of the case.

Question 2:

(a)   If the answer to question (1) is 'yes' why are judges and magistrates permitting expert evidence in so many cases?

(b)   Why is there an apparent reluctance to rely on the social work assessments of the local authority and the investigation by children's guardian?

I suspect that the answer to the first part of the question lies in the second. But I also suspect that the answer lies in part in the lack of resources available to both local authorities and CAHMS. This is a point strongly made in the Association of Directors of Social Services (ADSS) in *Position Statement: Expert Reporting in Public Law Cases*, para 1.3:

'Local authorities are finding themselves having to commission and purchase assessments and expert opinion, outside NHS provision from a relatively small number of clinicians/practitioners, operating in a national context, rather than from local health services. It is the local health services that are likely to have the information about the children concerned, knowledge of what's available locally and the capacity to plan and deliver a programme of therapy that may be indicated through any assessments and opinions they provide about the child. However, the ADSS experience is that in general, most local health service providers are not currently providing local authorities, guardians, parents and ultimately the Courts with the assessments and reports required for use within public law proceedings.'

The ADSS position statement addresses issues in my question (5) and I will return to it when considering that question. For present purposes, I fear that we may not have addressed the concerns set out by Dame Margaret Booth 5 years ago in her report, *Avoiding Delay in Children Act Cases* (July 1996). It is, I think, worthwhile giving extensive citations from what she said on the subject of local authorities:

'3.3.9   Evidence of social workers in court. A matter of major concern raised by every local authority consulted was the lack of credibility given by the court to the evidence of social workers. It was said that social workers find court appearances stressful and that many were terrified by the prospect. This has serious repercussions. Stress-related illness connected with court appearances was said to be commonplace and this could necessitate an adjournment of a hearing with consequence delay. Aggressive and hostile cross-examination could undermine the standing of the social worker and go so far as to taint the whole department in the eyes of the family so that future work was put in jeopardy. One local authority reported that social workers had resigned as a result of their court experiences.

---

[7]   Interestingly, in that case, one of the underlying purposes of the proposed report was to obtain for his carers better access to services provided by the local authority under the arrangements for the Placement of Children with Parents etc Regulations 1991 (SI 1991/893). The judge regarded that as trespassing on the proper role of the local authority post-care order.

[8]   This could be a statement endorsed by this conference; or it could be a statement of good practice from the President.

Because the evidence of social workers carries little weight, local authorities reported that they often felt compelled to instruct experts, despite the cost, to deal with matters which could otherwise be dealt with by their social workers who would speak with much greater knowledge of the child or family concerned.

3.3.10   Training in court skills for social workers. Training in all aspects of court work is essential for the social worker if he or she is to feel confident and able to avoid an adversarial stance. However, the social work qualification, which most social workers have, does not include such training and while some legal departments endeavour to provide in-house training, this is by no means widespread or regularly available. There is no general Interdisciplinary involvement in this area, although it was reported that the magistrates and clerks of one family proceedings court, which was not visited, do take part in court-based seminars for social workers which have proved to be very helpful. By contrast, a member of a solicitors' Children Panel who addressed a seminar for social workers met with such a poor response that the occasion has not been repeated. The recent publication by the Department of Health of its handbook for social services *Reporting to Court under the Children Act*[9] provides valuable practical guidelines, but Interdisciplinary training would still be of the greatest assistance.

3.3.11   Social workers and the guardians ad litem. The working relationship between social workers and guardians can be tense and difficult. It was reported by a number of local authorities that social workers frequently felt disadvantaged in court vis-a-vis the guardian ad litem whose evidence was perceived always to be preferred. One local authority observed that the philosophy appeared to be that the guardian is independent while the social worker is partisan. Some guardians reported similar difficulties in their working relationships with social workers.

...

3.3.23   The need for inter-disciplinary liaison. There is a very clear need for closer liaison between individual social workers and members of the other disciplines involved in Children Act work. It is not helpful to the court process or to the children and families concerned that social workers lack the necessary training to enable them to feel confident in an important aspect of their work, let alone that so many of them are intimidated by court appearances. Social workers need to be much more professional in this regard and to know what the court requires and expects by way of evidence. They also need to have a thorough understanding of court procedures. Equally, the judiciary and the legal profession need to have a good understanding of the role of the social worker and of the extent of his or her authority. There should also be a means whereby social workers and guardians ad litem can communicate informally and can discuss matters of dissatisfaction on either side frankly and speedily.'

I have included this extensive citation from Dame Margaret's report both because I think it goes some long way towards answering the questions under discussion and because I shall be interested to know the extent to which the conference feels that the issues she raises have been addressed. I have to say – this is an entirely personal and anecdotal perspective – that in the cases I have been hearing, largely on the Northern Circuit, the quality of social work and care planning has greatly improved in the last two years or so. I would like to think that this is in part due to *Divided Duties* and the Department of Health Circulars which followed. But I suspect that as the High Court gets the most difficult cases, it may be that more resources – possibly a disproportionate amount of resources – are given to these cases, to the detriment of cases in the county court and the family proceedings court. I never cease to wonder how local authority budgets stretch to accommodate some of the most difficult cases I hear – some lasting 3 weeks or more. But that is a different issue for another conference.

---

[9]   By Plotnikoff and Woolfson (Department of Health, 1996). This is an excellent book and should be required reading for all social workers engaged in this work.

The status of the social worker in care proceedings

In my experience, despite Dame Margaret Booth's report, the status of the social worker in care proceedings remains an issue. If one poses the question, are social workers expert witnesses?, one immediately highlights the difficulty we have got ourselves into by the perceived devaluation of the social work contribution to care cases relating to children. The social workers carrying the case on behalf of the local authority are, of course, its employees; they do not have medical/psychiatric/psychological qualifications; they have not been brought in from outside to advise from a standpoint of neutrality on identified issues in the case. But they are professionals who have made an objective professional assessment of the family and the children concerned, which they invite the court to accept. They accordingly give evidence as professionals and as part of what is – or ought to be – a multi-disciplinary process.

One of the reasons why I favour multi-disciplinary assessments of families and children as a means both of providing advice, help, support and recommendations where appropriate for treatment for children and families outside the court system, and as a means of identifying more efficiently those cases which should come within it, is precisely because it brings together the elements of the disciplines necessary to identify, analyse and treat the problems thrown up by family dysfunction. It is therefore extremely useful as a care-planning tool.

Where a multi-disciplinary assessment has resulted in the institution of care proceedings, I not only see no reason why the members of the team should not give evidence in the proceedings; it will be crucial to the outcome of the proceedings that they should do so. It will be when the multi-disciplinary team puts in its statement or reports that the court will have to decide whether any further professional evidence is required. It may well be that the multi-disciplinary assessment itself uncovers the need either for a particular therapeutic service or for outside expert advice which is not available to the multi-disciplinary team. Thus, the team itself might advise the court that further external input is required.

Social workers plainly have expertise in social work, and need to be afforded the status of witnesses who are professionals. They are not 'expert' witnesses within my definition, but they are professionals bringing their particular form of expertise into play.

Children's guardians are also usually social workers: they will not have more 'expertise' than experienced social workers. Why, then, is there a perception that courts favour children's guardians and afford them greater status than social workers? No doubt it is partly because the children's guardian is perceived to be independent, instructs a solicitor and represents the child. But (dependent on age and experience) their 'expertise' is the same. Both should be treated the same way, that is as professional witnesses giving the court the benefit of their expertise.

Once again, my personal experience is not one in which I have met professional antagonism between the social worker in the case and the children's guardian. Where the social services have developed a sensible care plan for the child and followed good social work practice, my experience is that the guardian has acknowledged that and frequently agreed with what is proposed. The guardian is the child's protection against poor social work practice: if the practice is sound, the relationship between social worker and guardian is usually, in my experience, reasonably harmonious.

There is a point here, however, which has to be made, and that is that the quality of much of the social work input into care cases is variable, particularly in the inner city boroughs, where turnover of staff is high, case loads are enormous, resources inadequate, pressures of work intense, and where sometimes crisis management is all that can be achieved. So all the agencies, including the government, which do not supply adequate funding, training or resources, all have a responsibility for a lack of confidence by the judiciary in social work assessments carried out by local authorities.

Questions 3, 4 and 5: The shortage of experts and the inadequacy of local services and CAHMS provision

The answer to these questions does not lie in the judicial sphere of competence. I was, however, extremely interested in the ADSS position statement, from which I have already quoted and which addresses these issues. This document makes a number of points. It identifies a need for 'joined up working', for example better co-ordination and collaboration between social services departments, health commissioners and health providing NHS Trusts in relation to the assessment and planning for children who may become the subject of care proceedings. It identifies the difficulty of obtaining reports and court attendance from clinicians who regard reporting and witness functions as falling outside their NHS contracts.[10]

The position statement goes on to argue that commissioning local health professionals to provide assessments or opinions is even more difficult where the family concerned is not currently receiving their services. As a consequence, the parties to care proceedings are obliged to make use of the relatively small number of external clinicians who conduct brief 'forensic' investigations, with the disadvantages that the expert in question will have a lack of previous involvement with the child or family and is unlikely to have any detailed knowledge of local facilities available. The document concludes that:

> 'As a result, recommendations made to the court about future treatment may not pay attention to what is available locally which the child can practically use; there may be unanticipated delays in securing what has been recommended; and when local services are subsequently engaged they may see a need to assess and form their own view of treatment requirements particularly if there has been no dialogue with the expert witness beforehand.'

The six bases upon which the position statement seeks to move forward are the following:

(1) continuity for children in the assessment, reporting and treatment functions;
(2) a shared commitment and responsibility – health, education and social services authorities – to understand fully the complex needs of children who are the subject of public law proceedings and to do their utmost to meet assessments and treatment within required timescales;
(3) locally based arrangements for multi-disciplinary teamwork between specialists;
(4) as far as possible, expert opinion that arises from multi-disciplinary teamwork between specialists;
(5) expert opinion being supplied by accredited clinicians and practitioners;
(6) a body with a responsibility for supplying the accreditation, setting universal standards, monitoring them and approving educational programmes associated with the function.

On the question of the shortage of key mental health clinicians, the position statement calls for the introduction of a mandatory, nationally agreed education and training programme in this area of work for child mental health specialists, the training to be consistent with wider measures designed to increase the supply and recruitment of such clinicians to work within multi-disciplinary teams. It also calls for 'some recognition on the part of all the professional bodies concerned' that this work is too important for the children involved to be left unregulated and outside the scope of NHS contracts.

---

[10] This is not something, I have to say, that I have ever encountered. That may be, however, because in the cases I try the treating doctors have usually made statements to the police covering their involvement with the children concerned, and when required come to court to give evidence on their statements.

I find the ADSS position statement a most stimulating and helpful document, and I hope that the conference will endorse its objectives. I would, however, like to make one or two observations on it.

First, I think that there is a risk of throwing the baby out with the bath water. There will always be cases where external expert opinions are not only helpful, but necessary. An obvious example is a disputed injury to a child where a second opinion on the interpretation of X-rays or brain scans is required. Equally, there are cases where a psychiatric assessment or paediatric overview from an outside perspective is extremely helpful. Issues addressed by expert evidence arise in the context of disputed care proceedings, and complex medical and psychiatric issues often require specific expertise to address them. One should always remember, in addition, that parents who seek to challenge a multi-disciplinary assessment may need to obtain permission for an external expert to scrutinise the work done by the multi-disciplinary team.

I have also to say that, as a matter of good practice, I regard it as extremely important for experts coming from the outside to make enquiries about and to familiarise themselves with locally available facilities for treatment or ongoing therapy. There is, plainly, absolutely no point in an expert making a recommendation for treatment if there is no facility for that treatment locally. It ought, therefore, either to be part of the instruction to the expert or a standard procedure for expert witnesses to make enquiries about local facilities as part of their assessments.

Contribution of the legal profession to the problem of the shortage of experts

A number of initiatives are in place. There is the judicial pupillage scheme, whereby registrars and consultants spend time siting with judges. This is time-consuming for the doctors, but I have found it extremely useful, and I am sure it is mutually beneficial. All the designated family judges should be encouraged to set up such schemes.

There needs to be a national register of accredited experts. At the moment there are very valuable local initiatives. The Liverpool initiative, organised by the legal profession with the assistance of doctors on the Northern Circuit, will publish its register next year. Funding has been a problem, and will remain so. Individual initiatives are greatly to be admired but, as the ADSS states, there needs to be a body with responsibility for supplying the accreditation, setting universal standards, monitoring them and approving educational programmes.

Question 6: Why are some doctors so reluctant to become involved in the forensic process?

Many of those reading this paper will know the answer better than I do. Many doctors see the work as taking them away from their clinical responsibilities. It is very time-consuming. Despite what I say in para 10, many doctors still see the courtroom as a hostile environment, and perceive cross-examination as a direct attack on their professional integrity. Add to this the need to travel, sometimes long distances, to attend court, and having to hang about before giving evidence or, worse still, to arrive at court to find the case has settled and nobody had told them.

As stated in para 10 these are all issues which the *Handbook for Expert Witnesses in Children Act Cases* tries to address. I hope that it has had some effect. But we will only really encourage the young registrar/consultant into this work if we can sustain the code of good practice we have developed. I look forward to hearing at the conference if there are any further ideas about how we can achieve this.

Question 7: Delay

The obvious concomitant of a shortage of experts is that those who are available are very busy and cannot undertake the task allotted by the court within the time-frame set down by the court. The court is then faced with three choices, all unsatisfactory: the first is to wait for the expert, thereby infringing the principle that delay in determining the case is contrary to the interests of children and adding to the stress on the parties and the children concerned; the second is to try to find another expert (who is likely to be in the same position or may not be as good); the third is to abandon the idea of expert evidence altogether.

The only answer, it seems to me, is rigorous case planning. This difficulty is particularly acute, in my experience, in cases involving 'split hearings', where the court makes findings of fact, and assessments follow based on those findings and the parties' reaction to them. However, whilst there are cases in which the court's findings exonerate the parents, and the proceedings come to a halt at that point, they are, in my experience at least, the exception rather than the rule. Accordingly, I see no reason why, when the case is in its early planning stages, the court should not identify the type of assessments likely to be necessary on the assumption that the court finds the facts in a particular way. If more than local authority social work assessments are then thought likely to be required, the expert(s) whose assessment(s) is/are likely to be commissioned can be approached at that stage and invited to be prepared to carry out work commencing immediately after the finding of fact hearing. That should provide sufficient notice for the expert(s); and since the date for the final hearing will have been fixed at an early stage, the expert(s) should have time to make his/their assessments in good time for the final hearing.

The other situation in which the problem can be acute is where an assessment or a report is ordered from an expert – perhaps jointly instructed – and the receipt of that assessment or report prompts one of the parties – usually the parents – to seek a second opinion. If the application is justified, there is the obvious risk that the timetable for the case will be thrown out; the final hearing will need to be vacated and substantial additional delay incurred.

There is no easy answer to this problem except to plan for it at the earliest possible stage, by giving a direction that the report has to be received sufficiently in advance of the date fixed for the final hearing so as to enable a second opinion to be obtained (usually on paper). If, in the event, the report is not received in time, any application to adjourn has to be heard with the 'delay' principle very much in mind, and can be refused if a fair hearing within Art 6 of the European Convention for the Protection of Human Rights and Fundamental Freedoms 1950 (ECHR) is possible and, as will nearly always be the case, it is in the interests of the child for the hearing to proceed.[11]

This, like so much of family work, all comes back to rigorous case management and case planning.

Judicial continuity

One area in which the higher judiciary seems to me to have failed is in achieving judicial continuity. The advantages of judicial continuity are, I think, self-evident. The judge has the case from the beginning or from a very early stage, and sets the timetable in accordance with his or her judicial commitments. The judge reads and knows the case as it develops: when it comes back for directions or because there is a crisis, he or she does not have to spend hours reading him/herself back into it. The prospect of adjournments are reduced, and the likelihood is that if there is a crisis, the judge will be able to accommodate an urgent hearing by reorganising his or her list. And, of course, where there is a split hearing, as has now been authoritatively stated by

---

[11]   In *London Borough of Croydon v R* [1997] 2 FLR 675 the local authority had obtained a psychiatric report making it clear that in the psychiatrist's opinion there were too many risk factors attached to the mother being able to care for her baby. The mother was given permission to obtain a psychiatric report, but the psychiatrist did not answer letters or file his report in time. Shortly before the hearing, the mother applied for permission to instruct another psychiatrist. That instruction would almost certainly have required an adjournment. The justices refused, and the mother's appeal against their refusal was dismissed.

the Court of Appeal, the judge who finds the facts must deal with the final hearing.[12]

For the High Court Bench, the difficulties of achieving judicial continuity are legion. This is because of the various responsibilities which the judges of the Family Division have: they must go out on circuit; they sit in the Court of Appeal, both Civil and Criminal Divisions; they sit in the Employment Appeal Tribunal and the Administrative Court. Timetabling a case round other commitments is thus very difficult, particularly when – as at present – diaries are only finalised a few months ahead.

For the specialist circuit bench the issue ought to be easier, since (for example on the Northern Circuit) judges plan their diaries a year ahead, and it is easier for judges to know their sitting patterns for family work.

In my view the judiciary needs to make a concerted effort at every level to achieve judicial continuity in care cases. I was shocked when sitting in London recently, dealing with directions in care proceedings, to see the number of judicial hands through which care cases had passed before reaching a final hearing.

This is an issue directly related both to the question of delay and to the question of expert evidence. A judge who has the case from the word go, who is in sole charge of its management, and who is going to take the final hearing will be in a far better position to ensure that the case is heard swiftly and to deal with applications for expert evidence arising both at the beginning and during its preparatory stages.

Question 8: The partisan expert and those who do not obey the rules

There are no longer, I think, paediatricians for whom it is an article of faith that parents do not injure their children, and that, accordingly, there has to be an innocent, alternative explanation to non-accidental injury. I do not think there are now any psychiatrists who believe that children should not be separated from their parents under almost any circumstances. At the other end of the spectrum, Cleveland demonstrated the dangers of inadequate and unscientific methodology as a basis for categorical diagnoses of sexual abuse.

With all the positive developments there have been in the field of expert evidence in child cases, it is, I find, very disappointing to see reported recently the case of *Re X (Non-accidental Injury: Expert Evidence)* [2001] 2 FLR 90 in which Singer J emphatically rejects the theories of Dr Colin Paterson on 'temporary brittle bone disease' in almost exactly the same terms as Cazalet J did in 1990[13] and I did in 1994.[14] What do we do with the experts who pursue their theses regardless, and in breach of the guidelines laid down by the courts for the proper presentation of expert evidence?

Singer J suggests that any application for permission for Dr Paterson to advise in a case should be transferred to the High Court and heard by a High Court judge. Whilst that solution should have the effect of blocking the instructions of Dr Paterson in an English case, my view is that this is not enough. Being heavily criticised for presenting misleading reports – with all the consequences which follow – by three High Court judges should in my view be sufficient to enable the General Medical Council to take action and to declare that such a witness should not be allowed to give expert evidence in proceedings relating to children.

The obverse side of a rota of accredited experts may, therefore, have to be a list of expert witnesses (hopefully very short) who are unreliable, or who mislead, or are persistently partisan or incompetent. This must, however, be a matter for the doctors to regulate.

---

[12] *Re G (Care Proceedings: Split Trials)* [2001] 1 FLR 872.
[13] *Re J (Child Abuse: Expert Evidence)* [1991] FCR 192.
[14] *Re AB (Child Abuse: Expert Witnesses)* [1995] 1 FLR 181.

Issues for discussion and possible resolutions

I invite the conference to consider the following propositions, decide whether or not they should be endorsed, and how they can best be implemented.

Practice

1. There should be a statement of good practice re-emphasising that when considering the directions to be given in every case, the court should give permission to instruct outside expert evidence only if that evidence is relevant to a particular issue in the case and necessary for the proper disposal of the case. This could be a statement endorsed by this conference, or it could be a statement of good practice from the President.

2. Whenever the court is considering the question of expert evidence it should have particular regard to the principle in s 1(2) of the Children Act 1989 that any delay in determining the question of the child's upbringing is likely to prejudice the welfare of the child.

3. Where an expert witness is asked to advise on the need for CAMHS services for a child, or where the witness forms the opinion that a child needs such services, it should be standard procedure for the expert witness as part of his or her assessment to make enquiries about the availability of local facilities.

4. The circuit and High Court judiciary should address the issue of judicial continuity with a view to one judge having overall conduct of a care case, from transfer up to final disposal.

5. All the designated family judges should be encouraged to set up judicial pupillage schemes to enable registrars and consultants to spend time sitting with judges in court.

Dame Margaret Booth's report

6. The continuing demoralisation of social workers needs to be addressed by training in all aspects of court work. Apart from in-house training (to which the legal profession could contribute) the judiciary, particularly the designated family judges, should take a proactive role by addressing social workers and holding regular discussions with the local directors of social services.

The ADSS Position Statement

7. The conference supports the ADDS statement and the six points set out at para 29.

8. The conference also agrees with the ADSS statement that, in the light of national shortage of key mental health clinicians, steps should be taken to introduce a mandatory nationally agreed education and training programme in this area of work for child mental health specialists.

9. The conference also agrees that training should be consistent with wider measures designed to increase the supply and recruitment of such clinicians to work within multi-disciplinary teams. It also calls for some recognition on the part of all the professional bodies concerned that this work is too important for the children involved to be left unregulated and outside the scope of NHS contracts.

ADSS POSITION STATEMENT

EXPERT REPORTING IN PUBLIC LAW CASES

1. Introduction

1.1 Expert evidence is being increasingly used in public law proceedings under the Children Act 1989. Expert evidence is commissioned by local authorities, by guardians ad litem and by parents in proceedings, and typically involves obtaining assessments and/or opinion from child and adolescent psychiatrists, adult psychiatrists, psychologists and paediatricians.

1.2 However, there are concerns about the availability and accessibility of this experience, its quality, and the relationship between expert assessments and subsequent care planning for the children who are the subject of the assessments.

1.3 Local authorities are finding themselves having to commission and purchase assessments and expert opinion, outside NHS provision from a relatively small number of clinicians/practitioners, operating in a national context, rather than from local health services. It is the local health services that are likely to have the information about the children concerned, knowledge of what's available locally and the capacity to plan and deliver and programme of therapy that may be indicated through any assessments and opinions they provide about the child. However, the ADSS experience is that, in general, most local health service providers are not currently providing local authorities, GALs, parents and ultimately the Courts with the assessments and reports required for use within public law proceedings. In summary, Section 27 of the Children Act and Section 26 of the NHS Act (collaborative arrangements) have failed.

1.4 The ADSS believes that these current arrangements are inconsistent, do not offer the best value for public resources and, crucially, do not lead to the best outcomes for children. Change is required and the purpose of this paper is to set out a general direction for this.

1.5 Government, professional bodies, the Courts and other interest groups all have an interest in this area. This paper is intended to make it clear what the ADSS sees as the way forward.

2. Policy context

2.1 It is very appropriate that this area of provision is reviewed in the current policy context. This context includes:

• A recognition that children and young people in public care are among the most socially excluded groups, initiatives designed to promote the health and development of children and young people looked after by local authorities, and a drive to ensure they have the opportunity to enjoy a standard of care as good as all children of the same age living in the same area (eg the Quality Protects programme and the recently issued draft guidance on the health care needs of looked after children).

- Emphasis on the importance of joined up working in improving outcomes for children. For example better co-ordination and collaboration has been called for between Social Services Departments, health commissioners and health providing NHS Trusts in relation to the assessment and planning for children who may become the subject of care proceedings. The revised *Working Together* Guidance also requires this collaboration and includes expectations about the need for liaison and agreements between agencies and professionals over assessments and reports in relation to child abuse cases.

- The promotion of children's rights – Article 24 of the Convention on the Rights of the Child states that: 'States Parties recognise the right of the child to the enjoyment of the highest attainable standard of health and to facilities for the treatment of illness and rehabilitation of health. States Parties shall strive to ensure that no child is deprived of his or her right of access to such health care services.'

3. Current arrangements for obtaining expert opinion

3.1 Social Services Departments seek expert opinion to assist them in planning and decision-making and in determining what may be in a child's best interests in matters that are before the court in care proceedings. This opinion is sought in a number of contexts:

Children already receiving assessment and/or treatment

3.2 Where a child, *the family or an adult considered a risk to the child* is already being seen by a professional/clinician, Social Services may ask them for advice or an opinion on certain issues to assist the process of assessment and planning. For the most part such collaboration occurs (ie the assistance obtained being provided being regarded as 'category one' work – work falling within NHS contracts). There can, however, be difficulties in obtaining a written report from the professional/clinician concerned and, should the case go to court, securing the professional's willingness to act as a witness. The reporting and witness functions are still regarded by many clinicians as falling outside of their NHS contract and any assistance obtained may be regarded as 'category two' work and thus charged for.

Children not currently receiving assessment and/or treatment and subject to legal proceedings

3.3 Greater difficulties exist in commissioning local health professionals or clinicians to specifically provide written assessments or opinion where the child or family concerned are not currently receiving their services. Attempts to obtain assessment and opinion in these circumstances are often unsuccessful because the health professionals/clinicians concerned regard the work as falling outside of their NHS contract, and/or they consider they do not have expertise in providing evidence in court and/or the requests would prejudice other demands on their time.

3.4 Whilst some local agreements have been made for such commissioning within NHS resources, the general experience of the ADSS is that Social Services Departments have significant difficulty in obtaining specialist opinion in this way and that Section 27 of the Children Act 1989, which provides a legal basis for such co-operation, is not effective in securing it in these circumstances.

3.5 The availability of multi-disciplinary teams at national centres of excellence (eg the London Teaching Hospitals) formerly provided an alternative means of obtaining expert opinion. However, a number of these teams no longer exist or accept external referrals for opinion in these circumstances.

The use of 'national experts'

3.6   In the absence of effective local arrangements, Social Services Departments, GALs and other parties to public law proceedings do make use of a relatively small number of clinicians who have developed particular expertise in *assessing* children, parents or whole families and supplying expert evidence in proceedings. These clinicians are often commissioned privately and do not undertake the work as part of any NHS contract. Whilst these arrangements *can* work there *are sometimes problems getting assessments from some distance away, causing problems for families where there are several appointments.* Evidence supplied in this way occurs outside of a proper regulatory framework where the standards of the work purchased by public resources are checked or can be reviewed. Generally, this work is not supplied by clinicians with nationally recognised accreditation. Additionally, most of the work done in this manner is undertaken by lone clinicians rather than being the product of multi-disciplinary teamwork.

Continuity for children

3.7   Perhaps the most serious drawback with the current arrangements lies in the fact that they occur as brief 'forensic' exercises. For the child this means fragmentation of intervention – the expert making assessments and recommendations about future care and treatment has not had previous involvement with the child or family, may have the briefest awareness of what is available locally in terms of treatment, and certainly has no power or authority to secure and provide for the child's future treatment needs. As a result recommendations made to the court about future treatment may not pay attention to what is available locally which the child can practically use; there may be unanticipated delays in securing what has been recommended; and when local services are subsequently engaged they may see a need to assess and form their own view of treatment requirements particularly if there has been no dialogue with the expert witness beforehand.

4. What is required in the future

4.1   The ADSS would like to see the arrangements for undertaking this work in the future based on the following:

- continuity for children in the assessment, reporting and treatment functions;
- a shared commitment and responsibility – health, education and social services authorities – to fully understand the complex needs of children who are the subject of public law proceedings and to do their utmost to meet *assessment and treatment needs within required time scales;*
- locally based arrangements for multi-disciplinary assessments/training;
- as far as possible, expert opinion that arises from multi-disciplinary teamwork between specialists;
- expert opinion being supplied by accredited clinicians and practitioners;
- a body with a responsibility for supplying the accreditation, setting universal standards, monitoring them and approving educational programmes associated with the function.

4.2   The ADSS recognises that professional bodies as well as Government have a role to play in bringing about this change. There is for example a national shortage of key child mental health clinicians. Steps should therefore be taken to introduce a mandatory nationally agreed education and training programme in this area of work for child mental health specialists. Such training needs to be consistent with wider measures designed to increase the supply and recruitment of such clinicians to work within multi-disciplinary teams.

There also needs to be some recognition on the part of all the professional bodies concerned that this function is too important in terms of the futures of the many children subject to public law proceedings, to leave it unregulated and outside the scope of NHS contracts.

4.3   The ADSS believes that Government has a leading part to play in encouraging this change. *The National Priorities Guidance* (1999–2002) included for child and adolescent mental health services (CAMHS) the following objective:

4.4   'To improve provision of appropriate, high quality care and treatment for children, young people *and adults* by building up locally based child and adolescent mental health services. This should be achieved through improved staffing levels and training provision at all tiers; improved liaison between primary care, specialist CAMHS, social services and other agencies; and should lead to users of the service to expect:

- a comprehensive assessment and, where indicated, a plan for treatment without a prolonged wait;
- a range of advice, consultation and care within primary care and Local Authority settings;
- a range of treatments within specialist settings based on the best evidence of effectiveness;
- in-patient care in a specialist setting, appropriate to their age and clinical need.'

4.5   The ADSS believes such guidance should also include an explicit expectation about local arrangements being established for expert opinion in public law proceedings.

4.6   Government also has the opportunity at the current time to encourage all health and local authorities to include arrangements for providing expert opinion in the three-year strategies health and social services authorities are charged to jointly develop. The Modernisation Fund and Children's Mental Health Grant provide funding opportunities for further developing what is required locally. More generally, there are opportunities within the Quality Protects programme for the Government to raise this issue as an item that should be jointly addressed through local action by social services and its partner agencies.

4.7   The ADSS also believes that as an additional measure the position on expert reporting and on some other related areas of co-operation between authorities, may also be improved if steps were taken by Government towards strengthening Section 27 of the Children Act 1989.

5. Recommendations

The ADSS recommends:

- that this paper is circulated to the range of professional groups and interested bodies concerned with expert reporting including the SSI, Royal College of Psychiatrists, Psychologists and President's Interdisciplinary Committee;
- that an appropriate forum is identified within which to discuss the paper and the points within on the way forward with a view to agreed action on the part of professional bodies and Government alike;
- that the impact Section 27 of the Children Act 1989 be reviewed by Government with a view to its strengthening further policy developments in this area.

DILEMMAS OF THE CORPORATE PARENT

Chris Davies CBE
Corporate Director of Social Services, Somerset County Council

Summary of paper

Starred milestones

Chris Davies made it clear in introducing his paper that it was not his intention to question the merits of the starred care plan proposal made in Re W and B; Re W (Care Plan) [2001] EWCA Civ 757, [2001] 2 FLR 582, but that he wished to pose two questions:

- *Once the power to review starred care plans is let loose, can it be reserved to a very small group of cases as identified by Lord Justice Thorpe and Lady Justice Hale? If so, he felt that it would be a positive development. However, he felt from his reading that this was unlikely to be the case.*
- *Even if the review mechanism is restricted to a small group of cases, are the snags which prevent fulfilment of care plans capable of judicial resolution?*

He expressed concern about whether looked-after children were helped by the involvement of ever more parties in their parenting, and queried whether it was right to invest more and more heavily in the quality control of child care than in getting the decisions right first time.

In his paper he set out key action points, showing what in his view needed to be done to get things right first time more often than at present. In particular, he highlighted the need to have more therapeutic intervention available for the children rather than relying solely on their placement. He was concerned about moves to bring more child and adolescent psychiatrists into the court process, due to the restriction this would place on their availability to do therapeutic work with children.

He also felt it important that social workers had more time to build effective relationships with children, rather than spending so much of their time in case management and dealing with the court process. He stated that most research showed that the criticisms children made of their social workers related in the main to the social workers not spending sufficient time with them.

Social work – recruitment and retention

Chris Davies considered that the main reasons why the recruitment and retention of social workers was proving so difficult were the following:

- *the public image of social workers;*
- *the sense that social work was too 'risky' a job (with particular reference to the 'scapegoating' of social workers following public enquiries into particular cases);*
- *the poor levels of pay, which had fallen well behind other similar professions, for example nurses, teachers and police officers;*
- *poor conditions;*
- *to some extent the way social workers were treated in the courts. He reminded those present that courts were not the natural territory of social workers and that court work was not their primary skill.*
- *the availability of more attractive alternative jobs, in terms of pay and conditions, with particular reference to the Connections scheme and CAFCASS.*

Introduction

The Court of Appeal judgment in *Re W and B; Re W (Care Plan)* [2001] EWCA Civ 757, [2001] 2 FLR 582, with its 'starred care plan' mechanism (currently suspended?), seemed to be taking us towards a much closer involvement of the judiciary in the 'parenting responsibilities' of local authorities. I want to look at some of the difficulties and dilemmas of the local authority as corporate parent, and, briefly, at what might make for better parenting and better outcomes for children looked after. I want to explore how starred care plans might help or hinder.

My suggestion is that they could assist the local authority to be a good parent, but they might also hinder its efforts. Is it too strained an analogy to suggest that the judiciary is like the non-custodial parent after divorce, previously feeling excluded and now gaining more influence over the life of the child? This could be for good or for ill. The local authority, of course, is the parent with custody!

So what are the dilemmas faced by the 'corporate parent'?

- There simply are not the people (foster carers, adopters, specialist therapeutic placements, skilled psychotherapists) to meet the needs of the most troubled children. These (relatively few) youngsters bounce from pillar to post of the care system, accompanied by an increasing sense of desperation in those around them. Eventually, too many graduate to adult mental health or criminal justice systems, whilst some surprise and delight us by making their own way (more or less successfully) as young adults or climbing back into the (more or less reluctant) bosom of their birth family. The former are our outright failures. They make us all feel bad. We must never close the door on them or give up hope for them. The problem is that the skilled people and capacity to help them simply is not there.

- We spend a lot of time dealing with the consequences of children's bad experiences and traumatic family breakdowns. We become exclusively problem-oriented. Adults who have been in care and ask to read their case-record (and I have sat alongside a few) are sad (and sometimes angry) that their bed-wetting and tantrums are described in detail, but no one recorded their goldstars for arithmetic or their swimming certificates. If a young teenager is living a chaotic lifestyle, staying out all night, misusing drugs, associating with older and undesirable 'friends', angry with the world, how do we move beyond the problems and focus on potential, ambition and hopes for the future? We know we must.

- Planning frameworks are in place which are thorough and comprehensive (the LAC system), *but*:

- they are very time-consuming and cumbersome. The evidence (sadly) is that social workers are spending more and more time on case management and less and less face-to-face with children, and that children want more time and attention from their social workers (viz recent research with adopted children);
- frameworks are overtaken by events in the desperate whirl of activity around crisis-ridden cases, where dealing with the latest placement breakdown and finding a safe haven is the dominant preoccupation. A sense of long-term direction can be lost.

- The local authority (LA) must act in the best interests of every looked-after child, but has several hundreds of them on any one day:

- a caring parent whose child is missing will be desperately worried and not rest until he/she is safe. As Director of Social Services, I want to know what is being done when a child is missing for more than a few hours. Sometimes I intervene myself. But to show the same concern as a birth parent for all 700 children who come through my council's care in a year (many of them unusually troubled) would be emotionally unsustainable. Is there clearly one individual for each child who carries that concern?;

– with eight or nine children living in a residential unit, there will sometimes be uncontrollable clashes, intolerably risky relationships or unmanageable chemistries, and one child will be moved in the interests of others and sometimes against their own – a decision a birth parent would very rarely face (the child care population includes, in Jean Packmans' terms , 'volunteers, victims and villains');

– unlike a birth parent, the LA does not have a purse with a fixed limit. It could always devote a larger share of its hundreds of millions of pounds annual spend to this one child. And yet every pound spent on child A is not available for child B, or to supply equipment for adults with physical disabilities, or to provide respite care to the spouse of an Alzheimer's sufferer. Sometimes plans are proposed for an individual child which would take huge sums away from other services (£150,000 pa for 2–3 years is not unheard of). Cost is a legitimate consideration, but there will be many different perspectives on what is a reasonable balancing of these considerations.

• The law requires LAs to share the parenting with birth parents, and the evidence is that keeping looked-after children in touch with their own families contributes to improved outcomes for them. But these parents tend to have had more then their share of troubles and can be people who have found effective parenting beyond them. Often there are conflicts between parents, and between parents and extended family or carers. Forging co-operative relationships focused on the needs of the child is far from easy.

• The corporate parent has to divide responsibilities between many individuals:

– a field social worker will hold the case accountability, but his/her supervisor will be quite involved, as might be a social work assistant with practical support tasks;

– there may be an independent reviewing officer and a leaving care personal advisor;

– if in a foster home, there will be a foster carer support worker and, if in a residential unit, at least 10 staff (changing over with every shift), an external manager, a statutory visitor, elected members and inspectors visiting;

– there will be an independent visitor for some children.

This list excludes all those outside the LA who may play key roles (psychiatrists, psychologists, children's guardians, etc), and all those in the list carry aspects of the parenting role. The risks of failure, with such divided responsibilities, must be high.

• Birth parents cope with their responsibilities in all sorts of ways. It is fortunate for us and our offspring that, as DW Winnicott told us, we only have to be 'good enough'. We cope with periods of misunderstanding, conflict and stress with our older children because we have years of 'building' on which to rely. But the LA takes over as parent, usually in crisis, with no 'history' to fall back on, and having to deal with children who often have lost all trust in adults who pretend to care. Birth parents can continue their interest and investment in their children as young adults because they are moving to another life-stage without the demands of young children to meet. The LA never stops having children! When the young adult moves on from his residential unit or foster home, his place ('bed') will quickly be filled. If he returns, we hope he will be welcome, but his room will not be there for him.

I make no apology for basing this commentary on the experience of the relatively small number of children who are 'failed' by us all. They are the ones who worry me constantly. But we also need a broader perspective. Many more looked-after children live stable and fulfilling lives with foster carers. In Somerset, 74% of children looked after for more than 4 years are in foster placements where they have been for more than 2 years – and that in an authority with a high rate of adoptive placement from care. Social workers, residential social workers and foster carers show tremendous commitment to getting the best they can for their charges.

But this litany of troubles, sadly, will not be unfamiliar to experienced family court judges. It is not presented to excuse or to seek sympathy. It is to try to understand why we are so prone to failure and how hard we need to work to avoid it; and now to go on to look at what this understanding suggests we might need to do to improve our parenting and its outcomes.

Key action points might be:

- to increase the numbers of foster carers and adopters able to meet the needs of the children who need placement;
- to have more therapeutic provision available, ie specialist residential settings, individual 'talking' and play therapists, and more resilient and responsive child and adolescent mental health services;
- to ensure that case-accountable social workers have the capacity to build effective relationships with children, and are supported by efficient systems which will facilitate effective planning and implementation;
- to develop skills in intervention with 'troubled and troublesome' teenagers, in engaging with end-of-tether and low self-esteem parents, and in managing complex systems around the child;
- to spend more time listening to children and their families about what they need from us and what they value in how we work with them;
- to use reliable quality assurance systems in the day-to-day management of our practice;
- to ensure that all those with responsibility in a child's life understand their role and responsibilities, and those of others, and that tasks are clearly allocated;
- to ensure that someone in every child's life cares 'unreasonably' for him/her and will fight his/her corner.

The list of troubles does not suggest, to me at any rate, that we should be spending ever more on checking, inspecting and regulating. That might be needed if there were signs that LAs were, for instance, failing to implement care plans out of carelessness or bad faith. But recent research sponsored by the Department of Health as part of its programme of evaluation of the impact of the Children Act concludes that 'the study did not find any deliberate flouting of the plan submitted to court. Nor did it find a lack of serious effort to put the plan into operation' (Harwin, p 63, above). Nevertheless, we are now investing in CAFCASS, which will cost much more than the services it replaces, and in the Care Standards Commission (much, much more). The starred care plan proposal would surely lead to far more costs to the judicial system and its servants. Japanese industry thrived when it realised that it was better to invest in the operatives so that quality was 'right first time', rather than in end-of-line 'checkers' who were there to find the poor workmanship. I have argued strongly in the past for rigorous inspection and proper regulation, but have we got the balance out of kilter?

To return to my first question, then, will the involvement of the courts in regulating LA's implementation of care plans help or hinder? Of course, it depends. To strain the analogy, the active involvement of the non-custodial parent helps when:

- the custodial parent:
- recognises the legitimacy of their involvement;
- feels that they enhance opportunities for the child;

- the non-custodial parent:
- respects the fact that the custodial parent bears the brunt of the responsibilities;
- is not destructively critical;

- is realistic about the limitations of their role and contribution;
- eases the burden of responsibility in practical ways,

and when both parents are committed to the child first and foremost, acknowledge their own limitations, and sink their differences.

When relationships are adjusting, there is always room for misunderstanding and bad feeling. I fear that judges may be offended by my analogy, but there is certainly room for misunderstanding by the custodial parent (local authorities) as to why the non-custodial parent (the judiciary) is now insisting on a stronger role in ongoing care arrangements. They say that this is to bring our arrangements in line with the European Convention for the Protection of Human Rights and Fundamental Freedoms 1950 (ECHR) and that this should not be seen as a signal of lack of judicial trust or confidence in care authorities. But that is not how everyone sees it. Hugh Howard, in the *Solicitor's Journal*, wrote, 'in the light of numerous cases where things have gone wrong, the judges have had enough ... at long last, the courts have taken back the right to control the future of children'.

Thorpe LJ said, 'there must be a considerable responsibility on the courts to ensure that any extension of function is used sparingly and collaboratively and not for the revival and perpetuation of adversarial issues'. But already Alistair MacDonald of St Phillip's Chambers has written:

'If the court can dictate which elements of the care plan are to be starred, in order to prevent an actual or anticipated breach of a Convention right, why could the court not order the addition of elements into the care plan in order to prevent the same? It is true that this would constitute a much stronger bridge across the divide. However, on the principles summarised above it is submitted that such a development must be a real possibility in the rare cases where the court considers the care plan to be in breach of convention rights but the local authority refuses to amend the same.'

Thorpe LJ, in his judgment, recalls that on the demise of the broader wardship jurisdiction ([2001] 2 FLR 582, at para [18]):

' ... the most general concentration of misgiving, certainly in the minds of judges, guardians and forensic experts, was the absence of any overriding mechanism for intervention in those cases where the care plan approved at trial was frustrated by unforeseen change of circumstance, lack of resources, neglect or by any other factor. There were equal concerns of unaccustomed frustration at the earlier stage of trial where the application for a care order was proved to the hilt but where the judge conceived that the care plan advanced by the local authority was not best calculated to promote the welfare of the child.'

In May 1997, this conference, according to Thorpe LJ, 'expressed grave concern', and developed a proposal much like the starred care plan. There was no claim that this was a response to the ECHR. It was clearly a response to the concerns of the judges. Lord Irvine, in the House of Lords, said that 'one problem is failure' (the Children Act) 'to trust the judges sufficiently'. Are we now failing to trust LAs? Thorpe LJ, in his judgment, asks (at para [23]):

' ... how does he [the judge] discharge this duty in the instances that I have cited above where his evaluation of what is best for the child conflicts with the outcome to which his order will almost certainly lead? All parties to the proceedings in which he gives judgment are equally entitled to a disposal which, at least in the estimation of the experienced specialist judge, is most likely to promote the welfare of the child. How is that entitlement delivered when the judge declares that he is obliged to make an order against his better judgement?'

But how does the LA fulfil its moral and statutory duty to act in the best interests of the child in its care if it is implementing a judge-made care plan which it does not believe to be in the child's interests?

Of course, there is a sound and constructive way forward. Thorpe, LJ, shows us that way (at para [32]):

'Even if the application is well founded the court must always be mindful of its limitations and at the same time respectful of the responsibility and function of the local authority. It is essential that the court should be acquainted with the services and resources of the local authority or authorities whose applications it regularly lists. The court should equally be aware of any budgetary constraints or staff shortages by which the authorities are currently affected. Courts must refrain from opinionated criticism as well as endeavours to achieve the unachievable. Any continuing interaction between the court and the local authority must be as far as appropriate collaborative and with no other objects than to promote welfare of the child and to ensure for the child and the other parties to the proceedings their Convention rights.'

Hale LJ describes much more succinctly than I have done, and with some sympathy, the difficulties LAs face (at para [60]):

'Even in a well-resourced authority with a wide range of good facilities, courts should beware a rosy tinted view of what can be achieved. Finding appropriate placements for children is getting more and more difficult. Foster placements are in short supply and there are fewer and fewer types of residential placements. At the same time, the needs of the children being placed are becoming greater. The more children are able to stay at home, with appropriate help and support, the more needy will be those who cannot do so. Finding foster placements, let alone adoptive families, for them is correspondingly difficult.'

And she reminds us of the cautionary conclusion of the *Review of Child Care Law* (HMSO, 1985) as to the contribution of the courts (at para [63]):

'The expertise of a court lies in its ability to hear all sides of the case, to determine issues of fact and to make a firm decision on a particular issue at a particular time, in accordance with the applicable law. It cannot initiate action to provide for the child, nor can it deliver the services which may best serve the child's needs … It is not only important that the reviewing body should itself have the power to deliver the care which it considers best for the child: it is also necessary that the body with day to day responsibility for the child should have a positive duty to "take a grip on" the case and make firm and early decisions without the temptation to pass responsibility to another body. The encouragement of positive attitudes and practices, as well as subjecting them to informed scrutiny, is more important than what could only ever be a limited form of judicial review.'

So why should I be concerned as a Director of Social Services about the 'starred care plan' idea? Why should I risk the wrath of the judiciary by raising these doubts? I would like to be able to agree with Hale LJ that (at para [81]):

' … such a limited process, in such limited circumstances, should not place an undue strain upon resources or drive a coach and horses through the careful division of responsibility established by the 1989 Act. The object is simply to seek to secure that the care system is operated in such a way as to comply with the Convention rights.'

And I would be much reassured if Thorpe LJ is right that (at para [31]):

' … the number of cases in which the duty to report and the power to review will arise should prove to be comparatively rare, certainly in relation to the number of applications for care orders that are issued. Obviously there would be a need to monitor the advent of this development to test the reliability of the speculation that only 200 applications a year would result.'

My worries are that:

- there is a more fundamental mistrust of LAs at work (do I misconstrue Sedley LJ's depiction of the courts as 'the rock' of decision-making and LAs as 'the sand'?);
- judges who have rued the day that they lost their powers in wardship will not be able to resist intervening much more widely than Thorpe and Hale LJJ expect;
- this will do little to address the fundamental problems which prevent us achieving good outcomes for children who are looked after;
- indeed, it may further split already confused responsibilities, convolute decision-making, and take resources away from direct help to the child;
- it could deliver to the judges power without responsibility, and to the LAs responsibility without power.

If starred care plans are used very sparingly, I will be proved wrong, and I will eat my hat with relish. I have no doubt that, used as Thorpe and Hale LJJ envisage, where the fundamental aim (reunification or alternative permanent family) is frustrated, then this will be a constructive development in the interaction between the judiciary and the executive in the public care of children. I am sure that other directors of social services, like me, would not just accept, but welcome that.

When the judiciary and the executive share the dilemmas of public parenting, respect each other's roles and responsibilities, and recognise that the child is the one who matters, we can achieve so much. I have been fortunate to work in just that way with excellent judges, and have valued the understanding, clarity of thought and authority they have brought to our efforts to restore stability to storm-tossed young lives. That, of course, is what this conference seeks to build. I look forward to it.

EXPERT WITNESSES

Pat Monro
Solicitor, Darlington & Parkinson

Summary of paper

Pat Monro made it clear to the conference that in her paper she was not advocating the use of more experts. Her view was that there should be far less use of experts, and that in many cases they were entirely unnecessary. Much more careful consideration should go into the circumstances in which experts were needed.

Social work assessments and expert evidence

She emphasised the need to re-skill social workers, recalling that in her early years of practice assessments were done by the social workers who retained a degree of respect. She was concerned that now experts were being used instead of social work assessments. In London this was generally because of the reduced numbers of social workers and high turnover of staff, leaving little option but to use experts to fill the gap.

She felt that the courts had played a part in the demoralisation of social workers as regards the court process. Social workers were generally not considered to be experts themselves. She advocated a change in judicial attitudes, and queried the kind of experience judges were seeking before they were willing to accept a social worker as having the competence to give expert evidence.

Approved list of experts

Pat Monro referred to the large amount of guidance and protocols available as to the use of experts, and expressed a wish instead for there to be one comprehensive guide to the instruction and use of experts.

She asked for consideration to be given to there being a court-approved list of experts. She referred the court to the Northern Circuit Expert Witness Initiative, and suggested a move to extending this nationally. She felt that such a list would assist not only with obtaining funding from the Legal Services Commission for a particular expert, but also with easing the concerns felt when using an expert with whom one had had no previous dealings. She further suggested that such a list of experts could be carried outside the Family Division into other areas and fields.

Alternative uses of experts

Pat Monro referred to the Civil Working Group proposals for there to be two types of experts:

- *a court expert, all of whose reports and advice was disclosable; and*
- *an expert who was used by a party merely as an adviser, whose reports and advice were not disclosable.*

She felt that this model was very attractive, and would assist a party both in obtaining advice as to particular areas of the case and in the cross-examination of the court expert. It would avoid people mounting an argument that their European Convention for the Protection of Human Rights and Fundamental Freedoms 1950, Art 6 rights had been infringed, but would not significantly increase costs or the length of hearings.

Before the Children Act 1989

One of the major concerns which had been voiced in the years prior to the Children Act 1989 was how to ensure, in care and related public law proceedings, that the court had the benefit of professional opinion concerning the interest of the child, expressed independently of the local authority and parents. This concern had been raised in the Field Fisher Report in 1974, which investigated the circumstances surrounding the death of Maria Colwell.

There was no widespread use of expert witnesses in public law proceedings before the Children Act. The majority of care cases were conducted in the juvenile court. Until May 1984, when the panels of guardians ad litem and reporting officers were established, the 'expert' evidence in the majority of cases was given by social workers employed by the local authority bringing the proceedings.

The period between 1976 and 1984 saw the development of the 'independent social worker'. MIND set up a panel of social workers prepared to act as experts in these cases. In the early 1970s, the panel named TRIAL (Register of Independent Advisors Limited) was established, to ensure that the court could have the benefit of expert opinion independent of the local authority. The members of this panel were mainly experienced social workers, but also included some psychologists. The Family Rights Group held its own register of social workers.

Child care lawyers increasingly used members from the panel to consider the services given to families, and the plans for the children. The Legal Aid Scheme required prior authority to be obtained for this expenditure if the case was conducted in the juvenile court. The experts used in these child care cases were somewhat hampered by the fact that they had no right of access to local authority records, and were frequently instructed for the parents, and therefore regarded as partial. There was no duty on the party obtaining the report to disclose it.

Complex cases, particularly those that involved an assessment of future risk to a child, were heard in the High Court, where the Official Solicitor would be appointed to represent the child. Since his staff were civil servants, with no training or expertise which enabled them to make social work assessments or to assess the plans for the child concerned, he would tend to instruct an expert witness to provide a report. This would inevitably be a child psychiatrist. It has never been entirely clear why experienced social workers were not instructed in appropriate cases, unless it was because of the attitude of the judiciary, who were generally not persuaded that social workers were 'experts'. This attitude was exemplified in the decision of Lord Justice Ormerod in a matrimonial case in the Court of Appeal, when he disapproved the use of an expert social worker, and indicated that the social worker could not be independent because one party paid him.

After the Children Act

Significant changes to this system were brought about with the implementation of the Children Act. A guardian ad litem was appointed to safeguard the interest of the child who was the subject of proceedings, unless it was not necessarily in her interest. Although the pattern of appointment varied enormously over England and Wales, guardians were to be found in the majority of proceedings. The regulations did not specify the qualifications expected of a panel member, but the DHSS Circular LAC 83(83)21 stated that they should be 'persons with qualifications in social work plus sufficient relevant experience'. In London it was necessary for a panel member to have at least 3 years' post-qualification experience as a social worker before becoming eligible for the panel, and there was a compulsory training course, which, in the London area, was a 3-day course covering legal and social work issues.

The child now had a welfare representative who would be regarded as an expert in relation to matters of general child care and development, and who had a right of access to local authority records (Children Act 1989, s 42). Where care cases required specialist knowledge which might be beyond the competence of the guardian, it was hoped that a parent wishing to challenge the local authority case would accept an expert appointed by the guardian, instead of seeking to instruct his or her own expert.

However, the use of expert witnesses increased. In 1999 BAAF published research into the use of experts in care proceedings.[1] It found that all parties had increased their use of experts. The reasons for guardians doing so were identified as follows:

- some of the concerns about the undervaluing of social work expertise by the courts had contributed to guardians' increased use of experts;
- the policies and practices adopted by some local authorities had contributed to the increased use of experts by guardians;
- complexity of cases;
- the case demanded the diagnosis of a mental health state.

Contrary to popular debate, guardians in the survey did not identify the 'spiral' or 'domino' effect as a major reason for the increase in use of experts.

Guidance on use of experts

There has been a considerable amount of judicial guidance and directions in relation to the instruction of experts.

- In 1991 Mr Justice Cazalet set out a statement of the principles which applied to experts in family proceedings.[2]
- The Children Act Advisory Committee report for 1994/95 set out a draft letter for the joint instruction of an expert. The same report noted relevant case-law in which guidance was given as to meetings of experts;[3] functions of the expert and judge;[4] letters of instruction and information to be provided to experts appointed;[5] duties of experts; and expert evidence on credibility.[6]
- In 1994 Mr Justice Wall set out propositions which should govern the grant of leave and consequential directions for expert evidence in children cases.[7]
- In the Final Report of the Children Act Advisory Committee in June 1997 additional case-law on experts' meetings was noted.[8]

The Children Act Advisory Committee produced the *Handbook of Best Practice in Children Act Cases* in June 1997. Section 5, on experts and the court, was stated to apply equally to experts appointed in public and private law cases. This summarised much of the guidance which had previously been issued, and urged advocates to consider an application for leave to instruct an expert at the earliest possible stage of the proceedings.[9] It also referred practitioners to the

---

[1]   Brophy, Wale and Bates, *Myths and Practices: A national survey of the use of experts in childcare proceedings* (BAAF, 1999).

[2]   Note: *Re R (A Minor) (Experts' Evidence)* [1991] 1 FLR 291.

[3]   *Re C (Expert Evidence: Disclosure Practice)* [1995] 1 FLR 204.

[4]   *Re AB (Child Abuse: Expert Witnesses)* [1995] 1 FLR 181.

[5]   *Re M (Minors) (Care Proceedings: Child's Wishes)* [1994] 1 FLR 749; *Re T and E (Proceedings: Conflicting Interests)* [1995] 1 FLR 581.

[6]   *Re S and B (Minors) (Child Abuse: Evidence)* [1990] 2 FLR 489; *Re FS (Minors) (Child Abuse: Evidence)* [1996] 2 FLR 158, CA.

[7]   *Re G (Minors) (Expert Witnesses)* [1994] 2 FLR 291 at 298.

[8]   *Re CS (Expert Witnesses)* [1996] 2 FLR 115.

[9]   *H v Cambridgeshire County Council* [1996] 2 FLR 566.

Expert Witness Pack which was produced by the Expert Witness Group[10] and which includes:

- several pro formas;
- draft letters of instruction and acceptance;
- checklist for solicitor and expert;
- guidelines and a model *curriculum vitae* for expert witnesses;
- a model format for experts' reports.

Mr Justice Wall, with His Honour Judge Iain Hamilton, has written a *Handbook for Expert Witnesses in Children Act Cases.*[11]

The Law Society has produced guidance for its members on the instruction of expert witnesses.

Experts in civil proceedings

The development of rules governing the instruction of experts in civil proceedings has very much mirrored the development of practice within the Family Division.

The impact of the Woolf Report 'Access to Justice'

In his *Interim Report on Access to Justice* (June 1995) Lord Woolf stated that:

> 'the need to engage experts was a source of excessive expense, delay, and, in some cases, increased complexity through the excessive or inappropriate use of experts. Concern was also expressed as to their failure to maintain their independence from the party by whom they had been instructed.'

The basic premise of the new approach as set out in the Woolf report was that there should be no expert evidence at all unless it will help the court, and no more than one expert in any one speciality unless this is necessary for some real purpose. He recommended a case management system in which the court would have complete control over the use of evidence, including expert evidence.

Civil Procedure Rules

The Civil Procedure Rules 1998 (CPR) came into force on 26 April 1999. The Rules 'are a new procedural code with the overriding objective of enabling the court to deal with cases justly' (CPR, r 1.1(1)). CPR Part 35 followed the recommendations on the use of expert witnesses which were made in the Woolf Report. Part 35 limits the use of oral expert evidence to that which is reasonably required; it requires that, where possible, matters requiring expert evidence should be dealt with by a single expert; and permission of the court is always required either to call an expert or to put an expert's report in evidence.[12]

- The duty of the expert is to the court, irrespective of who instructs or pays him/her.
- No expert may be called, or expert report submitted without the court's permission.[13]
- Expert evidence is to be in a written form unless the court directs otherwise.

---

[10]   Family Law, 1997; Expert Witness Group, c/o Dr Eileen Vizard, St Luke's Woodside Hospital.
[11]   Family Law, 2000.
[12]   Brophy, Wale and Bates, n 1 above.
[13]   In *Re A (Family Proceedings: Expert Witnesses)* [2001] 1 FLR 723, Wall J stated that in family proceedings it is wrong for one party, without the knowledge of the other party or the court, to commission an expert's report. An expert must know the terms of the court order permitting an expert's report to be obtained, and should not accept anonymous instructions.

- A party may put written questions to an expert, whether a single joint expert, or instructed by another party; such questions must be submitted within 28 days of service of the report, and must be for clarification purposes only, unless the court gives permission or the other party agrees. If the expert does not answer a question, the court may order that the instructing party may not rely on the evidence of that expert, and/or may not recover the expert's fees from the other party.[14]
- The court may direct that one expert only may give evidence on a particular issue, and may, in the absence of agreement between the parties, select the expert from a list prepared or identified by the parties, or direct that the expert should be selected in such other manner as the court directs.
- The court may direct a discussion between experts for the purpose of identifying the issues, and where possible reaching agreement. The court may direct that the experts prepare a statement for the court showing the areas of agreement and disagreement, and reasons for disagreeing. The content of the discussion between the experts shall not be referred to unless the parties agree. Any agreement reached between the experts is not binding on the parties unless this is expressly agreed.
- An expert, without notice to the parties, may file a request for directions to assist him in carrying out his function as an expert.

Practice Direction

The Practice Direction, which supplements CPR Part 35, requires the expert report to be addressed to the court, and details the information which should be contained in the report. The report must be verified by a statement of truth, and must comply with the requirements of any approved expert's protocol.

Duties of expert witnesses

The duties of expert witnesses have been considered in a plethora of cases, in particular *The Ikarian Reefer*[15] in which Mr Justice Cresswell analysed the duties and responsibilities of expert witnesses. Judge Toulmin QC extended this analysis in *Anglo Group plc v Winther Brown & Co Ltd*[16] in which he identified eight principles relating to expert witnesses, which reflected the requirements of the CPR.

Pre-action protocols

Following the Woolf Report, Pre-action Protocols were established in relation to personal injury and clinical negligence cases. The Employment Appeal Tribunal has recently issued guidance on the use of expert witnesses.[17] These are intended as guidance until more formal rules emerge, and provide a framework for use in cases where one or more parties regard an expert as necessary.

Draft code of guidance

The Civil Procedure Working Party has produced a draft 'Code of Guidance on Expert

---

[14] In *Mutch v Allen* [2001] EWCA Civ 716, CA, the court stated, 'this is a useful provision, enabling a party to obtain clarification of a report prepared by an expert instructed by his opponent or to arrange for a point not covered in the report, but within his experience, to be dealt with. In a given case, were it not possible to obtain such clarification or extension of a report, the court for that reason alone, may feel obliged to direct that the expert witness should testify at trial'.

[15] *National Justice Compania Naviera SA v Prudential Assurance Co Ltd* [1993] 2 EGLR 183, [1993] 2 Lloyd's Rep 68.

[16] (2000) 72 Con LR 118.

[17] *De Keyser Ltd v Wilson* [2001] All ER (D) 237.

Witnesses'. The Working Party attempts to draw a division between the role of the expert as 'advisor to the parties' and 'assistant to the court', in the event of a dispute. 'Advice' is defined as meaning 'things said and done (including any draft report) by the expert outside the litigious process'. Such advice would not be disclosable to the other party on the ground that it attracts legal professional privilege. However, once an expert is instructed to prepare a report for the purposes of court proceedings in accordance with CPR, Part 35, then his report and any advice given thereafter may be disclosable if the court so orders. Discussions between experts are covered. A concise agenda for experts' discussions is encouraged, suggesting, as far as possible, that questions raised within it are 'closed', ie capable of being answered 'yes' or 'no'. The agenda is to be circulated 28 days before the meeting, and agreed 7 days before. Attendance of lawyers is allowed for but strictly for the purpose of 'assisting the experts in their discussion'.

Academy of experts: code of guidance

The Academy of Experts has issued an extensive Code of Guidance for experts and those instructing them.

The future

Issues to be addressed

- Some members of the judiciary are sceptical about the appointment of an expert unknown to the court. In particular, the judiciary is sometimes hesitant to accept that a social worker may be an expert in a particular field, and of more value than a medically qualified expert.
- It is perceived that some judges appear to place disproportionate weight on the views of experts well known to them.
- There are insufficient well-qualified people, still in clinical practice, available to prepare reports.
- The usefulness of an expert report may be outweighed by the consequent delays in timetabling. The cost of such reports, although secondary to the interests of the child concerned, may be considerable.
- Experts frequently wish to call a meeting of professionals before commencing work. The purpose of such a meeting is usually so that the informal views of other professionals can be obtained. Such a meeting, if not attended by the family, or minuted for distribution, offends the principle of openness which must obtain where an expert is to be seen as independent of the parties.
- Where a multi-disciplinary team is involved in the preparation of the report, this adds to the costs, and usually requires a number of people to be available for cross-examination. It is often difficult to ascribe the views in the report to a particular worker.
- Where there is a single joint expert, the parties will have no alternative view against which to test the opinions of the expert unless allowed to instruct another expert, possibly for the purpose of advice only.
- Now that CAFCASS has been established, with the current uncertainty about how many experienced guardians will join the service, it remains to be seen how the practice of instructing experts will change. If those acting as guardians do not have experience, expertise and sufficient training to make their own assessments of a family situation, then it can be expected that the use of expert witnesses will increase, with the attendant problems of delays and additional costs.
- The courts have been anxious to avoid a proliferation of experts, and 'shopping around'. There are also indications that the judiciary wishes to take more control over the instruction

of experts. In *Re X (Non-accidental Injury: Expert Evidence)*[18] Singer J was critical of the evidence and conduct of a particular specialist, and stated that future applications for leave to seek a report from him should not be granted without prior scrutiny by a Family Division judge. (This expert has been criticised twice previously by the judiciary.) However, a restrictive approach to the instruction of experts, both by the courts, and the Legal Services Commission (which may refuse to authorise an increase in a costs limitation to cover the fees), may lead to challenges under ECHR, Art 6. Decisions of the court to date have been in respect of decisions taken by other European courts with an inquisitorial system. However, in *Bönisch v Austria*[19] the principle of equality of arms has been held to have been infringed where there was unequal treatment between the court-appointed expert and the expert witness for the defence in a criminal trial. It is implicit in the court's judgment in *H v France*[20] and *Mantovanelli v France*[21] that where expert evidence is indispensable to a fair trial, either the court should call such evidence or legal aid should be provided to enable the parties to do so.

Proposals for change

- More multi-disciplinary training would assist a better understanding of the respective roles of those involved in proceedings.
- Part 35 of the CPR should be made applicable to family proceedings.
- There should be detailed codes of practice and guidelines to tie in with Part 35.
- Consideration should be given to the establishment of an approved list of experts (such as the Public Service Interpreters' list).
- In standardising guidance and practice, care should be taken to avoid being over prescriptive. This can lead to 'practice by numbers' and prevent lawyers from exercising professional judgment as to the best way to represent their client and ensuring the right result for the child concerned.
- In the BAAF research in 1999, the conclusion stated that certain issues needed clarification. These were that:

– the joint instruction of experts will not be appropriate or achievable in all cases;
– the existing body of child welfare knowledge is neither static nor uniform and consultants do not always necessarily agree with the local authority. On that basis and in the interest of social justice, legal procedures for the appointment of experts should not reduce the opportunities for that breadth of relevant knowledge to inform decision-making with regard to the future care and well-being of very vulnerable children.

These issues remain important ones for consideration in any revision of the guidance and directions.

---

[18] [2001] 2 FLR 90.
[19] (1985) 9 EHRR 191.
[20] (1990) 12 EHRR 74.
[21] (1997) 24 EHRR 370.

THE USE OF EXPERT WITNESSES:
USEFUL OR USELESS?

Jenny Stevenson MA, AFBPsS, MBA,
Chartered Consultant Clinical Psychologist
Dr Arlene Vetere PhD, AFBPsS,
Academician, Academy of the Learned Societies in the Social Sciences,
Chartered Clinical Psychologist, Tavistock Clinic, Principal Lecturer in
Systemic Psychotherapy, University of East London

Summary of paper

Dr Arlene Vetere

Dr Vetere stated that the intention of her paper was first to suggest that courts are not always able to make the best use of expert witnesses, and secondly to critique the practices of some experts.

To assist the courts to make better use of expert witnesses, she made the following suggestions:

- that greater attempt be made to use experts strategically for the more complex cases;
- that a more targeted use of experts might mean that they could be retained for a longer period, to consult on the care planning and implementation process, and be involved in reviews;
- that this would help to prevent the practice and use of 'snapshot' assessments.

In relation to the practices of some experts, she suggested:

- that expert witnesses make use of regular consultation to their own process, given the often profound effect of their opinions on people's lives;
- that they acknowledge the situated nature of their knowledge, and actively grapple with the implications of being subject to the same social and cultural discourses as the subjects of their reports;
- that they engage with those they assess over a period of time, allowing them to assess the capacity for attitudinal and behavioural change, thus avoiding 'snap-shot' assessments.

Overall, Dr Vetere expressed the wish to see the assessment process helped to be more reflective, thoughtful and transparent.

Jenny Stevenson

Jenny Stevenson expressed the concern that evidence of the continuing professional development of experts was rarely sought. She felt that if there was no such evidence, that person should not be seen as an expert.

She felt that training for court work should be included in the experts' own general training. She sought its inclusion by the relevant Royal Colleges, and believed that until this was addressed, people would continue to seek 'sticking plaster' solutions to this issue.

She emphasised the need for data, to provide feedback to experts on such matters as what their job was and how plans based on their opinions had been implemented. Without such data and evaluation, it was in her opinion not possible to affect the practice of experts.

Introduction

We have responded to this title as two psychologists who have considerable recent experience in the family courts, both in private and public law proceedings.

The Over-use of Expert Witnesses? : A Psychological Perspective

by Dr Arlene Vetere

The title seems to predispose the answer, and invite a potentially polarised debate. I shall pose the question somewhat tangentially – does the court system use expert witness assessments appropriately and to the best effect? This may seem an odd question in the light of the recent recommendation in the Woolf reforms for joint instruction and the clear directive that experts' responsibilities are to the court. However, I hold some misgivings about the practices of some expert witnesses and our present use of expert witness assessment. It is likely there will be some difference of opinion as to what constitutes the most appropriate use of expert witness assessment. I shall offer some thoughts and try to weave into this discussion consideration of the implications of two major pieces of legislation, the Children Act and the Human Rights Act.

The Children Act requires us to hold the needs of the child paramount whilst striving to work in partnership with parents. The Human Rights Act protects the right to a fair and public hearing in a reasonable time, and the right to respect for private and family life, which can be breached to protect the rights and freedoms of others. These two pieces of legislation have complementary aims, but hold within them, and between them, important areas of tension and relative degrees of uncertainty. Arguably the push within child care proceedings and the wider legal system is for certainty and this is where the expert witness comes in, to help the decision-making process move forward to the best possible conclusion.

However, within modern psychology, the notion of 'expert' is problematic. Observers are conceptualised as part of the system under observation, so that patterns and processes observed by the expert are only some of many that could be identified. There is an interaction between the observer, the method of observation and the people under observation, which gives rise to a fundamental philosophical problem. We cannot know what would have happened in the observers' absence. Experts, as observers of human behaviour, are subject to the same cultural and societal discourses as are the people under observation, introducing sources of bias into the observation that sometimes defy quantification. We could argue that bias in assessment is a cross we have to bear and that our responsibility is to try and understand these sources of bias and reflect on how they operate in our observations and assessments. However, my concern stems from the belief that many experts do not acknowledge sources of variance in their data and conclusions, and act as if their knowledge is objectively knowable, rather than socially constructed.

The worst excess, for me, is when the expert witness assessment does not take account properly of the impact on parenting of wider social processes such as poverty, violence, ill health, migration, and poor housing, and how these processes get inside people's heads, so to speak, and impact directly on their competence, well-being and sense of self-worth. In my experience most parenting assessments are carried out by middle class professionals on working-class parents. This is the way of the world, but I would like to see some reflection on these class and cultural divides in the expert reports, that thoughtfully considers where different opportunities and standards might operate in people's lives, in a class-based way.

Thus, for me, assessment of parenting abilities and the potential for change needs to be carried out in a way that allows the proper exploration of the ability to change. One or two meetings with parents, accompanied by one observation of a contact meeting is not sufficiently rigorous to allow the systematic exploration of the instructions in the face of the inherent problems in the assessment process. Time is needed to develop a working alliance with the parent(s) to assess whether they can work in co-operation with professionals and have the ability to see professionals as potentially helpful. I am not recommending that experts develop therapeutic relationships with parents, but there is no doubt in my mind that a full assessment has therapeutic potential, in that it can facilitate attitude change in the parents.

The Framework for the Assessment of Children in Need and Their Families reminds us that assessment is a process and not a single assessment event, and that assessment needs to be based on partnership with families and young people. Assessment should be grounded in knowledge derived from theory, research, policy and practice, and, I would add, a critique of the manner by which we claim to know. There is room for improvement. Expert witness reports can become more scholarly documents and deconstruct policy and practices that have no evidence base.

Since the advent of the Woolf reforms, I have increasingly been invited to 'experts' meetings'. I welcome this change in practice as it helps to identify areas of agreement and disagreement between the different perspectives. However, in the light of the Human Rights Act, our practice could take a step further, by inviting children's guardians and experts to take part in collaboratively devising care plans, harnessing the strengths within the different positions. If key indicators or progress are to be identified within care plans, experts can be consulted for their view. Such a process makes transparent the consideration of the balance of rights in any particular case.

Arguably, the Human Rights Act will focus attention on post-adoption contact, on sibling placement, and privilege sibling relationships in recognition that they may well be a child's longest-lived relationships. Such attention will demand familiarity with the literature on sibling relationships, because practice has lagged in these domains for all professionals involved in the legal process.

All of this leads, in my view, to the conclusion that experts should receive consultation and/or supervision on their assessment practice. Thus is practice open and accountable. It could be argued that adversarial questioning has a role to play in holding experts accountable for their opinion and their evidence base in that it makes us think. Too often though, in my view, it does not do that, as defensiveness becomes the primary psychological response, especially in the face of questioning from barristers trained in the criminal courts, who come into the family courts looking for work. I am not convinced that this is the best approach to decision-making and understanding.

To finish my half of this paper, I shall comment on the idea that experts are over-used within the court system. They may well be. However, a decision would need to be taken earlier on in the process that an expert opinion was not needed. Thus, those who decide would need to be trained to make such judgments, particularly in complex cases, where mental health issues are present and where a parent may have learning disabilities. In my experience, when I am asked to provide an assessment where a parent has suspected or borderline learning disabilities, I find I am often called in too late. For example, local services have offered help to the family without tailoring it to the specific learning needs of the parent, and fail to understand that the parent cannot generalise his or her learning, and may well struggle to maintain that learning without regular top-up support. This example illustrates that sometimes key professional people in families' lives do not have requisite training or experience. Under the Human Rights Act, social workers will be expected to demonstrate fairness and involvement of all relevant parties in assessments. Thus, the involvement of the expert witness brings another perspective, with all its constraints and affordances, and helps triangulate available sources of information. I would like to see experts encouraged to critique the wider system under observation, whilst maintaining a reflexive stance in the face of their own biases.

Delay in Proceedings? – The Use and Over-use of Expert Witnesses

by Jenny Stevenson

I have outlined below some key issues which I hope will focus our thinking both on the practicalities and implementation regarding current court practices as well as considerations of current and future policy.

Some key issues appear to be as follows.

(1) The court process itself can act as a catalyst for change within some families, and the additional input from an expert witness can further reinforce desirable change. Many families have unfortunately accommodated too much of social services' remonstrations over the years and have demonstrated little change in the face of such exhortations. However, when legal advice is latterly sought by the local authority and court proceedings are initiated, this can, in some cases, provide the catalyst for significant change. The involvement of an expert at such a time is very useful in that there is not only a clear observation of pre- and post-change, but also ongoing advice from an expert on how to promote such change, measure it, etc.

(2) Each party's voice in proceedings is rightly heard and promoted, not just the children's. The joint-instructed expert, who is often asked an opinion about various family members' functioning, can provide a useful overview, recognising each member/party's perspective. In a legal forum it is appropriate that all parties are served in such a way as to facilitate informed participation. The use of an expert in proceedings, in particular via joint instruction, tends to promote this principle.

(3) The expert has very particular expertise and/or experience. From a psychological perspective, the psychologist has particular expertise and information about cognitive/intellectual abilities and capacities, as well as expertise and relevant information as to memory functioning, attentional deficits and strengths, attitude formation, and so forth. This information is well grounded in theoretical frameworks as well as a robust knowledge/research base. Such information is often highly relevant to the case and therefore to the court's decision-making.

(4) Current cases coming before the courts are increasingly complex. Given the level of complexity, chaos and fragmentation often encountered in these cases, it is understandable and beneficial to have the view of an expert witness. It is appropriate and necessary for the court to obtain input from experts in various disciplines. The question of divergent views is a red herring but it is important in that it would seem that when divergent views occur, even following a full exploration in an experts' meeting prior to final hearing, such divergence is all too often treated as an event to be avoided. I consider that this is a fundamental misunderstanding of the role of the expert witness and indeed the role of the court proceedings. It can be argued that divergent views indeed are a healthy indicator that there has not developed an over-cosy relationship between the various professional parties – the guardian ad litem, the expert witness, and the local authority representatives. Consistent convergence of views would be of greater concern than divergence.

(5) It cannot be assumed that other workers involved in the case are experienced and skilled in child care matters. There has always been this possibility, but inexperience, for example, on the part of social work staff is much more commonplace than in former years. Staff shortages in most social services departments have meant that workers involved in highly complex child care cases are frequently inexperienced not only in the complex matters of

the actual case but also in the court arena. Whether or not it is appropriate, expert witnesses are frequently 'filling the gap'. It is also the case when inexperienced workers are involved that an expert assessment is requested inappropriately. For example, I have recently been asked in two cases when I was ready to begin an assessment on two families, to carry out my assessment contemporaneously with a residential assessment being undertaken. While I can appreciate that 'parallel planning' has merits, this approach to assessment is confused and time wasting. Social work staff need to liaise fully with their legal representatives and, if there is doubt as to the appropriate timing of an expert assessment, it would be best to approach one or two known local experts and seek relevant advice.

(6)   Experts themselves must be aware of the need to provide objective, well-supported evidence rather than a subjective, partisan view. It would seem to be that there are particular problems with this from within the disciplines themselves. For instance, my own psychology colleagues from a learning disability speciality often provide a highly subjective report about a parent with whom they are involved – they fail to fulfil the court requirement of the provision of a considered, balanced and objective view. Given that within the disciplines themselves of psychology and psychiatry there is poor understanding at the interfaces of child health and adult services, it is hardly surprising that all too often a confused and contradictory picture is put before the court. I would also add (and know that this is controversial) that I have difficulty in understanding how a clinician directly involved in the treatment of a patient/client, where the clinician is charged with a professional responsibility to promote that client's welfare and needs, can easily provide an objective view.

(7)   There are many 'flying' experts in the disciplines of psychology and psychiatry who are happy to see a patient/client on one, or perhaps two at the most, occasions and then provide a report. This is an inappropriate and fragmented use of what psychology has to offer – psychology has a much larger part to play not just based on tests and psychometrics. I think that this is particularly relevant in terms of child care proceedings and an assessment in relation to children's lives, since a much more detailed comprehensive holistic picture is required of children's lives than in the adult services' arena. 'Flying' experts may be quick and cheap but all too often their involvement results in ill-founded generalisations and partial assessments.

(8)   There is frequent and increasing talk of delay in child care proceedings. What is avoidable and unavoidable delay? Certainly the setting of a court timetable at the outset of proceedings appears to be an important principle to be upheld. Given that all parties are working to a known timetable, it would seem that the setting up of a 3 months' timescale for experts to undertake an assessment and produce a completed report is a reasonable one.

(9)   Related to this is that experts themselves are frequently wrong-footed by failure to receive a promised letter of instruction and court bundle on time. All too frequently the letter of instruction is delayed by several weeks, not only creating chaos in the expert's timetable but immediately introducing a delay of several weeks. This is not a delay introduced by experts but rather a failure of the respective solicitors to work efficiently to a court timetable. Also, specific instructions to an expert need to be reasonable. Three and four pages to an expert of specific questions sometimes in excess of 30 in number is plainly ludicrous. Specific instructions need to be succinct and tailored to specific areas in the case requiring particular information. A plethora of questions not only irritates the expert, who immediately wonders whether the other parties involved are doing any assessments at all,

but clearly serves to de-skill the other professionals involved. Instructions to an expert need to be precise, concise and focused.

(10) There needs to be much greater clarification as to why, and not just when, an expert is being brought in. There is all too often evidence of a kind of 'scatter gun' approach of bringing in an expert because a case is complex or particularly noteworthy/notorious, etc, rather than clarity of thought leading to an expert's view being requested to provide information and an assessment on specific issues.

(11) There now appears to be further delay arising in cases when adult/parent(s) request further or additional assessments claiming rights under the new Human Rights Act legislation. Some of these requests appear to be blatantly tactical in that expert assessments have usually already been completed and are before the court giving an adverse view of the adult/parent(s) in question. It seems a 'last hope' strategy that the adult/parent is then advised to seek additional assessments using the Human Rights Act framework. When such additional assessments are allowed, it is difficult to square this with the paramountcy of children's needs.

We have both been reminded when compiling our papers that George Bernard Shaw noted that 20 years' experience was oft times one year's experience repeated 20 times; and that in the context of increasing requests for clear measures of outcome and evidence-based practice he also recommended that we should all be obliged to appear before a board every 5 years and justify our existence … on pain of liquidation.

PLENARY FIVE

THE SKILL OF REPRESENTING CHILDREN AT A TIME OF CHAOS

Vivienne Reed
GALRO Panel Member

Summary of paper

Vivienne Reed focused in her paper on the guardian ad litem's skill in holding a child at the point between stability and instability, during the time of chaos in the child's life brought about by the issue of public law Children Act proceedings by the local authority. The skill of guardians was shown in their ability to prevent a child from plunging into instability (for example when their placement breaks down or social worker is changed), or in the event that the child is plunged into such instability, to limit the damage to the child this causes.

One particular matter the guardian needs to assess is the balance of empowerment versus protection of the child. The aim is to empower the child by providing him or her with the information he or she requires to make sense of the court process and the future, yet to protect him or her from the court process itself. The time this takes cannot be limited.

The guardian must also consider the provision of therapy for some children during the court process. Generally, medical practitioners do not want to take on children in a psychotherapeutic capacity whilst proceedings are ongoing, yet often the child needs some therapy which the guardian is unable personally to provide. Vivienne Reed's experience was that play therapy was generally the most suitable at this stage.

The continuity the guardian provided to the child was of great importance, particularly given the shortage of social workers and therefore on occasions the lack of continuity of social worker in the case.

Overall, Vivienne Reed felt that what the guardian could bring to the court process was emotional intelligence. The guardian had to look at the external environment in which he or she was working, and consider the impact of this on the child.

'Children and adults participate in a process in which the future is unknowable'

Introduction

This month I leave CAFCASS to become operations manager for the new National Adoption Register run by Norwood Ravenswood, a voluntary child care agency. I therefore welcome the opportunity to write a reflective paper on working as both a manager of public law and as a practitioner representing children in public law proceedings. It is a privileged ending to what has been a privileged experience over the last 10 years.

This reflection concentrates on case studies that either have involved me as a practitioner or that I have reviewed as a manager. When I accepted this commission I was told that I was not to include anything too clever! So with that instruction I have not placed the cases in a theoretical framework and have concentrated on practice. It is a child-focused piece of work and demonstrates the skills that public law practitioners need in supporting children through the court process. There is still so much more work to do in representing children, and for every rewarding case there is one where the outcome is far from satisfactory for the child.

If there was ever a time of chaos for a child, it is during the court process in public law proceedings. Although the procedure of instigating proceedings for either local authorities or parents is the same, there is no familiar patterns or predictable outcomes. Chaos creates an environment whereby there is no certainty, and inflicts change on the individual. The changes that occur during proceedings are radical, happen quickly and are often continual throughout their currency. The Children Act 1989 requires the guardian to ensure that children according to their age and understanding are involved in this process. Public law practitioners need therefore to hold children during chaos at a point that is in between instability and stability. This point may be repeated several times during this embroiled period. At no time during proceedings is it a stable time for children, but practitioners without the necessary skills can plunge a child into instability. Sometimes this is unavoidable but the skill is to limit the damage that instability can bring to the child. In my experience it is at this point that the child is most receptive in understanding the process, and it is at this time that continuity and consistency from the guardian is required. The strength of the service over the last 10 years has been a stable workforce that has ensured that children have received a professional and high-quality service.

In this paper I am going to address how the guardian has to balance the different variables in a case. Although the aim is to stabilise the child to enable them to reach adulthood in an environment that will assist them to reach their potential in all areas of life, the reality is all too often very different. Usually, children in specified proceedings have already been damaged and have suffered significant harm. The impact of this significant harm, whether physical, sexual or emotional, together with the uncertainty of the proceedings, will have profound effects on a child. A skilled practitioner needs to assess the level and characteristics of the harm suffered by the child and make a judgment as to how he or she will conduct the case and engage with the child in ascertaining his or her wishes and feelings. Sometimes it is a new experience for children to be the focus of attention and to be empowered in contributing to any decisions that affect their lives. For some children it is impossible for them to understand or process the volume of information available during proceedings. Some children do not have the emotional or developmental capacity to understand, while others may understand the court process but not the consequences of the process.

Holding a child at the point between stability and instability

Legal representation and safe practice for the child

Guardians have a huge responsibility in choosing a solicitor for a child, and they are reluctant to experiment with children by appointing someone they do not know or who has not been recommended to them. Solicitors have a duty to see children, often alone, as they have to make a decision on whether a child can give instruction. Although this is mostly in consultation with the guardian, the solicitor will advise the court if he or she feels that a child satisfies the judicial guidance to enable the child to attend court, give evidence and have sight of the papers in the case. As a manager I have supported guardians in their reluctance to use untried people because, in child protection terms, they would be safer appointing the lollipop lady. There are no checks or balances a guardian can make as to the suitability of a solicitor because of the following:

- solicitors are not required to have police checks;
- solicitors must inform the Law Society if they have broken the law, and there is no other mechanism for this;
- there is no assessment of quality available to users of the service.

The following case study illustrates an example of unstable legal representation of a child. This situation could potentially have plunged a child into instability during the currency of the proceedings. It indicates the need for the Law Society to employ a safe practice policy and enable there to be a mechanism for CAFCASS to make safe practice checks.

Case Study 1: Trusting Legal Representation

A guardian was appointed to a child aged 11 years old. The court had already appointed a solicitor to the care proceedings. The guardian accepted the legal representation for the child as they had met and formed a relationship with one another.

During the currency of the proceeding the solicitor changed firms three times, which caused disruption in that the guardian had to withstand pressure from two of the firms who wanted to reappoint a solicitor in their company to the case. One of the firms even withheld the legal aid certificate while it tried to negotiate a change.

There was no explanation to the guardian of why the solicitor left, and no good reason as to why the child should suffer instability by changing solicitors.

The guardian needed to keep the child's welfare central to the argument about a change in solicitor, but had no way of verifying that no change was in the child's best interest. Guardians are required to take the services of a solicitor on trust. For this child the outcome was right for the child, but there is no informed risk assessment a guardian can make about solicitors leaving firms to assess whether there are any child protection issues which need addressing.

When a child is in desperate need of therapeutic support during court proceedings

The most chaotic and volatile applications to court are first applications. These are the bulk of the work of a guardian. Applications under s 31 (care and supervision) of the Children Act represent the most complex of cases and take longer to complete than most applications. The following case study describes a boy of 10 years. Ben was subject to care proceedings for 18 months. It describes his frustration with the adults involved in the process and illustrates how the guardian needed to make sense of the process for him and was required to negotiate with the local authority to meet his therapeutic needs.

Case Study 2: Ben's Chaos

Ben decided that he wanted to sack his guardian and had told his grandmother this. It was a compliment in a way because he clearly understood the role of the guardian and decided that he wanted to see her more often.

The guardian wrote to Ben, concerned that he felt neglected, and went to see him the following week. The guardian explained that she would visit him only when there was a purpose to her visit, for example if a doctor needed to be appointed to the proceedings, someone in court was saying something different from before, or there was a change in his own circumstances, such as a new place to live or a new school to attend.

Ben's reply was quite profound, he wanted an explanation as to what would happen if he had the purpose and he wanted the guardian to visit. Ben was in chaos, he felt confused and frustrated by the proceedings. He had lived for 9 years with his heroin-addict mother, punctuated with respite breaks with his maternal grandparents. Although he was living with his grandparents under interim care orders he could not understand why he could not return to his mother as he had in the past.

Case Study 2: Ben's Chaos (continued)

Ben was frustrated because he wanted to be with his mother and saw his placement with his grandparents as a holding situation until his mother managed her drug addiction. Although rehabilitation was to be attempted, it was felt that the assessment needed to be over a period of time to test the mother's resolve to remain drug free. The placement with his grandparents was at breaking point and, for Ben, alternatives to living within his family offered nothing and would have been destructive to his development.

The guardian negotiated with Ben the frequency of her visits to him but realised that he needed something extra, which was not her gift to give. Ben needed therapeutic help to assist him over the rehabilitation assessment period, but no child and family clinic will accept a child for therapy while they are in care proceedings. The only therapy that can bridge the therapeutic gap for a child who is at the point between instability and stability is play therapy. It is my experience that play therapists have been able to shore up placements during this chaotic time and help children make sense of their anger and frustration about the court process.

The guardian negotiated on behalf of Ben with the local authority to fund a play therapist. Ben had been listened to, and his purpose of being able to express his feelings more frequently was satisfied by a therapeutic intervention on a weekly basis. The message from Ben was that wishes and feelings needed to be worked with continually during the proceedings and not only at the final hearing.

'Bursting a child's bubble'

Often, public law managers and practitioners reflect on whether stability can ever be achieved for a child in some of the most complex cases that are before the courts. Sometimes it is a compromise, and other times we have to 'burst a child's bubble' by not giving him or her what he or she wants, because what the child wants is just not there. Or we know that what we are leaving the child with is far from satisfactory and the likelihood of him or her finding stability is nil. In some cases we have no alternative than to sacrifice the wishes of an older child to ensure that the younger brothers or sisters have a chance of stability. Public law practitioners in some cases have had to leave a child in the knowledge that chaos might prevail because the child is too damaged or too old for a suitable placement to be found to meet his or her needs. There is no easy way to explain this to the child.

The public law practitioner must, in the reports, express the wishes and feelings of a child under a separate heading and often this is the part of the report that children see. The guardian must be skilled in this direct work with children to enable the child to cope with the entire proceedings. The relationship with the child has become a combination of dealing with both the child's immediate and future needs. Practitioners are increasingly separating out wishes and feelings because, where difficult decisions are being made, it is easier to impart this to the child using this separation. For example:

> 'You wish to live with your mother and want her to be part of your life again but you feel that she won't be well enough to look after you because she has to go to hospital such a lot. You wish you could remain with your foster carer but you feel that this is impossible because you have been told that another placement is to be found for you.'

The above example is a somewhat simplistic approach to unpacking the complex world of a child, but is seen as adopting a more developmental and incremental approach in direct work with children. I believe that we still have a long way to go. As proceedings are becoming longer and more complex, the position of the child in public law proceedings, in my view, is becoming of more concern. It is those concerning cases that guardians take to support groups or move their manager to tears at appraisal meetings.

Children can be victims to the system and the process. The following case studies illustrate where the care system failed the child: in the first the guardian trusted the local authority care plan; in the second a child was empowered within the court process but the consequences for her were devastating. Both children were left in chaotic circumstances after the court process.

Case Study 3: The irreparable damage to Christy

When Christy was 6 years old she was made the subject of a care order. She had suffered significant emotional harm whilst in the care of her mother. Her mother showed high criticism and low warmth to the little girl and, in turn, Christy took on the role of carer for her mother who suffered from mental health vulnerabilities and epilepsy.

During the court proceedings Christy's mother had shown some improvement in her parenting capabilities. A central London teaching hospital medical team wanted to continue with the parenting treatment programme. The care plan gave an undertaking that if the treatment was not successful or the mother refused treatment the child would be removed and a permanent placement sought. The guardian agreed to this so that the proceedings could be concluded and delay was prevented. At that time a competent social worker and team manager were responsible for the case.

Three-and-a-half years later the mother applied for a discharge of care order. During her investigations the guardian found that the care plan had not been followed and the treatment plan had broken down some weeks into the care order. Christy had remained with her mother for 3 years before being given a respite care placement, even though the school had brought to the attention of social services the fact that Christy was distressed and unhappy. Directly after the care order had been made the competent social worker became a guardian and the team manager was promoted. For 12 months Christy did not have a dedicated social worker and, as a result, her circumstances deteriorated.

For Christy the discharge of care proceedings was difficult and emotionally draining. She was 10 years old and was at a school for children with emotional difficulties. The guardian was told by the consultant psychiatrist that Christy would not recover from the emotional harm meted out to her from her mother, and the family placement team of the local authority felt that she would be difficult to place and could not give a timescale for placement. Christy was very confused and unable to express clear wishes and feelings.

The mother withdrew her application under cross-examination because she said that she was too ill to care for Christy. Although the guardian wanted to ensure that the local authority took radical steps to expedite a permanent placement for Christy, there was no legal way she could remain in the case. The only way forward for the guardian was to ask the judge to release the papers in both the care proceedings and the discharge of care proceedings to enable the Official Solicitor to consider the issue of negligence against the local authority. The pursuit of a negligence claim was beyond the understanding of Christy, and the guardian left the child with no satisfactory outcome.

Case Study 4: Louise – A victim of the court process

Louise, aged 14 years, and her sister Amy, aged 12 months, were subject to care proceedings. Louise had alerted social services to the neglect and emotional abuse she had suffered over the years and did not want her sister to suffer in the same way. Her wishes and feeling were that she wanted to be placed with Amy within a foster care.

Louise met the judicial test of being able to attend court, give evidence against her mother and read reports and statements before the court. Louise played an active role in the proceedings but the judicial test does not take into consideration the impact of the significant harm the children had suffered. Louise had had 14 years of emotional abuse and neglect. Therefore, her self-esteem was low and, during the protracted proceeding, she became self-destructive and at one time was admitted into secure accommodation.

The placement for Louise broke down and the local authority plan for Amy was adoption. The loss for Louise was twofold and long lasting. She not only lost her sister but her extended family as well. Her mother died shortly after the proceedings were over and the extended family members refused to speak to Louise at the funeral.

Louise became a victim because Amy's interests were paramount and, in retrospect, the adults in the process did not recognise this in the context of whether it was in the interest of Louise to participate in the proceedings.

Conclusion

This paper, I feel, has identified that the role of the guardian has developed from indicating the future needs of the child after proceedings, to one of supporting children through complex and protracted hearings. The guardian has become an agent who has to hold the child at the point between instability and stability and make decisions on what is the best for the child during, as well as after, the court process.

Over the last 10 years guardians have had to consider the changes in the environment and how this has impacted on the welfare of children. There is a national crisis in the recruitment of social workers, and local authorities can no longer guarantee continuity of service; this has impacted on the delivery of care plans.

This paper also illustrates the point that the empowerment of children needs to be handled sensitively and address the impact on the child. Child care cases have created an industry, and the process can become a product that becomes an entity in itself. This entity can create an environment in which the child becomes a victim of the product rather than the process being an instrument to enable the child's welfare to become paramount.

CHILDREN, SAFETY AND PARENTAL CONTACT IN PRIVATE LAW PROCEEDINGS

Rukhsana Farooqi Thakrar LLB (Hons), MA, CQSW,
Diploma in Humanistic Counselling,
Accredited Social Work Practice Teacher, Children's Guardian,
Children and Family Court Reporter, CAFCASS

Summary of paper

Rukhsana Farooqi Thakrar explained that she had selected the case which formed the basis of her paper because it raised a number of important issues.

The effects of domestic violence and its impact on children were increasingly recognised, but she felt that within the private law sphere it was difficult to bring domestic violence to the fore in the courts. She also highlighted the difficulties of dealing with communities which were often misunderstood.

In this case, she felt there had been clear evidence of domestic violence. Her recommendation was for a referral to the Domestic Violence Intervention Project (DVIP) – a pilot project which provided in-depth risk assessments and support for victims of domestic violence, followed by contact if appropriate at the Coram meeting place.

Rukhsana Farooqi Thakrar felt that the DVIP was an excellent means of dealing with such cases, and expressed the hope that similar projects be set up throughout the country.

Introduction

The significance of domestic violence within the family and the related child protection issues is increasingly gaining recognition. There are an increasing number of publications addressing this issue, and research of child psychiatrists, psychologists, social work academics and information from practitioners working with children and families is providing a wealth of information about the adverse effects on children who witness domestic violence. The courts are making a conscious effort to consider the seriousness of domestic violence in contact and residence disputes.

The research from academics such as Marianne Hester (Professor of Sociology and Social Policy, University of Sunderland, Co-Director, International Centre for Study of Violence and Abuse) and David Quinton (Professor of Social Policy, University of Bristol) indicates that men often take advantage of post-separation contact in order to continue abuse against their ex-partners. The level of fathers' contact tends to diminish over time. If contact is to benefit children, domestic violence has to be eliminated.

In practice it is still very difficult to obtain risk assessments of perpetrators of domestic violence in order to assess the risk they pose to children and to their ex-partners through contact with the child and the motive for contact with the child.

The former Court Welfare Service in Middlesex has established a safe contact project with the Domestic Violence Intervention Project (DVIP) and Coram Child Contact Service for

Domestic Violence in Child Contact Disputes.

A referral to the DVIP involves a recommendation in the children and family court report for a risk assessment whenever domestic violence has been established which might make contact arrangements unsafe.

Domestic violence is established when the courts have made a finding of fact on evidence.

If domestic violence is disputed, the court should be asked to establish the facts at the earliest opportunity.

The following case example shows how difficult it has been to use the safe contact project, and the need to increase awareness of this project in order to establish other similar projects for the benefit of children.

Vikash

Vikash is aged 5 years. His mother and father married in India. They are both Hindu. The father has spent all his adult life in London and has his own business. The mother was born in India and spoke no English when she joined her husband a number of months after the arranged marriage.

The mother's story was that she was subjected to extensive physical and emotional abuse from her husband who already had a partner in London. The mother alleged that she would be locked up and prevented from going out. She was not allowed to have friends and would be beaten by her husband and his family if she stood up for herself.

She did have sexual relations with her husband from time to time as his family wanted a grandchild. She alleged that she received no support from her husband when she was pregnant. She had a very difficult pregnancy. After Vikash was born she stated that her mother-in-law was so pleased that she took Vikash from her and took over the parenting role. Her husband was absent from the home most of the time and did not assist in the parenting of Vikash. He also, according to her, found it difficult to contribute financially.

She was forced to go to work to make a financial contribution. It was by starting work that she was able to talk to others about the ongoing domestic violence. She described the violence occurring in front of Vikash and her mother-in-law who remained silent. Eventually she was able to flee the home in a planned way with Vikash with the help of Southall Blacksisters. This is a support group for Asian women who are active in promoting awareness of the effects of domestic violence on Asian women. She remained in an Asian women's refuge with Vikash for a considerable amount of time.

Her husband eventually tracked her down by instructing his solicitor to use an enquiry agent. She was served with an application for contact and residence. The father denied all allegations of domestic violence and alleged that the mother had mental health problems. He wanted residence of Vikash. He denied having a girlfriend and maintained that he lived with his parents and that his wife was lying. He stated that he would like his wife to return. If she did not return then she should go back to India. He was clear that Vikash should return to his care.

The father was angry because he had helped his wife come to this country. He was also angry that other Asian women had helped to remove his son from his care. He felt that the system would be biased against him.

He described a close relationship with Vikash and stated that the mother had physically abused Vikash in the past. He had made a referral to the local social services office, which took no action against the mother.

I received the request to write a report on the issue of contact and residence after the parties had attended a conciliation appointment at the Royal Courts of Justice. The court had already ordered supported contact between Vikash and his father at a contact centre. The parties and the court had wrongly assumed that contact at a contact centre would be supervised. The court had not made a finding of fact that there had been domestic violence, despite the mother fleeing to an Asian women's refuge.

In the course of my inquiries the mother gave a comprehensive description of the domestic violence. A letter from her previous employer and a worker from an advice agency which had given advice to the mother on immigration issues supported this account.

The major problem for the mother was that her employer, who was an Indian woman who had seen bruising on the mother's face, and the advice worker were frightened of the father and his family. They were not prepared to have their identities revealed to the court. In addition, the mother explained that her family in India were suffering pressure from the father and his family. She felt that she had bought shame to herself and her family. She also believed that she was denying her mother-in-law her only grandson.

Vikash informed me that he remembered his mother crying and his father shouting at his mother. Despite this he wanted to see his father and he wanted to see his grandmother.

Vikash exhibited no fear of his father in the observed contact between him and his father. The father had bought Vikash a new toy lorry and Vikash amused himself playing with the lorry and other toys in the office whilst his father sat and watched. The father did not join in the play with his son. He preferred to engage in conversation with me. It worried me that the father did not engage in play with his son and preferred to have a discussion with me.

The mother agreed that I could observe contact between Vikash and his father in the home and also observe contact between Vikash and his maternal grandmother. The mother informed me that she had given detailed information to her solicitor about the domestic violence, and her solicitor had failed to prepare a statement. She felt under increasing pressure to agree to contact away from the contact centre both by her solicitor, and by the father who would wait at the end of contact and argue with her outside the contact centre. She explained that she had no relatives in this country and she did not wish to deny Vikash his right to see his maternal grandmother. Her main concern was that her husband's family might try to take Vikash from her permanently, undermining her parenting and relationship with Vikash.

In the observation of contact the main interaction was between Vikash and his maternal grandmother. Vikash was close to his grandmother. She informed me away from Vikash that she had cared for Vikash prior to Vikash leaving with his mother. She wanted her daughter-in-law to return home with Vikash. She denied that there had been domestic violence towards her daughter-in-law by her husband. She also denied that he was living elsewhere with another partner. She informed me that Vikash had lost weight and she was concerned about the care that Vikash was receiving from his mother.

Vikash informed me when I saw him in the office on his own that he wanted to visit his maternal grandmother and his uncle and aunt who also visited the home. He also informed me that his father was collecting him and dropping him at his grandmother's home and would not stay with him.

The issues raised by this case were as follows:

- The mother was unable to speak English.
- She had no family support in this country, and was isolated and vulnerable.
- She stated that her family was under pressure in India as a result of her leaving her husband with Vikash, not allowing her mother-in-law to have contact with Vikash and bringing shame to the family.
- The court, prior to the request for a welfare report, had ordered contact in a contact centre, which was not supervised. This meant the mother was under pressure from her husband who would pester her after contact and speak to Vikash in Urdu so the volunteers at the contact centre could not understand what was being said.
- The mother alleged that her husband swore at her and called her derogatory names in front of Vikash.
- She decided not to stop the contact between Vikash and his father in the contact centre

because she believed that the court would criticise her for this. In addition, the father made threats against her family in India.

- In the report for the court I recommended that the father should be ordered to attend the DVIP for a risk assessment as to the safety of contact and how this could be managed. An assessment would also be made concerning his suitability for an approved violence prevention programme. If the recommendation was accepted, the following procedure should be followed:

– the DVIP would need an adjournment of 6 weeks to prepare and file its report from receipt of papers from the court. CAFCASS would not be expected to file a further report during this period;
– the court would need to order the release of all relevant court papers (including my report) and Legal Aid papers to the DVIP to assist in conducting the risk assessment. These should be sent through the applicant's legal representative;
– papers should also be released at this stage to the Coram Family Supervised Contact Centre, which would make a pre-assessment of the suitability of its centre for contact should that be recommended by the DVIP and ordered by the court.

- I recommended that the court should make a decision that domestic violence was established. In my report I stated that it was my opinion there was evidence that domestic violence had occurred.
- The difficulty was that the father's influence in the community meant that witnesses of the domestic violence were reluctant to come to court, although they provided information to me in my enquiries.
- The court ordered the mother's solicitor to prepare a statement outlining the domestic violence so that a hearing could take place on the finding of fact.
- The mother's solicitor failed to produce such a statement. The mother informed me that she had provided the solicitor with all the information. It later transpired that the solicitor did not have time to prepare this statement.
- The matter was returned to court.
- The mother's solicitors apologised to the court for failing to produce the requested statement.
- The father's solicitors applied to the court to have me removed from the case on the basis that they thought that I was biaised against the father for making the above recommendation. The court refused this application.
- The mother was persuaded by her solicitor to agree to contact taking place out of the contact centre on the basis that the father found it difficult to travel to the contact centre due to his self-employment.

The court ordered that contact take place once a Sunday from 12 pm to 6 pm. The father would collect Vikash from his mother outside the local library. The court also ordered me to write an addendum report addressing the question of residence and contact.

The mother compiled with this order and Vikash commenced regular contact whereby his father would collect him from the library and take him to his mother's home.

When I saw Vikash for the purpose of the addendum report Vikash was clear that he wanted to continue to see his maternal grandmother. He told me that sometimes his father would not stay with him after picking him up from the library.

The father was unhappy about the length of contact and he wanted contact to move to weekend staying contact. He wanted to collect Vikash from a different location which was nearer to his home. He also wanted the matter to be sorted out of court.

The mother informed me that she recognised that Vikash enjoyed contact with his grandmother and she wanted to promote this. She informed me that her husband continued to make derogatory remarks about her, and Vikash would tell her the comments made about her. She was unwilling to take the matter further and wanted to agree to the father's demands. She was afraid of the repercussions on her family if she proceeded with the court case.

She also informed me that the father had found out where she lived and had come to her house to demand to see Vikash and swore at her in front of Vikash. Despite this she still promoted contact between Vikash and her mother-in-law.

The issues raised in this case are that the mother clearly in my opinion had suffered domestic violence from her husband.

The court did not make a finding of fact from the start and ordered contact to start at a contact centre. The understanding was that this contact was supervised.

The contact at the contact centre was not supervised contact but supported contact. The father spoke to Vikash in Urdu and pestered the mother after the contact.

The mother was advised by her solicitors to encourage contact, although my report recommended a risk assessment of the father following a finding of fact and that the court should order the mother's solicitors to provide a statement outlining the violence. The mother's solicitors failed to do this. The mother agreed to contact outside the contact centre after pressure from the father's solicitors. I advised against this in the discussions outside court. The parties reached an agreement and presented this agreement to the court. I raised my objections to this agreement.

The father continued to disparage the mother in front of Vikash. The mother was clearly encouraging contact because she was receiving pressure from her family in India and advice from her solicitor that this was the best course of action. She had become totally demoralised with the court process.

Vikash's wishes and feelings must be seen in context: he was only 5 years old and his mother was under extreme pressure. She felt no choice but to promote contact. Although the father may not have posed a direct physical threat to Vikash, indirect ill effects might have resulted, for example deviant attitudes to women or denigratory feelings towards his main carer.

It was clear in this case that the father expressed deviant attitudes to women and undermined the mother in front of Vikash. His mother (maternal grandmother) also held this view.

The Safe Contact Project may have recommended that the father undertake an approved violence prevention programme. The aim of this would be to achieve long-term attitudinal and behavioural change. It is also designed to protect victims and children from further violence, and from what might be inappropriate referrals for contact.

It is hoped that in time pilot schemes such as the Safe Contact Project will become more widespread and used to promote the interest and welfare of children such as Vikash.

References

Jaffe P, Wolfe D, Wilson S and Zak L, 'Similarities in behavioural and social maladjustment among child victims and witnessed to family violence' (1986) 56 *American Journal of Ortopsychiatry* 142.

Sturge C and Glaser D, 'Contact and Domestic Violence – The Experts' Court Report' [2000] Fam Law 615.

Material from the Children, Safety and Parental Contact (an international conference on domestic violence), Camden, London, 18–19 November 1999.

Material from CAFCASS (formerly Middlesex Family Court Welfare), DVIP and Coram Family.

SPEECH BY CHAIRMAN OF CAFCASS

Anthony PM Hewson
Chairman, CAFCASS

Introduction

This is the first time I have attended the President's Interdisciplinary Conference. I shall present an update on CAFCASS – since I am reliably informed that you want facts not visions!

Today CAFCASS is 182 days 'old' – 6 months. Amanda was kind enough yesterday to refer to the enormity of our task and if you don't mind I'm going to start at that point, but before I do so I want to record a 'disclaimer'. I am not going to spend any real time – it's a waste of your time and my energy (reserves of which feel pretty low at the moment) – talking about the past and who might or might not be to blame for our current situation.

I will simply say this – it isn't a personal opinion, it is that of the Board and it is already well recorded in the Lord Chancellor's Department: we have inherited a position that nobody wanted. None of us on the Board or executive team, not our staff, not the Lord Chancellor's Department and certainly not either of our key stakeholders, yourselves or, more particularly if I may say so, the children and families we exist to serve, wanted what we have inherited.

I will start with money and I will be frank. It is absolutely clear now that in a number of key areas – whatever the Home Office, Department of Health and the DETR thought they were transferring to CAFCASS before 1 April 2001 – the reality is different. Entirely different. We have 'more' of most things. That means the cost of the service at 1 April 2001 is more than was agreed – based on best estimates and assumptions. Now we have the reality and we are where we are. We have to get on with it.

We are starting this task by demonstrating in the best way we can – the actual costs at 1 April 2001. We have to have that money if we are to run the same service that existed on that date. I don't see it as a 'negotiation'. I see simply the facts. I will do everything within my power, and I know I am supported by all my colleagues on the Board, to support whatever processes are required to recover the monies properly due to us. It isn't a case of robbing anyone – it's simply that the estimates of transfer and some of the assumptions made do not match reality. Put another way, to ensure there is no misunderstanding, some or all of those Departments I've mentioned are better off by the amount we are short. The Lord Chancellor has assured me personally that when we present the information (this in itself has been a hugely time-consuming project to gather together) which will be in the next week/10 days, he will robustly pursue our claim directly with the Departments concerned. It is substantial sum – I believe it will be between £6 million and £9 million in an overall operating budget of £72 million. The matter is clearly urgent.

Now I want to turn to the very difficult and challenging issue regarding children's guardians. First, on behalf of the Board, we accept and understand that we failed to consult about the possibility that the Board might decide that it would not offer any contract of self-employment. I want to say that we are sorry about that. We have learnt a difficult lesson. We now need to move on. On Wednesday this week I received some proposals from Susan Bindman, Chair of NAGALRO (she is with us here today) on a process we might adopt for moving forward. We will consider that proposal very carefully indeed alongside our own ideas. We want to do this as quickly as is practicable; but one message I have put out since receiving Mr Justice Scott Baker's judgment is that we are now going to take proper time and space for reflection. We have been driven by a whole series of events, and the time has come to think carefully about what we are doing both to ourselves and the service. This need not take a long time but I am not prepared to be hustled into any more hasty decisions. We got it wrong last time. In the best interests of those we exist to serve we have a duty and responsibility not to get it wrong a second time. Its frankly unthinkable. There are considerable obstacles ahead and the nature of those obstacles has not changed as a result of the judgment. We need to be realistic. We need to be focused and more than anything else we need real and sustained dialogue. This is where my 'first' focus lies – in achieving an agreement for a process of real dialogue. Real dialogue is the only way we will be able to establish trust and confidence – an absolute prerequisite to reaching any understanding.

Turning now to other priorities. We have a huge range of work to be undertaken and it has become increasingly clear that our 'start-up' resources are wholly inadequate for the many tasks needed. In our submission in the 7–10 days I spoke about earlier we will identify the essential requirements to conclude the start-up phase properly. I believe it will take until October 2002 to attend to all start-up priorities. What I mean by this is work on governance, achieving a well-thought-through corporate plan, refining our business plan, determining the key information systems, establishing credible National Standards and a robust complaints procedure, working on human resource policies, building a proper Board secretariat, and sorting out our communications – and these are just a few of the priorities we now have to tackle. I spent a day here before this conference started with Diane Shepherd, our Chief Executive. We made substantial progress in trying to get things in the right order and agreeing the resources that are necessary to manage effectively our current difficulties whilst at the same time building an efficient and effective infrastructure. This is the key – we have to do the two together.

Finally, I want to conclude by spending 2 minutes on why I believe – no matter how hard the going at the moment – we have to press on and succeed. Over the next few weeks and months our single most important priority is to ensure that the service to children and families is maintained at the level it was at on 1 April 2001, whilst building an infrastructure that will deliver the improvements in service we all want CAFCASS to deliver. I am not blind to the challenges ahead. In our first group meeting yesterday, Phillip Curl said that there had been an increase of 25% to 35% per annum in care cases in Norfolk. CAFCASS has a cash-limited budget. Now I am not suggesting that just because we hear a comment like this we need additional funding, but, and it is a big but, just imagine if even half of that is going on all over the country. Imagine the resource planning arrangements we need in place just to manage the increase – even if we had the money. The infrastructure arrangements we will put in place over the next year will be designed to capture data like this very quickly so that we can plan the way forward. We have to plan everything we do very carefully indeed.

In the next 5 weeks I will meet with seven different organisations, all of whom are engaged in working with children. More particularly I will be gaining a better understanding of how we should ensure that the views of children can be valued and central to our thinking when we are building services for them. One of these organisations is Article 12 – an organisation run by children with an adult support worker. The children have invited me to join a 'conference call' next week because they want to include me in the process of working out how our meeting will work. They have asked me to think about what I want out of the meeting. Now I am thinking about how one might interest a group of children in contributing to our corporate plan! It is an interesting challenge but perhaps emphasises the focus we intend to adopt on ensuring that children help develop every aspect of our work. They are our primary clients and through working with them we will be able to work more effectively with yourselves.

I want to close with an important message. I am pleased that by and large the service offered to the courts is continuing without too many problems. We are aware of specific hot spots, some of which emerged during the summer, and I want to take this opportunity to thank the President personally for her support, particularly in ensuring that we are kept in close contact with areas where an increase in delay, because of our current difficulties, is becoming a problem. I hope that by working with NAGALRO and others over the next few weeks we can ensure that at the very least the status quo that existed on 1 April is maintained. But in accepting the status quo, and in accepting the wholly inadequate infrastructure in each region to support our staff – employed or self-employed – we are not building a new vibrant culture which is necessary to deliver our aspirations. What we are doing in simple terms is allowing – by default – a whole series of different cultures to evolve. It is a slow process, it isn't too late, but we need to take care now if we are to deliver what I am given to understand all our stakeholders aspired to – long before I came along. We must – we absolutely must – properly resource CAFCASS. We cannot accept for very much longer the creation of a series of 'hybrid' cultures if we are to build an organisation that will deliver what all our stakeholders believed they were going to get.

Let me close by assuring you that my personal commitment – and that of my Board and executive team colleagues – whilst rather battered by the vagaries of the last few months, remains intact. We are resolute about the need to build a properly structured organisation with values that support the aspirations we all hold. I sincerely believe that our colleagues in the Lord Chancellor's Department want that too, and I hope that in the next few weeks we will finally be able to tackle the job we all want to do.

Thank you.

PRESIDENT'S RESPONSE

The President thanked Anthony Hewson for coming to the conference at such a fraught time in CAFCASS's existence. She felt that he had been brave to come and share his views.

She emphasised to the conference that we all have to work with CAFCASS. The concept of CAFCASS was very good, but the teething problems at the moment were acute. It was up to all of us to be helpful and tolerant towards CAFCASS, to assist it in getting through this crisis.

She emphasised that none of us can do without CAFCASS, or guardians ad litem. She hoped that the current crisis would be short-lived and that CAFCASS would be able to go forward to provide for all of us the service it wants to and can provide. We all had a duty to help in achieving this.

PLENARY SIX

INTERNATIONAL ADOPTION

Professor Carolyn Hamilton[1]
Director, The Children's Legal Centre

Summary of paper

Professor Hamilton talked to the conference about her recent experiences in Romania where she is in charge of redrafting Romania's national and intercountry adoption legislation. This experience had led her to reconsider her personal views on the Hague Convention on Protection of Children and Co-operation in Respect of Intercountry Adoption.

Her work in Romania was funded by the Department for International Development and was intended to last 3 years. It resulted from the Romanian Government's application to join the European Union. Part of Romania's accession criteria is reform of its child welfare system; the United Kingdom is its mentor state for accession.

Romania ratified the Convention in 1994. Despite the hope that this would bring about improvements, Professor Hamilton felt that this had not happened. Romania had been pressurised by many western countries to provide children for intercountry adoption. A points system had been developed whereby western agencies provided funding for the Romanian child protection system in return for a certain number of children being placed for adoption through them. Corruption had entered the system, with officials, parents and institutions being bribed. The number of children adopted intercountry had significantly increased, yet without any real improvement in the local child protection system for those remaining.

Professor Hamilton considered the main aims of reform of the system to be:

- *removing money from the system;*
- *removing the incentive to place children for intercountry adoption;*
- *removing the ability for the agencies to identify and place children;*
- *making adoption part of a fully integrated child and family service, in the hands of local authorities;*
- *putting in place a system for promoting the development of family support and prevention.*

Although Professor Hamilton recognised that intercountry adoption could be in the interests of some children, she felt that its existence and the buoyancy of demand militated against the best interests of Romanian children generally due to the reduction in planning for children and consideration of alternative placements and family support systems, and the lack of incentive to develop integrated child services within the country. The result for the children left behind is institutionalisation. The impact for Romania in the future, given the number of children being adopted away from the country, is potentially huge.

Recognising that steps had to be taken, Romania placed a moratorium on intercountry adoption in June 2001. Since then, many western countries had placed immense political pressure on them to release further children.

Professor Hamilton's particular concern was that the Hague Convention sanitised a system which

---

[1] Professor of Law, University of Essex, Barrister, 17 Bedford Row, and Director, The Children's Legal Centre.

was not in the best interests of children, rather than reforming the system for their benefit. She felt that the Conference must address this issue.

Conference discussion arising out of the paper

- *Peter Harris (former Official Solicitor) raised the issue of the significant difficulty of controlling importing states involved in intercountry adoption.*
- *Vivienne Reed (GALRO Panel Manager) queried how many Romanian families were waiting to adopt Romanian children. She was concerned to ensure that children were put first, and felt that they should not be kept waiting for permanence. She emphasised the need for the availability of good quality childcare whilst the children were waiting.*
- *Professor Judith Harwin (Brunel University), who has worked with UNICEF in Eastern Europe, stressed that there was a much larger problem across the whole region, including a huge rise in intercountry adoption in many Baltic states. More work had been done in looking at regulation in Romania than in the other countries. She felt that the issue of intercountry adoption was particularly difficult to resolve, but that the economic position of the countries was a very important factor to address. She believed that national adoption allowances would be of great benefit. She queried whether it was possible to provide better regulation of the Romanian points system, which in principle had been a benign policy. She felt that Professor Hamilton had been over-pessimistic about the attempts to put a social work infrastructure in place in Romania.*

Introduction

The Hague Convention of 29 May 1993 on Protection of Children and Co-operation in Respect of Intercountry Adoption (the Convention) is a rather less familiar instrument in the United Kingdom than the Hague Convention on the Civil Aspects of International Child Abduction 1980. Although the United Kingdom has signed the Convention, it will not ratify it until early 2002. There are, however, currently 42 contracting states[2] and it has been noted that the Convention has outstripped the Convention on Child Abduction in the speed of its development.[3] The contracting states include both states of origin – the net exporters of children as well as the receiving states – the western states. Spain, Canada, the Scandinavian countries, the Netherlands, France, Israel, Austria and Italy are all contracting states.

Purpose of the Convention

The Intercountry Adoption Convention can be seen as a companion instrument to the UN Convention on the Rights of the Child, fleshing out the bare bones of Art 21(c) of the UN Convention. This Article requires that states parties to the Convention 'ensure that the child concerned by intercountry adoption enjoys safeguards and standards equivalent to those existing in the case of national adoption'.

The prime objectives of the Adoption Convention are:

---

[2]   Thirty-one states have ratified the Convention and a further 11 have acceded. Fifteen states are signatories but have not as yet ratified mainly because the adoption procedures and structures have not been put in place. On 20 September 2000 the Senate of the United States approved a resolution of advice and consent to US ratification of the Convention, and passed detailed implementing legislation also passed a few days earlier by the House of Representatives. President Clinton signed the legislation on 6 October 2000, but it is expected to take 2 years before the implementing legislation is put in place, the ratification is deposited and the Convention comes into effect.

[3]   See Duncan, 'The Hague Convention on Protection of Children and Co-operation in Respect of Intercountry Adoption, its birth and prospects', in Selman (ed), *Intercountry Adoption: Developments, Trends and Perspectives* (BAAF, 2000).

(a) to establish safeguards to ensure that intercountry adoptions take place in the best interests of the child and with respect for his or her fundamental rights as recognised in international law;

(b) to establish a system of co-operation amongst contracting states to ensure that those safeguards are respected and thereby prevent the abduction, sale of, or traffic in children;

(c) to secure the recognition in contracting states of adoptions made in accordance with the Convention.[4]

This paper examines the implementation and impact of the Convention in Romania. The objectives of the Convention listed above are concerned with the regulation of intercountry adoption and the stamping out of abuses that were obvious before the Convention came into being. It can be argued, however, that the fact of better regulation of intercountry adoption has made the practice more socially acceptable and has created a market in children, leading to an ever-increasing number of children being adopted intercountry. The major fault of the Convention is that it has no ability to ensure that the states of origin develop a well-functioning domestic, functioning, child protection system that can meet the needs of children. Neither can the Convention ensure that, over time, in-country rather than intercountry placements are found for every child needing a home.

Romania has faced considerable international criticism in relation to the intercountry adoption of its children, ever since the fall of the Ceaucescu regime. The problems are well known, and it is not intended to rehearse them in detail in this article. They have been outlined in a number of reports by a variety of organisations, both governmental and non-governmental, over the course of the last decade.[5] They include improper financial gain, children being placed for intercountry adoption when other in-country alternatives exist, inflated prices being charged for children, and the general development of a commercial market in children. The Government of Romania has announced that it is committed to addressing these abuses,[6] and to reforming its adoption laws. The author has been a member of a team funded by the Department for International Development providing technical assistance to the Romanian National Authority for Child Protection and Adoption in its redraft of Romanian adoption law.

As has been well documented, the fall of Ceaucescu led to a huge rise in unregulated intercountry adoption from Romania. Indeed, in 1991 Romanian children accounted for more than one-third of intercountry adoptions worldwide.[7] It was well recognised that the children of Romania needed protection from unregulated adoptions, and it was hoped that the implementation of the Hague Convention would put an end to the abuses and to the alarming flow of children out of the country. That hope has not been realised.

Under both the Hague Convention (preamble and Art 4) and the UN Convention on the Rights of the Child (Art 22), intercountry adoption is to be a last resort where a suitable placement cannot be found in the state of origin. This does not reflect the reality of the situation in Romania. The numbers of children adopted intercountry from Romania has risen steadily. In 1992 the numbers recorded[8] were 135. By 1995 the number had risen to 1,057. There was a small dip to 1,048 in 1996, but by 1999 the number was 2,117, and in 2000 the number of adoptions was near the 4,000 mark. The official numbers are, however, likely to be a significant underestimate of children adopted intercountry. For instance, in 1999 the official figures record

[4] Duncan, ibid.

[5] See Order No 543 (1998) of the Parliamentary Assembly, Council of Europe, *International Adoption: Respecting children's rights* (Doc 8592), Social, Health and Family Affairs Committee, Council of Europe; report by DCI and ISS; Report of a Group of Experts on the Implementation of the Convention on the Rights of the Child regarding inter-country adoption (April 1991). See also Ambrose and Coburn, *Report on Inter-Country Adoption in Romania* (USAID, January 2001).

[6] Announcement of Prime Minister Nastase, 12 July 2001.

[7] Duncan, 'Regulating Intercountry Adoption – an International Perspective', in Bainham and Pearl (eds), *Frontiers of Family Law* (Chancery Lane Publishing, 1995).

[8] Romanian Adoption Committee website – www.gov.ro.

that there were 739 intercountry adoptions to the United States. However, the US website notes that on 15 December 1999 it granted the one-thousandth visa that year to parents adopting a Romanian child intercountry.[9]

Problems on ratification

The Romanian Government faced considerable difficulties when it ratified the Convention in 1994.[10] These included high levels of institutionalisation of children, the existence of a thriving 'market' in children accompanied by a continuing demand from the West for young white children for adoption, the lack of a system for matching children to adoptive parents, and a failure to eradicate improper financial gain within adoption. Furthermore, and most importantly, Romania lacked an effective, integrated child protection system which would have prevented children coming into the care of the local authority, and which would have been able to offer children alternatives to institutionalisation other than intercountry adoption.

Following ratification, the Government introduced policies which, in hindsight, were ill-advised and exacerbated the difficulties surrounding intercountry adoption. The Government sought to regulate the role of private foundations and agencies. Private bodies were allowed to continue working in adoption provided they were Romanian registered agencies (generally partnered with an overseas agency or a Romanian branch of the overseas agency) or, alternatively, if they were foreign agencies that were accredited by the Romanian Government. The accreditation requirements were minimal. Further, a bilateral agreement was reached between the United States and the Romanian Government whereby any organisation which was accredited in the United States would be regarded as accredited to work in Romania. Thus, the Romanian Government carried out no check on American agencies and foundations. Neither were the Romanian agencies licensed in any meaningful way. No quality standards were set and the organisations were not monitored. Agencies and foundations mushroomed, with around 75 domestic agencies and 25 foreign agencies in Romania offering intercountry adoption services at the beginning of 2001.

Government of Romania Decision No 245 of June 1997 *concerning the licensing criteria for private organisations which work in the field of protection of children's rights through adoption* provided that private organisations licensed to carry out activities in the field of protection of children's rights through adoption could undertake the following tasks:

(a)   inform, support and counsel the persons interested in adoption;

(b)   carry out the necessary steps in order to draw up and solve the adoption files at the competent authorities;

(c)   assess and survey persons interested in completing adoption in co-operation with competent authorities both before and after adoption approval has been granted.

This Decision was augmented by Government of Romania Decision No 506 of 26 August 1999 *regarding the methodology of assigning the task of finding an adoptive parent or a family and of supervising the adoption for the children registered with the Romanian Adoption Committee.* This Decision permitted authorised private bodies and foreign adoption agencies to assign children to adoptive parents in co-operation with local authorities The number of children a private body could assign depended on how many children were allocated to it for this purpose.

An Emergency Ordinance was introduced in 1997 which put in place what became known as the 'points' system for the allocation of children for intercountry adoption.[11] The number of children allocated to a Romanian or foreign agency depended upon donations, sponsorships

---

[9]   See www.usembassy.ro.

[10]   Law No 84/1994. The Convention came into force on 1 May 1995.

[11]   Government Decision No 502/1997.

and programmes performed in the field of children's protection. This included payment for foster parents, the promotion of domestic adoption, the provision of maternal assistants, etc. The 'points' system was amended in Decision 506/1999 of 26 August 1999,[12] but continued until the moratorium on adoption was announced by the Romanian Government on 21 June 2001.[13]

The purpose of the points system, introduced in 1997, was to fund and improve child protection programmes. It might have been expected that with the increase of moneys in the child protection system, and the development of programmes on prevention, rehabilitation, fostering and national adoption, the numbers of intercountry adoptions would have fallen. Although little research was carried out on the effectiveness of the programmes funded by overseas 'points' money, anecdotal evidence was that little money found its way into the child protection system. Further, there was evidence that the private bodies used a portion of the money to provide foster parents for children who had already been identified as destined for intercountry adoption, thus ensuring that they spent as short a time as possible in institutional care. There is little evidence that money went towards effective prevention programmes, and some evidence that there was resistance from local authorities towards agencies working to reunite small children with their families.[14]

The linking of expenditure on 'child protection services' and the allocation of children for adoption resulted in an ever-increasing number of intercountry adoptions and a corresponding lack of development of local authority child protection services. Local authorities did not develop effective child protection programmes, and central government did not focus on the need to create and adequately fund such services; thus, a child protection system which addressed abandonment, worked with families and promoted good parenting simply failed to materialise. In many areas child protection was left almost entirely to the private bodies. The points system did, however, provide an unedifying spectacle of disputes between agencies over which of them a child belonged to for the purposes of matching, of children on occasions being matched with two different sets of overseas parents, and of appeals by agencies arguing that the money paid entitled them to more children than they had been allocated.

The costs of adoption and improper financial gain

In general, the allocation of children for goods, money or services is undesirable and open to abuse. There has been little transparency within Romania as to the destination of money received from international adopters, and much anecdotal evidence of bribes being paid at all levels to ensure that a child is allocated for intercountry adoption to a particular agency. Further, as money followed the child in intercountry adoption, but not in a domestic adoption, there was little incentive on the part of local authorities to develop and increase domestic adoption.

Up until the moratorium in June 2001, Romanian children could be found advertised for

---

[12] It was also amended by Emergency Ordinance No 192 of 8 December 1999.

[13] The Romanian delegate announced that the points system had been abolished at the Special Commission Meeting on Inter-Country Adoption held at The Hague, 28 November to 1 December 2000. Although there does not appear to be any published governmental decision to this effect, we were informed by the President of the National Authority that the points system had been repealed. This information was also contained in a national Romanian newspaper of 7 February 2001. We have proceeded on the assumption that the points system has in fact been repealed.

[14] See The Child Welfare and Protection Project, *Mid-Term Evaluation*, Wulczyn, Orlebeke and Haight, (Chapin Hall Centre for Children, 2000). The authors note the reluctance of Constanta Child Protection Commission and the Cluj Child Protection Commission to allow NGOs to work on reintegration or domestic adoption with children under the age of 6, but especially under the age of 3. They also note that some children had already been placed for international adoption and the Commission for Child Protection decided to keep these children with that plan, rather than having the project pursue integration.

adoption on the internet. The International Adoption Centre, a US-based organisation,[15] charged around $23,500 for a Romanian child, with little clarity as to what expenses and fees were covered by this payment. United Families, another American organisation,[16] also advertised children on its website.[17] According to the website, the cost of a Romanian child from two Romanian organisations varied from a low of $25,845, to a high of $39,280. (Roma children came cheaper at $15,590.) However, would-be adopters were warned that 'prices may vary'. Of this figure, $20,000 to $30,000 was referable to a United Families placement fee. This money was intended to be paid into child protection programmes in Romania. However, unofficial estimates were that only $3,000 of this money was actually spent on child protection in Romania in order to obtain 'points'. The destination of the remaining $17,000 to $27,000 per child remained unaccounted for.

The involvement of agencies

While the use of accredited private bodies to perform the functions of the Central Authority is permissible under the Hague Convention,[18] the use of such bodies in states of origin, even if they are 'not-for-profit' organisations, is debatable. The Romanian Central Authority has insufficient resources to supervise such bodies, and no experience in setting quality standards or accreditation procedures. The very reason for the existence of such private bodies in Romania is intercountry adoption. Their funding is dependent upon them placing children with paying overseas adopters. These private bodies have had no involvement or indeed any funding to work in the field of national adoption. In the absence of effective national adoption services, but a highly organised, well-funded intercountry adoption service, it is perhaps inevitable that the most adoptable children were placed for intercountry adoption. Data from the National Child Protection Agency (now the National Authority for Child Protection and Adoption) shows that for the first 10 months of 2000, the average age of a child placed for domestic adoption was 3 years. The average age of a child placed for intercountry adoption in the same period was approximately 10 months.[19]

The role of western states

While the necessary controls, to ensure that intercountry adoption was in the best interests of the child and was a placement of last resort for the child, were not adequately in place or enforced by Romania, the fault could not be said to lie upon the Romanian Government alone. The receiving states must also take responsibility. Knowing the abuses that were taking place, receiving states were still permitting their nationals to apply to adopt children from Romania. Receiving states also continued to issue visas to adoptive parents to remove children from Romania right up until the moratorium was announced, knowing that adopters had paid a sum of money hugely in excess of what might be termed expenses. The failure on the part of receiving states to monitor the activities of their agencies, to prevent the advertising of children on the internet by their accredited bodies and to restrict the sums of moneys being demanded and paid to their own domestic agencies is serious. The activities of some agencies exploited children, the adoptive parents and, sometimes with the help of their governments, placed a considerable pressure on the Romanian state to permit increasing levels of intercountry

---

[15]   www.adoptlaw.org/tiac-htm/12fee.htm.

[16]   www.members.aol.com/UnitingFamilies.

[17]   The website contained adverts for children available from Copii Fericiti and Totul Pentru Copii, as well as from Ajutorul Chrestin Bin Romania (all of which are Romanian private bodies).

[18]   See Art 22.

[19]   *National Authority for Child Protection and Adoption Statistics 2000.*

adoption. That political pressure was maintained by some states even after the moratorium was announced in June 2001.

There has been little discussion amongst receiving states, and indeed here in the United Kingdom as we move towards full ratification of the Convention, of the impact that ratification, accompanied by the growing demand for small children for adoption, places on states of origin. Indeed, it is arguable that the very existence of the Convention promotes rather than simply regulates intercountry adoption. While intercountry adoption had its roots in altruism and humanitarianism, today it is at best a service for children, but in many instances is a service to provide parents with children.

The major problem for states of origin is that ratification of the Convention is not tied into development of a child welfare system. Although ratification by states of origin which have not developed such a system has been welcomed by the Hague Conference, it can be argued that the implementation of one without the other is an undesirable state of affairs. The evidence of Romania is that ratification of the Convention, where this is not accompanied by a functioning child welfare system, promotes and increases intercountry adoption. Its existence has allowed local authorities to move a child through the child protection system to final placement at speed. Not only is there no cost to the local authority, unlike a domestic adoption, but in the case of Romania there has been a financial gain. Payments are not sanctioned by the Convention, but even if no money accompanies an intercountry adoption by way of a 'donation', the Convention still allows the payment of expenses relating to the adoption. It is still cheaper for a local authority to send a child for intercountry adoption than it is to find a domestic adopter or retain the child in a children's home or with foster parents.

Reforming the law in Romania

The first imperative in reforming the adoption system was to cut any direct or indirect link between foreign intercountry adoption agencies and Romanian intercountry adoption agencies. The second was to remove the financial incentives that were present in the system. The third was to reduce the need for intercountry adoption and to boost national adoption. To achieve this it was deemed necessary to put intercountry adoption back into the hands of the Romanian Government, both central and local, and to develop a state-funded-and-run integrated child welfare system. Although the Convention allows the use of accredited agencies and private bodies to carry out the functions of the Central Authority, it was decided not to permit their use in the new draft legislation. Given the past history, and the lack of resources to run an effective accreditation system or provide adequate monitoring and supervision of the activities of such agencies, it was decided to limit the role of such agencies very strictly. Under the draft legislation such agencies would only be allowed to perform certain specialised tasks that the local authorities were unable to do themselves, and only under contract to the local authority. This would include preparing a child for intercountry adoption, managing the process of transfer once an adoption order had been granted, and preparing a life story book for the child.

It was seen as essential in order to address corruption and financial abuses that the processes of identifying a child as in need of intercountry adoption should be completely separated from the selection of an appropriate intercountry adoptive family. Up until March 2001 accredited private bodies would identify children in need of adoption and select a parent from amongst the files provided by a partner or parent agency overseas. Thus, an application by an adoptive parent might not be vetted or reviewed by anyone other than the agency to which the parents had paid a large fee. The only restrictions placed on the approval of potential adopters were those imposed by their home state.

Under the new draft legislation, all applications must be made through the Romanian Committee for Adoption, which is the Central Authority. All applicants will need to comply with the criteria for both national and international adopters to be set down by the National

Authority for Child Protection and Adoption. Adopters will be asked to pay the expenses of adoption, which will be fixed and known to adopters before they apply. Donations will not be sought, nor will they be permitted. The cessation of financial contributions to child protection from agencies is likely to result in a diminution of services in some local authorities. In particular, it is likely to lead to a drop in the number of foster carers being available for children. This posed a dilemma for the Working Group working on the draft legislation. There was an inevitable debate as to whether a system should be set up similar to that in China, where adoptive parents are asked to pay a sum of money that represents a donation to the children's home or children's services. This was ultimately rejected, partly because of the lack of enthusiasm for such a system from the Hague Conference Special Commission, which met in November 2000, and partly because of the need to remove all financial incentives from the system. Some of the shortfall in services will be met by the European Union through the Phare Programme. It is also anticipated that, when it is accepted that money will not follow a baby, and that there will be no financial reward for any person or body giving up a baby for adoption, the numbers of babies being abandoned and taken into care will reduce considerably.

The demands on social workers will, inevitably, rise. Local authorities will be required to draw up care plans for all children in their care and to seek a national adoption placement for each child. The removal of private bodies from the field of adoption may well result in short-term skill shortages. Most local authorities do not have staff who are skilled and experienced in adoption. Any reform of the law therefore has to be accompanied by the provision of training and the requirement of additional social workers.

Intercountry adoption will still be retained and recognised as a possible placement for a child, but only as a last resort. Before seeking an intercountry placement a local authority will be under a duty to satisfy the Central Authority that it has complied with all the procedures laid down in the draft legislation and that it has not been possible to find a national adoptive parent for the child. If the local authority decides that intercountry adoption is an appropriate placement for the child, and the Central Authority is satisfied that a national placement cannot be found, the Central Authority will transmit the details of up to five sets of appropriate intercountry adoptive parents according to set procedures, and the local authority will undertake matching.

Conclusion

In the United Kingdom, ratification of the Convention is seen as a way of making it easier for parents to adopt intercountry, rather than addressing intercountry adoption abuses. This is the reality of the Convention, which has led to an increase in worldwide intercountry adoption. In 1993 the number of children adopted intercountry was 16,027; by 1997, the figure was 23,199; and in 1998, the figure was 30,709. In the United States alone there were nearly 20,000 intercountry adoptions last year.[20]

The shortage of white babies for adoption worldwide places a great premium on such children. It has been noted by UNICEF that, worldwide, there are 50 prospective adopters for every available child.[21] The pressure on states of origin to keep the availability of children for adoption flowing can be immense, particularly where a child welfare system is virtually non-existent, or is poorly resourced and staffed.

---

[20]   The United States does not have the highest rate per capita of population. This distinction belongs to Sweden, which, since the end of the 1960s, has received over 40,000 foreign children. See UNICEF, *Innocenti Digest*, 'Intercountry Adoption'.

[21]   See Parliamentary Assembly, Council of Europe, *International adoption: respecting children's rights* (Doc 8592).

The contracting states to the Hague Convention might need to take a long, hard look at whether the Convention is really meeting its objectives. Is it truly safeguarding children, or is it simply creating a market, making it easier for parents desperate to adopt to find a child? The adoption rate in Romania has risen from 185 per 100,000 live births in 1995 (the year after ratification of the Convention), to 326 per 100,000 in 1998. The only countries with higher rates are Bulgaria and Russia. Romania cannot, in the long term, afford to lose its children. The fertility rate is dropping, and is said to be below replacement rate. One of the primary aims of the new draft legislation will be to keep Romanian children in Romania, safeguarded by an effective welfare system and legislation which ensures that intercountry adoption is truly a last resort.

PLENARY SEVEN

FEEDBACK FROM SMALL GROUPS AND DISCUSSIONS

The small groups were asked to provide topics for discussion by the conference primarily arising out of the papers given, and suggestions for change where appropriate.

Group A

Discussion topic

Group A focused on the need for the collection and exchange of data across the family justice system, particularly the following:

- *Statistics*: practical ways were needed of providing better statistical information about children and litigation, including the number of cases handled, and the length of time cases took both nationally and in different care centre areas. The Group queried whether the local Family Court Business Committee (FCBC) should have the responsibility for the collection of such data and the exchange of this with other committees. It felt that the FCBC would be a useful mechanism for doing this, but that there should be a national mechanism for then collating and disseminating the data so that both a national and local picture would emerge.
- *Feedback*: there was no mechanism in place to allow the professionals and judiciary involved in cases to learn from experience as to the practical outcome of their involvement. The Group suggested that the FCBC could be used to require the local authority concerned to provide information on implementation of care plans, although not on a specific case basis.

Conference response

- Chris Davies CBE (Director of Social Services):
- *Statistics*: He believed that quite a lot of statistics had already been collected, for example by the Department of Health, but that they were not presented in such a way as to allow people to make positive use of them. He suggested that we look at what had already been collected and set up exchanges of information between different areas of the system.
- *Feedback*: He felt fairly sure that directors of social services would be happy to set up a system for the provision of some sort of follow-up report to the care judge in every case where a care order had been made, if the courts would find that helpful and if the content and format of the information required was clear. He suggested that an update take place 12 months after the making of the care order, setting out the child's present situation, what problems there had been and what the future was felt likely to hold. He personally was very willing to join in such an enterprise, and was prepared to consult more widely to see whether other directors felt the same.

- The President, Dame Elizabeth Butler-Sloss:
- *Statistics*: The President felt that in the medium term we should look more critically at what data should be collected, how it should be collected and how it should be used. She

- suggested the provision of statistics to the FCBC as to the length of time cases were taking, with encouragement to improve the situation.
- *Feedback*: She was interested in getting feedback for the FCBC, which might include feedback from directors of social services as to what happened in cases where a care plan was not implemented, and the reasons why not. She queried whether requests made by the FCBC would generate the required energy in local authorities to provide this information.

- Arran Poyser (HM Magistrates; Courts Service Inspectorate) sounded a note of caution about feedback, stating that in consultation with judges prior to the Care Planning Guidance 1999, they felt that such a system would not work. He particularly raised practical difficulties, including how to identify and find the relevant judge, how to ensure that the files were in the same place as the judge, and the concern that, given the rapid fading of judicial memories, such a report would merely create an anecdotal view rather than a detailed analysis of the position.

- Dr Danya Glaser (Great Ormond Street) felt that experts would be equally interested in finding out about the outcomes of cases in which they had been involved. She suggested a pilot scheme initially, which identified cases at random to be followed up at a later date. It was important to be clear about what outcome data was required. The focus should be not just on fulfilment of care plans but also on welfare outcomes for the children with the suggestion that the views of children themselves be obtained. She further suggested that it be decided in advance who should be provided with follow-up information, and proposed judges, counsel, solicitors and experts involved in the cases.

- His Honour Judge Hedley (Liverpool Combined Court Centre) stated that he frequently asked for feedback following cases, and felt that social workers were generally very happy to provide this. He considered such feedback to be useful not only for himself, but also for the family involved as evidence of a continuing interest in the case.

- Lord Justice Thorpe felt that there was sufficient momentum regarding feedback to justify a pilot scheme, and suggested putting together a sub-group within the Interdisciplinary Committee from social services, the judiciary, experts and practitioners to set up the pilot, subject to the approval of the President.

- Lady Justice Hale emphasised that her group (Group C) was concerned that the feedback should not be regarded as part of the case or as judicial follow-up of the case along the lines of *Re W and B; Re W (Care Plan)* [2001] EWCA Civ 757, [2001] 2 FLR 582. The Group felt that it should be a research study of the value of feedback to the people involved in the case, and should cover a random selection of cases, not just the ones which troubled judges. It was important to see both success and failure.

- Mr Justice Wall endorsed Dr Glaser's suggestion that the children's views should form part of the feedback. He referred to the statutory requirement in Scotland to review children in care on an annual basis, which was generally done by means of a letter from the social worker. He felt that the value of this review was put into question by the fact that it did not seek the child's views.

Group B

Discussion topic

Every effort must be made to re-elevate social work expertise and the weight attached to internal assessments conducted by social services departments. This message, both to the judiciary and to practitioners, might be strengthened by the provision of more interdisciplinary training for social workers in courtroom and witness box skills. The model operating in Somerset which provides an intensive 5 days' training, supported by local judges, magistrates and practitioners, might be usefully adopted by other local authorities. If greater reliance were placed upon multi-disciplinary local assessments the use of external expertise (usually from a consultant child and adolescent psychiatrist) might be reduced.

Conference response

- Lord Justice Thorpe asked Liz Evans to give the conference details of the scheme run in Somerset. He particularly felt that the element of interdisciplinarity was important, with barristers and judges providing part of the training.

- Liz Evans (Glastonbury Social Services) told the conference about the 5-day training course run by Glastonbury Social Services for social workers with 18 months' PQE. The structure of the course was broadly as follows:

- *day 1*: the social services legal department, a district judge and barristers explained to social workers what they were looking for, and the 'tricks' of the profession, including skills of cross-examination. Reading material and case studies were provided;
- *day 2*: participants worked on a case study, focusing on writing assessments and the identification of significant harm;
- *day 3*: role play, with a district judge hearing a case, barristers cross-examining witnesses and the legal department representing the social workers. The role play was stopped at various stages for feedback on how to improve;
- *day 4*: cross-examination on care plans;
- *day 5*: a bench of magistrates worked with the social workers on the care plans, looking at the complexities for example of contact, and closed and open adoptions.

- Peter Harris (former Official Solicitor) felt that what was being sought was not so much the re-skilling of social workers as the recognition of their existing skills and the elevation of their status by recognising the expert knowledge and skills which they could provide to the court.

- Judge Susan Darwell-Smith (Designated Family Judge, Bristol) felt that the Somerset scheme was very worthwhile, particularly in its use of interdisciplinary co-operation, and thought that it would be very helpful if all FCBCs nationally could provide feedback on the schemes happening in each area.

- Mr Justice Bodey emphasised the need to find a practical way of raising the morale and profile of social workers. He believed it important to retain the best social workers in day-to-day social work practice rather than them moving to management, and suggested the introduction of consultant social workers along the lines of the consultant nurses being introduced.

Group C

Discussion topic

Group C raised concerns about the new Adoption Bill, in particular regarding the following:

- safeguards for consent: given the powerful legal consequences which consent to placement and adoption would have, the Group was concerned about safeguards both for giving and evidencing consent;
- the threshold for orders in non-consensual cases (including cases dispensing with consent);
- alternative ways of achieving stability/permanence: the Group supported the special guardianship order as an appropriate solution when total transfer of the child was not appropriate but stability was important. It also felt it necessary to look at why so few long-term foster parents did not want permanence, and what would encourage them to commit more than at present;
- the need for targets for stability rather than targets for adoption: the Group was concerned with whether local authorities were to have incentives for adoption rather than incentives for stability. It felt that incentives for stability were very important but that incentives for adoption should be only as part of those for stability.

James Paton, in giving his paper on adoption, had stated that suggestions for amendment could be taken into account by policy makers, and for this reason Group C considered it important to seek to influence decisions about the Bill by raising its concerns at this stage.

Conference response

- Pat Monro (Darlington & Parkinson Solicitors) expressed concern that the Government had dropped the requirement for seeking consent from a child over the age of 12. She felt that this requirement should be reinstated.

- Lady Justice Hale raised concerns about the application of the welfare-based test for dispensing with parental agreement. She also referred to situations where parental consent was not sought or was refused, and the local authority applied for a placement order; the non-return provisions then meant that the local authority could hold onto a child without an order.

- Gillian Schofield (University of East Anglia) was in favour of having a range of options supporting security and stability, and particularly highlighted the proposed special guardianship orders. She proposed the use of more s 91(14) orders to secure long-term foster placements.

- Danya Glaser queried whether it was necessary to continue with 6-monthly reviews of children in long-term foster care. She felt that it was not in the children's interests to be questioned every 6 months about their circumstances, being inconsistent with a feeling of permanence.

- Cathy James (Department of Health) agreed to pass on the conference's concerns to James Paton.

- It was also decided that Lady Justice Hale would crystallise the main points of concern in writing for the Department of Health. The Resolution which she subsequently drafted is appended to this chapter.

Group D

Discussion topics

Group D raised three matters for discussion:

(1) The Group would support an amendment to the Children Act to enable the court to review the operation of a care plan post-care order in certain specified circumstances.

(2) The Group invited the President to consider reinforcing important aspects of good practice relating to experts by issuing a Practice Direction or widely disseminating a good practice guide, including:

- the need for expert evidence to be established;
- the identification of the issues the expert witness is to address;
- the specification of the date by which the letter of instruction is to be dispatched to the expert and the lodging of a copy of the letter with the court.

(3) The Group felt that the President's Interdisciplinary Committee needs to value diversity by broadening its membership and/or the attendance at the conference, and should give consideration to this as a theme for the next conference.

Conference response

As to (1) above:

- Lord Justice Thorpe stated that the House of Lords was going to list the appeals in *Re W and B; Re W (Care Plan)* [2001] EWCA Civ 757, [2001] 2 FLR 582 in November. It was certain that the Department of Health and Lord Chancellor's Department would look at the policy questions which then remained.

- Mr Justice Wall expressed Group D's perception as being that this was an area of the Children Act where amendment had been pressed for, for a long time. He felt that the conference should continue to press for amendment. This was generally agreed.

- Jane Held (Vice-chair ADSS Children and Families Committee) shared some of the concerns expressed, but considered that there might be equally appropriate ways of managing the outcome of cases without continuing the involvement of the court. She suggested the initiation of a separate discussion involving a number of key people in the case, to consider how to progress matters.

As to (2) above:

- The President stated that she was considering asking designated family judges in care proceedings to encourage district judges to be much more hands on in case management, particularly as to:

- why an expert was needed at all;
- what were the material issues;
- why the social worker and guardian ad litem could not give evidence without the need for an expert;
- limiting the use of experts to unusual cases requiring unusual help.

- She believed that there was a diversity of practice around the country and would consider providing guidance, although not by way of a Practice Direction.

- Senior District Judge Gerald Angel (PRFD) expressed the difficulty judges often felt at hearings, given the pressure they were under to appoint experts, but stressed that such pressure ought to be resisted. He agreed that a Practice Direction would be inappropriate, but felt sure that guidance would be generally welcomed.

- Dr Clare Sturge (Northwick Park Hospital) suggested some control between the court making the direction and the instructions being received by the expert, in particular as to the number of questions the expert was asked.

- Danya Glaser felt that experts would find it very helpful to obtain the view of judges as to the usefulness of their evidence in resolving the case, in particular what the judge felt the expert contributed over and above the rest of the evidence. She also suggested inviting the expert to be a consultant to the case at an early stage, to assist on matters such as whether an expert view could add anything to the case and the evidence or information which needed to be obtained. Such an early approach might obviate the necessity for a full expert's report in many cases.

As to (3) above:

- Mr Justice Wall expressed the views of Rukhsana Farooqi Thakrar (a member of his Group) in acknowledging that as most of the conference were middle class and white, there was potentially limited insight into the position of ethnic minorities. It was important to take such a criticism on board.

- Lord Justice Thorpe accepted the validity of the point, and queried how it should be addressed. He emphasised that the work of the Committee depended on the willingness of individuals to give their time. The Committee had found it very difficult to engage various groups who clearly had a role to play, particularly paediatricians and the police. He emphasised that the Committee was an open body, and that all were encouraged to support its work and contribute to its diversity.

- Rukhsana Farooqi Thakrar stated that she knew of people from a black perspective who she believed would be prepared to contribute to the work of the Committee.

- Dr Judith Trowell (The Tavistock Clinic) suggested that young people be invited to the next conference to share their experiences. She hoped that with appropriate encouragement they would attend.

- Dr Clare Sturge referred to the number of children in the case system from ethnic minorities and mixed backgrounds, and suggested that the Committee devote a whole conference to looking at how to deal with this issue.

Group E

Discussion topic

What, if anything, can or should be done regarding the apparent lacuna whereby a *'Gillick-*competent' child, or a child over 16 years, can be treated (eg for anorexia) in the face of his or her refusal, by virtue of consent given by someone or some body with parental responsibility, without such child having a guardian or other independent person to protect his or her interests?

Conference response

- Mark Powell (Association of Lawyers for Children) expressed the concern of Group E about children falling halfway between the Mental Health Act and the Children Act, particularly those who were *'Gillick* competent' but whose refusal to treatment could be bypassed by their parents. He felt that there was a need for more than just a voluntary advocacy service for these children, and queried whether this was an area which CAFCASS could take on in the same way that the Official Solicitor had taken on such cases in the past, in order to provide a form of statutory help for these children.

- Laurence Oates (Official Solicitor) felt that this issue was one which should be given much wider currency in the NHS, in relation to the way that the NHS Trusts and doctors behaved. In many cases, such circumstances arose before the case came to court. The concern was what went on in practice without the case going to court. He referred to various well-known circumstances in which the NHS may not allow parents to override a child's refusal, for example heart transplants for 15/16 year olds. He considered that the issue was whether the case should come to court. At that stage the court would act in the best interests of the young person, making it likely that the court would uphold the right of the doctor to treat if in the interests of the child's welfare.

- Mark Powell emphasised that his concern was for cases which did not come to court, where the young person was left with no independent support.

- His Honour Judge Hedley referred the conference to the Children's Rights Advisory Forum which had been set up at Alder Hey Hospital, and which was made up of 50% consultants and 50% lay members (of which he was one). The Forum was charged with advising in these sorts of cases where there were no ongoing court proceedings. Advice was given as to whether the case should go to court. The Forum was convened at the request of the child, parents or doctors. He considered such schemes, although not perfect solutions to this problem, were a helpful step in the right direction.

- The President considered that this was a matter which hospitals themselves needed to look at, but was a very important point. The number of such cases which came before High Court judges was very small, generally life or death situations (for example involving Jehovah's Witnesses). The question was what ought the court's duty to be to *'Gillick-*competent' children: is there an overriding duty to preserve the child's life, or is it the child's right to die?

- Dr Brian Jacobs (Maudsley Hospital) stated that the area where the Mental Health Act and Children Act overlap is very complex. Practitioners were generally experts in one or the other, not both. He would not assume that CAFCASS would have both sets of skills, but felt that it would be laudable for CAFCASS to take on such cases for children who were in need. Generally he considered that there was a need to become more familiar with mental health legislation.

- Dr Judith Trowell referred to the framework within the Mental Health Act for a second opinion and right of appeal, and queried whether there was a way of building this into the Children Act perhaps by way of a Children's Rights Forum. The power and lack of safeguards in the Children Act caused her concern, but she felt that social services were generally anxious about the potential stigmatising effect of using the Mental Health Act as an alternative.

Group F

Discussion topic

Acknowledging the finite pool of expertise available in children proceedings, Group F invited a more creative use of existing resources, for example:

(1) wider use of multi-disciplinary forums (to include parents if they wish) with a view to reaching a consensus about difficult or disputed aspects of medical treatment for a child, thus avoiding the need for court intervention;

(2) more extensive use of family group conferencing in care proceedings to make better use of the family's own resources, eg in supporting the parents or, if living at home is not possible, offering alternative accommodation;

(3) more input from experts as to their role in particular proceedings with experts expected to comment on the way in which they can best be used and to indicate when they consider that it is not appropriate or necessary to instruct them at all.

Conference response

As to (1) above:

- Mrs Justice Black referred the conference to the Alder Hey Children's Rights Advisory Forum mentioned by His Honour Judge Hedley, and recommended wider use of such schemes.

As to (2) above:

- Mrs Justice Black considered that multi-group conferencing could be used to support families, and particularly parents, in providing a greater understanding of the care process.

- Christine Field JP queried whether family group conferencing was universally available within the care system.

- Jean Clydesdale (Team Manager, Harlow) explained to the conference the Family Group Conferencing Scheme piloted in Essex, which endeavoured to provide a family group conference prior to care proceedings to see if it was possible to keep the child within the family, and to avoid care proceedings entirely. The scheme was also used within the youth justice system.

- Chris Davies CBE believed that there was patchy use of family group conferencing by local authorities. The essence of such a conference was to put the material concerns to as many of the wider family as it was possible to assemble, encouraging the family to come up with a plan to deal with the concerns and to provide reassurance to the local authority to go along with their plan. He felt that these conferences often brought out plans not previously considered by the local authority and which could be very powerful. However, they were not appropriate in every case.

As to (3) above:

- Mrs Justice Black believed that increased input from experts could tie in with raising the status of social workers, with the expert confirming that the evidence he or she would normally be asked to provide could instead be provided by the social worker, and raising points which should be considered by the social worker in his or her assessment.

- Peter Harris felt that using experts in this way was overlapping with the role of solicitors. Solicitors are already advised to consult the expert as to whether their expertise is necessary or appropriate. This was a matter which should properly be dealt with at the directions appointment, rather than the expert having to raise this later.

RESOLUTION ON THE ADOPTION AND CHILDREN BILL

1.   The conference was united in its concern about two aspects of the Adoption and Children Bill introduced in the last Parliament:

   (a)   the serious consequences for parents of giving consent to placement, and the need for formal safeguards to ensure that consent is freely given with full knowledge of the consequences and speedy access to a court in cases of withdrawal or disagreement with the agency;
   (b)   the lack of a threshold of significant harm for making placement orders without consent. Combined with a lowered threshold for dispensing with consent to adoption, this might permit compulsory placement for adoption where compulsory care or supervision would not be permitted.

   These were thought to have serious implications for children accommodated by local authorities, fundamentally altering the relationship between the authorities and their clients, and putting parental confidence in social services and the care system at risk.

2.   The conference was, however, also united in welcoming many other aspects of the Bill, including in particular:

   (a)   the recognition that the complete and irrevocable transfer of a child from one family to another involved in full adoption is not appropriate for every child who requires a stable and secure home throughout his childhood. The conference was glad to learn that targets and incentives would promote this security and stability (terms preferred to 'permanence') in a number of ways, including but not limited to full adoption;
   (b)   the wider range of legal methods of providing stability and security appropriate to the needs of children and their families. These would have to take account of the needs of long-term foster parents who do not at present wish to apply either for adoption or residence orders and encourage people to come forward as special guardians.

PROSPECTIVE

THE WAY FORWARD

The Rt Hon Lady Justice Hale

The new dawn

Taking stock, it might be helpful to remind ourselves of what the Children Act 1989 was originally trying to do. I think there were five main interlocking aims. Experience and research have shown that these were sound and have largely been successfully achieved.

Reform and codify the substantive law

The Act started life as two separate law reform exercises: the Government's child care law review and the Law Commission's review of private law. Each aimed to end the chaos and injustice of different substantive law in different courts and different proceedings. It was often impossible to get all the issues about the same child tried in the same place at same time. Happily for us all, the Government's delay in legislating for the child care law review meant that both public and private law could eventually be tackled together.

Create a new family justice system

Bringing all the substantive law together made it possible to bring together all the courts in a joined-up family justice system, with the procedures the same or virtually the same throughout. The Act itself pointed the way towards new procedural approaches, with its requirement for timetabling and consequent expectation that courts would actively manage cases.

The creation of a new system coincided with a new enthusiasm for interdisciplinary co-operation, not only between the medical, mental health and social work professionals, but also between the professionals and the courts. The impetus came from the professionals who joined together in the (sadly now defunct) Council for Family Proceedings, stimulated by the intellectual and promotional work of Mervyn Murch and Douglas Hooper, and actively encouraged by the President of the Family Division. The Act brought with it new formal structures for interdisciplinary co-operation, spearheaded by the Children Act Advisory Committee and an enthusiastic judiciary, which promoted both good practice and procedural innovation (some of which would later be copied in the Civil Procedural Rules).

Unify children's services

Bringing together all the local authority responsibilities to provide and monitor social services for children and their families exposed the full extent of these for the first time (it would have been very helpful if the National Health Service and Community Care Act 1990 had done the same for community care services for adults). It also did away with the distinctions between handicapped or disabled children and children in need of protection. The hope was that all would be seen simply as children in need of help. This brought with it the principle of working in partnership with, rather than opposition to, parents and families.

Clarify boundaries between courts and service providers

This too was a consequence of providing one substantive law for all. Was it to be modelled on wardship, with the court at least nominally in charge, able to direct the local authority what to do, and able to keep the case under review? Or was it to be modelled on the Children and Young Persons and Child Care Acts, where the court had a role after a care order or parental rights resolution only if the local authority brought all contact with the parents to an end? The Act, as is well known, chose a middle course somewhat closer to the statutory than to the wardship model. The new features were a greatly enhanced contact jurisdiction, detailed guidance for local authorities on involving both parents and children in decisions about their care, and a new complaints mechanism for all users.

Separate the family and criminal justice systems

Most of this would not have been possible without the initially controversial decision to separate the family and criminal justice systems. No longer would the child protection system, or children's services in general, be the poor relation to the juvenile justice system for offending or misbehaving children. This was controversial because it undid more than a century of bringing them closer together. But separating the two systems did not necessarily entail a more punitive approach to juvenile offending.

New Act, new issues

But one set of changes always throws up new issues to tackle (as Amanda Finlay put it, you slay one dragon to find another set of teeth baring themselves at you). This conference has highlighted a few.

Completing the code

In bringing all the substantive law relating to child care and upbringing together, the Act missed out adoption law. Even then, it was obvious that adoption had become largely part of the child care system rather than a transaction between families mediated by adoption agencies. Hence, the next joint venture between government and the Law Commission was the adoption law review, trying to bring about a similar modernisation. As with the Children Act, however, the enthusiasms of law reformers and policy makers do not always catch the attention of legislators until there is some political catalyst. The Prime Minister's personal crusade to increase the use of adoption has played much the same role in bringing forward the Adoption and Children Bill that the Cleveland crisis played in bringing about the 1989 Act.

This gives the opportunity to bring together the two systems of law and make them work properly together, both at the substantive and at the procedural level.

At the substantive level, the Bill introduced in the last Parliament is very welcome in recognising that in English law adoption is for the whole of life – not only for the adopted child, but also for the adoptive parents and their families. It is the total transfer of the child from one family to another. There is still a need for this in some cases. But if so, we should not pretend that some things amount to adoption when they do not. There should be alternative machinery for giving children security and stability (more accurate terms than 'permanence') throughout childhood: parental responsibility orders and agreements for step-parents; and special guardianship for foster parents and other non-parental carers. The details may need further consideration so that they do not introduce inconsistencies and injustices, but the additional flexibility to tailor legal relationships to actual relationships must be a good thing. Of course, the families' understanding of such nuances can be rather different from professionals' understanding, and the families may well be right. They may attach more weight to the need for local authority financial and personal support while wishing to escape from local authority interference and insecurity. We need to understand more about long-term foster carers' needs and why they do not apply for residence orders now. We need to think about how to encourage new forms of care, perhaps by recruiting special guardians. But the idea of targets for stability, rather than targets for adoption alone, is welcomed.

As to adoption itself, integration with care proceedings must be a good thing. Worries about the previous Bill focus more on provisions which are not consistent with the current system. Is it acceptable under the European Convention for the Protection of Human Rights and Funadmental Freedoms 1950 (ECHR) to have consent to placement conferring parental responsibility upon the agency without any obvious means of resolving disagreements? If consent to placement will have such important consequences, what will the safeguards be? Is it acceptable for local authorities to be able to keep children without prior court authority if they intend to apply for a placement order, against parental wishes? Is it acceptable for a court to be able to give permission to place when it could not make a care or even a supervision order? How can the threshold for making a placement order be lower than that? This is allied to the proposed criteria for dispensing with parental consent: do they mean that the requirement will be meaningless in practice? Can this fulfil the proportionality requirement in Art 8 of the ECHR?

The President has already demonstrated how much might be achieved under the present law, with new arrangements for adoption cases: confining them to specialist courts (also having care jurisdiction) and providing for timetabling and court case management.

Fine-tuning (or rescuing) the family justice system

The challenge of tackling delay and drift while also trying to ensure that the right decisions are made remains enormous. The Civil Procedure Rules have borrowed some of our ideas and even improved upon them. But ordinary civil proceedings are easy compared with children's cases.

(1) They have pleadings: however often amended, people know at least the outlines of the dispute at the outset. This is not so in many children's cases. If we asked local authorities to plead their case at the outset we would risk endless applications to amend as the case went on.

(2) They are retrospective: compensating for a wrong which has already been done before the proceedings started. Children's cases are prospective: although the care threshold must be crossed, once crossed there are many ways in which people may seek to change a child's life for the better (although we have also to accept that there may be some children whose lives cannot be made much better and for whom our only hope is that we do not make matters worse and that in time they may be able to make sense of what has happened to them and learn to cope with it).

(3) Assessments of the appropriate level of compensation may change radically (up or down) during the case, but the nature of the liability usually does not. Children's cases are changing all the time as the often chaotic lives of the main actors change about them.

(4) This includes the child: the subject matter of ordinary civil proceedings is neither an active player in the continuing story nor a participant in the case. Proper attention to the developing wishes and feelings of the child is essential in any children's case. Proper machinery is needed to do this: CAFCASS is a good thing in principle, so we must all try to be patient while it sorts out, after taking over, the things which should have been sorted out before it began.

For all these reasons, children's cases cannot be just like ordinary civil proceedings. The goal of an orderly beginning where the issues are clearly laid out, a middle where the evidence is collected, shared and presented, and a conclusion when judgment is given (preferably arrived at by negotiation and agreement rather than by the court) cannot always be met. It is not surprising that many cases last longer than intended, or that the best-laid plans of timetable and directions have to be overturned.

But that does not mean that we should not try to meet the goal. It is one thing if the nature of the case changes beneath us; it is quite another thing if, for example: the courts' own administrative constraints add to rather than solve the problems; or changes in relationship between local authorities and the NHS add to the difficulty and expense of obtaining the necessary professional assessments; or parties who were originally content with joint instructions change their minds when they see the result.

It is important to remember that the proceedings are only part of the process. Recent research is revealing how unstable children's lives are while proceedings are pending, with an appalling number of moves. This is because their admission to care is so often a response to crisis, in which they have to go to whichever placement is available, however unsuitable for their particular needs. We need to encourage less crisis intervention, better planned and prepared proceedings and better planned and prepared placements. Then there might be fewer cases where the proceedings themselves are the assessment process, rather than an adjudication upon the assessments already done.

We still need formal and informal interdisciplinary structures linked to the family justice system. The demise of the Children Act Advisory Committee was a bad thing, however bravely and effectively Wall J has tried to fill the gap. The demise of the Council for Family Proceedings was also a bad thing, because these professionals still need to get together. Along with the police and paediatricians as notable absentees from this gathering I would put the education services – always in the forefront of everyday contact with the children but so rarely engaged in deliberations such as these.

Achieving quality services

The major amendments and modifications to the 1989 Act so far have been in the Care Standards Act 2000, the Children (Leaving Care) Act 2000, and the Carers and Disabled Children Act 2000. The family justice system has not had much to do with the development of standards and targets in children's services. I hope that we are all now much more aware (even before Chris Davies' paper) of the constraints and difficulties facing social services departments. No amount of judicial haranguing will solve the problems of recruiting and retaining good social workers, but solving these is more likely to achieve better services and protection for children, their families and carers, than is more litigation and more court hearings.

In the end, there is no substitute for good, well-informed judgments by all the professionals concerned, but, above all, social workers. I was delighted to hear the calls to re-skill and restore respect for social work expertise during this conference. I hope that this is what will come out of the Laming inquiry rather than more blame, shame and claim. One product which would be a great help to the family justice system would be a clear statement of what the core expertise of social work with children and their families is, so that we all know what we can expect a social worker to know and to be able to do.

Redrawing the boundary

Both the procedural and the quality problems are bound up with the fundamental issue of the division of responsibility between courts and local authorities in making decisions about children. It is one thing for the court to be managing the case, another thing for the court to be managing the child. Perhaps courts would be better at case management and timetabling towards an early conclusion if they were not so concerned about the ability of local authorities to look after the child.

Those of you who were at the President's Interdisciplinary Conference in 1997 which resulted in *Divided Duties*, or whose memories stretch even further back to the debates before the child care law review, may have been surprised to find me not only participating in the Court of Appeal's decision in *Re W and B; Re W (Care Plan)* [2001] EWCA Civ 757, [2001] 2 FLR 582, but even supplying the human rights case for doing so. I was relieved to learn that whatever the House of Lords may say, at least one academic expert in children's rights thinks that I was right. I found myself between a rock and a hard place: Thorpe LJ with his memory of what could be achieved under wardship and the frustrations of the medical profession and guardians ad litem ringing in his ears; and Sedley LJ with his detailed knowledge of what could go wrong under the previous legislation gained through the Tyra Henry inquiry.

Courts are for determining rights and duties, usually but not invariably in the context of a dispute. It is wrong for anyone's rights to be taken away by an administrative authority. Even if there is no objection, some rights are so important that it is wrong to allow them to be taken away simply by consent. This is especially so where the rights in question relate to another human being – a child – and where the child himself is also the possessor of rights.

Courts are not for looking after children. Courts cannot deliver care plans. Only people can do that. Courts are not for deciding upon levels of public funding or for allocating the public funding available between the many different calls upon it. Ultimately only politicians democratically elected and accountable can do that. Hence, courts have never been in the business of telling service providers exactly what they must do, as opposed to telling them what they may do.

The basis for the decision is clear: the local authority may otherwise be infringing the Convention rights of parents, carers or most importantly the child. In my view, the most important points in *Re W and B; Re W (Care Plan)* [2001] EWCA Civ 757, [2001] 2 FLR 582 were:

(a) the recognition of positive obligations towards children whose family lives have been interfered with or even destroyed by necessary action to protect them; and

(b) the recognition that ss 6 and 7 of the Human Rights Act 1998 demand a merits-based remedy if Convention rights are infringed to which the child must have access. Whatever else the House of Lords does about 'starred' care plans, about which I do have some reservations, I hope that it does not upset either of these important principles (the latter followed in the prison babies cases).

These were not meant to be a recipe for intervention in every case: merely in those where there was a real fear that these rights would not be complied with. But (asks Rupert Hughes, father of the Children Act) what is the court to do if the remedy is invoked? It cannot magic resources – especially not the people resources on which it all depends – from the air. It cannot do much to force local authorities to do so. I do not have a convincing answer.

My real hope is that the possibility of a return to court if things go badly wrong could encourage courts to loosen the reins rather earlier than they often do at present. That may be over-optimistic. We may end up in an even worse position than before, with courts hanging onto cases endlessly, resources tied up in more and more assessments, and still no action.

But the way in which the court manages the case is closely bound up with the point at which the court expects to bow out. That is why my plea is for as much clarity as possible about the nature of the problem and the likely solution to it as early as possible in the case. There is, after all, only a limited number of options:

(a) the child is to live at home but with the help and support of social services: as Judith Harwin has argued, this should usually be under a supervision order (because a care order expects too much of both the social workers and the family), and we should be prepared to give these teeth and make them work;

(b) the child is to be placed away from home throughout his childhood: the court should make a care order, sometimes but not always with a placement order under new legislation;

(c) the child is to be looked after by the local authority but with a view to returning home if things improve: the court should make care order coupled with appropriate arrangements for contact to help keep everyone up to the mark;

(d) it is not clear what the medium or long term holds, but it is clear that the child cannot go home for the foreseeable future: should the court hold onto things until at least the medium term is clear, or should the court accept that nothing is ever certain in the life of a child and hand over to the local authority but with the possibility or even the requirement of returning if problems arise? These are the hard cases to manage.

At least if there was more clarity at the outset about the desired outcome within those broad options, the parties and the court might have a much better idea of what they needed to know before the decision could be taken. There might be less temptation to use the court process as the assessment procedure. This, in turn, would lead to earlier identification of the issues upon which external expert help is needed. The approach to outside expertise should differ according to what the court needs to know. Factual decisions as to the nature and cause of a child's injuries or disabilities are different from assessments of family relationships, parenting skills and the capacity to change.

Keeping the family and criminal justice systems separate?

Given the procedural problems raised by the case of Thompson and Venables, the increasing use of prison service establishments which cannot meet the needs of young offenders, and the issues raised by Susan Bailey and Mark Hedley, some may wonder whether the separation between the criminal and family justice systems should be reconsidered. There is no clear divide between the welfare and punishment approaches to youth justice: all are part of a continuum of responses designed to serve the developmental needs of the child. The family justice system is now so well established that there is less danger of the needs of the criminal justice system for offending children swamping the needs of the family justice system for abused and neglected children.

But there are still dangers of being swamped in other ways, through resources such as secure accommodation being taken over by the criminal justice system, leaving less room for the very damaged children who need it for other reasons. More attention could be given to making sure that the right children are fed into the right system – through careful assessments and diversion – and then making each system as responsive to their needs as it is possible to be, consistent with their different purposes and principles. But they are two separate systems serving two separate purposes, and they should remain separate from one another.

A wish-list

The wish-list I devised at the start of this conference has stayed much the same by the end:

- get the Adoption and Children Bill right this time and, once the legislation is right, consolidate it all to produce a new code;
- reinvent the interdisciplinary machinery and the Children Act Advisory Committee;
- sort out CAFCASS but be patient;
- re-skill and restore respect for social work;
- use but don't abuse *Re W and B; Re W (Care Plan)* [2001] EWCA Civ 757, [2001] 2 FLR 582 – to promote children's rights;
- Keep the faith!

CONCLUDING COMMENTS

The Rt Hon Lord Justice Thorpe

In closing the conference, Lord Justice Thorpe expressed the hope that the matters discussed and conclusions reached would be disseminated widely amongst the various professions who were represented at the conference.

He reminded the conference of the focus on interdisciplinarity which he had proposed in opening. He felt that the advantages of this for family justice were clear. He referred to the practical difficulties identified at the conference by the various professionals involved, which might easily have been dissolved or diminished had there been in place the interdisciplinary support structure which had been pressed for, for so long.

What was needed was a consultative council at national level which could disseminate information and advice to care centres throughout the country, and receive information as to problems or difficulties in return. He hoped that those present at the conference who were involved in family policy making could persuade ministers of the huge potential achievement of such a structure.

Lord Justice Thorpe further recognised that the effective working of such a structure depended not just on government support, but also on the commitment of the individuals involved. It was often not within the contracts of these individuals to assist in encouraging interdisciplinarity, but through their dedication and commitment to the family justice system there was sufficient enthusiasm to make such a structure work.

Lord Justice Thorpe expressed the hope that all those working for change within the family justice system would continue in their work, despite the difficulties and frustrations involved. He thanked all those who had given their time to attend the conference.